The
POWER
in the
PEOPLE

The POWER in the PEOPLE

Felix Morley

With a new introduction by
Michael Henry

Transaction Publishers
New Brunswick (U.S.A.) and London (U.K.)

New material this edition copyright © 2010 by Transaction Publishers,
New Brunswick, New Jersey. Originally published in 1972 by Felix
Morley.

This book is printed on acid-free paper that meets the American National
Standard for Permanence of Paper for Printed Library Materials.

Library of Congress Catalog Number: 2010001593
ISBN: 978-1-4128-1342-6
Printed in the United States of America

Library of Congress Cataloging-in-Publication Data

Morley, Felix M. (Felix Muskett), 1894-1982.
    The power in the people / Felix Morley.
        p. cm.
    Originally published: Los Angeles : Nash Pub., 1972.
    Includes bibliographical references and index.
    ISBN 978-1-4128-1342-6 (alk. paper)
        1. Constitutional history--United States. 2. United States--Civi-
    lization. 3. Political science--United States--History. I. Title.

JK31.M64 2010
320.973--dc22

                                                    2010001593

THIS BOOK IS DEDICATED

TO THE MEMORY OF

JAMES MADISON

Contents

Introduction to the Transaction Edition

"In grasping for the shadow of democracy we are losing the substance of self-government."
—Felix Morley

Felix Morley, who died in 1982, would have been thoroughly dismayed but not at all surprised by the government-expanding consequences of the 2008 election because this is precisely what he devoted most of his eighty-eight years to analyzing, to predicting, and, as much as possible, to resisting. Indeed, it would be no exaggeration to say that he thought of himself as a combatant in a long-running civil war between advocates of centralized State power and advocates of individual freedom, a struggle that he believed had significantly accelerated and intensified in his lifetime.

One of the major contributors to the Libertarian branch of the Conservative movement in the mid-twentieth century, Morley was born in 1894 in Bryn Mawr, Pennsylvania as the second son of immigrant Quaker parents. His father Frank taught mathematics at the Quaker institution of Haverford College until 1900, when he became the chair of the mathematics department at Johns Hopkins University in Baltimore. This move was fortuitous, because it made it easy for Morley to be present at the 1912 Democratic convention in Baltimore that nominated the Progressive Woodrow Wilson on the forty-sixth ballot, the occasion on which, as Morley recalled more than sixty years later, "the virus of American politics entered [his] bloodstream."[1] It was to prove a permanent infection.

Because Morley wanted to understand the world as much as possible he devoted considerable time to living, working, and traveling in Europe, as well as other parts of the world, particularly during his twenties. After graduating from Haverford College and studying at Oxford as a Rhodes Scholar (an honor he shared with both of his brothers, Frank and Christopher), he launched his professional journalism career in 1922 when he became an editorial writer for the *Baltimore Sun*. Three years later he was offered an assignment in China that afforded him an opportunity to travel in Asia. Some time after his return to Baltimore he decided that he wanted "a truly international listening post." He went to Geneva on a Guggenheim Fellowship to write a thorough study of the League of Nations, which was published in 1932 by The Brookings Institution (which also gave him a Ph.D.) as *The Society of Nations: Its Organization and Constitutional Development*. The following year he was offered the editorship of the *Washington Post* by Eugene Meyer, who had bought it with the intention of elevating it from a local city newspaper to one of national significance. This perfectly suited Morley's own editorial policy, which was "to make the paper something of an American version of the famous Manchester *Guardian*. That is to say, its outlook should be international; its philosophy independent and liberal in the classical sense of the word; its foreign correspondence informative and impartial; its editorials well reasoned, well written and forceful; its adherence to strictly Constitutional government unquestionable."[2] In 1936 he was awarded the Pulitzer for his editorial writing. No admirer of Roosevelt or the New Deal, which he considered disastrous in its consequences for the liberty of Americans, he adhered to a hierarchy of loyalties that would probably seem quaint to most contemporary editors: "Supreme loyalty, of course, was to his God and to the Christian tradition under which he had been reared. Next to that and generally in accordance came his country, meaning not the President nor any part of officialdom but the ideas and ideals that had been so clearly written into the Constitution."[3] Adherence to the Constitution would be one of his lifelong concerns.

Early in 1940 he was offered the presidency of Haverford College, and although he was reluctant to leave the *Washington Post* at a time when it looked as though the United States would be drawn into World War II, he decided to accept the offer. However, given his commitment to the good of his country, this hardly represented a withdrawal into private life. Since he had been born and reared in the Quaker tradition Morley most likely had a predisposition toward a more pacifist, isolationist foreign policy, but his reasons for opposition to war in general seemed to be rooted primarily in a concern for war's harmful effects on American freedom rather than in purely pacifist principles, and he did not think that the United States could accomplish anything constructive by entering yet another European war (after the "hideous blunder" of World War I). However, despite his non-interventionist position and the pacifist views at the college, after Pearl Harbor Morley realized that "Haverford could not successfully oppose the authoritarian pressures which protracted hostilities foreshadowed" but must cooperate "in what would undoubtedly be a totalitarian effort,"[4] and he pursued policies and established programs that enabled the College to survive the inevitable drop in enrollment and made the College's contribution to the war effort "as constructive as possible."

By the end of 1943 he had put Haverford College on a sound financial footing and was considering other options. Although he remained as president for two more years, he also joined with Frank Hanighen and William Henry Chamberlin in the launching of the (initially) weekly journal *Human Events* early in 1944, with Morley providing editorial supervision and a third of the analytical essays, and leaving everything else in the hands of Hanighen. The name *Human Events* was taken from the opening sentence of the *Declaration of Independence* "which asserts that it was proper for the American people 'to assume among the powers of the earth' a 'separate and equal station,'"[5] and reflected Morley's admitted greater interest in human events than in human beings. He wrote later that his ambition was that *Human Events* should serve as "a vehicle to help restore the vitality of American political thinking" and to promote a durable peace.

In his prospectus for *Human Events*, dated January 1, 1944, Morley informed potential subscribers that the publication would "examine and interpret those international developments which, while wholly beyond the control of our own electorate, are nevertheless holding the future of this Republic and of all its citizens."[6] The two catastrophic

World Wars had, he believed, "distort[ed] and impoverish[ed] our national life" without creating an effective world community and had also created the twin dangers of tyranny, "a domestic counterpart of National Socialism," through the substantial growth of government power that diminished both individual freedom and the vitality of local government, and a trend toward military alliances that would reduce America's independence and freedom of action as a nation. He feared the development of American imperialism, something he considered incompatible with the country's federal system of government, and thought that the only isolationism to be truly concerned about was "the increasing disregard of that political philosophy which prompted the establishment and insured the development of this Nation." Looking ahead to the postwar world, Morley believed that *Human Events* would help to fill the need for careful thought about America's place in the world and the ways in which it could exercise moral leadership, but, above all, for "rededication to our own neglected creed." He did not, of course, believe that all of the danger to the American heritage came from outside, for he saw most of it coming from within the country. The analysis of this insidious internal threat later became the subject of two of his books, *Freedom and Federalism* and *The Power in the People.*

Morley was to remain with *Human Events* for the next six years, until he and Hanighen disagreed at the beginning of the Cold War about the policy toward the Soviet Union. Although Morley and Hanighen had opposed the wartime alliance with the Soviet Union because of its avowed interest in destroying free enterprise, after the establishment of Soviet hegemony in Central Europe Morley came to the conclusion that the United States had to accept the situation and seek a *modus vivendi* with the Communists. But, according to Morley, Hanighen "believed that it would be both justifiable and profitable to swing Human Events into a clearly anti-Soviet orbit, even though this meant more 'entangling alliances,' militarization, and centralization of government, which we had heretofore opposed." This disagreement Morley saw as "the first premonitory break in what had been a united and fundamentally isolationist Conservative front," a break that leaned toward "National Socialism" and moved "away from the restoration of the balanced Federal Republic to which we both aspired."[7] Unable to resolve this policy disagreement with Hanighen Morley terminated his connection with *Human Events* in early 1950.

At this mid-century point the modern Conservative movement was just beginning to awaken as a response to the dramatic change in the concentration of power in Washington through the New Deal and the necessities of waging a world war. Morley was one of the early figures in this movement that would, through much debate, disagreement, and struggle, eventually lead to the unsuccessful Goldwater campaign and the later and successful Reagan presidential campaign. *The Power in the People* which was begun in the mid-forties, around the time of the publication of Hayek's *The Road to Serfdom,* appeared in 1949. The second of his books that grew out of the central concern of his life's work, resistance to the steady undermining of freedom since the founding of the Republic, and that he considered his "major contribution to American political thought," *Freedom and Federalism,* appeared in 1959, some twenty-two years after he began to work on it. No admirer of Roosevelt's New Deal, he had reluctantly voted for FDR in 1936, but he began to collect the material for *Freedom and Federalism* on March 9, 1937 after listening to the "fireside chat" in which Roosevelt defended his proposal to pack the Supreme Court with six new appointees who would presumably be more compliant to his legislative plans that were, Roosevelt said, intended only "to make democracy succeed." To Morley the syllables of the word "democracy" were like a palimpsest that barely concealed the underlying text of dictatorship.

The belief that democracy is the harbinger of dictatorship was, of course, scarcely original with Morley. The ancient Athenians, proud pioneers in direct democracy, were so concerned about the danger of return to rule by an ambitious *tyrannos* that they instituted the practice of ostracism to banish any man too power-hungry for democracy. Many of their political practices, such as short terms of office and the prohibition of the same man holding an office for successive terms, were designed to limit any one person's ability to accumulate power. Plato's critique of democracy and its tendency to degenerate into despotism in his *Republic* is well known. That it was the Athenian democracy that had executed Socrates was only the beginning of Plato's reasons for detesting it. Democracy's love of excessive freedom and equality, rooted in envy, meant that the substance of order and good could never be more than an unstable balance of competing irrational desires. Furthermore, Plato would surely have agreed with the terse formulation of the revolutionary Shigalyov, in Dostoevsky's *Demons,* that "starting from unlimited freedom, I conclude with unlimited despotism." Within the soul unlimited freedom means that the most depraved and power-hungry appetites are free to enslave the rest and in the polis the appetites of the citizens, unmoored from the guidance of reason, are willing to surrender themselves to anyone or anything that promises easy gratification. For this reason Plato considered democracy only slightly less corrupted than despotism because of its complete lack of self-mastery.

The context of Morley's own argument against democracy is, however, modern political philosophy, and particularly the philosophy of Jean-Jacques Rousseau. Much of his critique of democracy in *Freedom and Federalism* uses Rousseau's concept of the General Will, which one commentator calls his *"bête noire,"*[8] to analyze the corrupting effects of democracy, and *The Power in the People* also discusses the theories of Hobbes and Locke. Morley argues that Locke clarified the "vital distinction between Society and State that Hobbes had so completely missed"[9] because Hobbes assumed that human beings are entirely incapable of exercising self-control. In order to survive the chaos created by the anarchic passions Hobbes believed that human beings must subordinate or enslave themselves to an Absolute Sovereign who is not reason but an absolute and arbitrary will ruling the violent and egocentric passions by the force of terror. According to Hobbes the only way in which human beings can live together in some semblance of peace is by conferring

> all their power and strength upon one man, or upon one assembly of men, that may reduce all their wills, by plurality of voices, unto one will: which is as much as to say, to appoint one man, or assembly of men, to bear their person; and every one to own and acknowledge himself to be the author of whatsoever he that so beareth their person shall act, or cause to be acted, in those things which concern the common peace and safety; and therein to submit their wills, every one to his will, and their judgements to his judgement. This is more than consent, or concord; it is a real unity of them all in one and the same person, made by covenant of every man with every man, in such manner as if every man should say to every man: *I authorize and give up any right of governing myself to this man, or to this assembly of men, on this condition; that thou give up thy right to him, and authorise all his actions in like manner* (II, 17).

This insistence that human beings, mastered by their passions, are so incapable of living together in order that they must be completely subordinated to the one will of the Sovereign, which purports to be their will, is the crucial difference between Hobbes and Locke, for Locke believed that both within and outside society individuals are in fact capable of self-government, of choosing to conform themselves to the natural law. Therefore he could advocate a minimal government whose sole function was protecting the vast majority of law-abiding citizens from foreign invasion and from the predations of the minority in society who were not self-governing. Morley recognized the considerable Lockean influence on American political thought, including the distinction between society and state, along with the political effects of the Puritan Revolution and the Glorious Revolution of 1688 in England, as well as other arguments proposed to justify the emphasis on individual freedom over the "divine right" of kings. Unlike Hobbes, Locke assumes that in the social contract individuals do not hand over or abdicate responsibility for self-government. Without the self-government that Hobbes considered impossible, chaos and absolute sovereignty are the only options; a democracy would inevitably collapse into chaos. For Hobbes anarchy is chaos, but for Locke it is an essentially orderly life in the mostly peaceful state of nature.

While Morley recognized the significance of Hobbes and Locke for American political thought, he was more interested in tracing the growth of government and the decline of freedom to what he saw as the subversive influence of Rousseau's concept of the General Will, which appears in his *Social Contract* where he explains "the problem" as that of finding "a form of association which will defend and protect with the whole common force the person and goods of each associate, and in which each, while uniting himself with all, may still obey himself alone, and remain as free as before." This is clearly derived from Hobbes' notion of the surrender of individual wills to the Sovereign but there has been a shift of focus from self-government to the useful fiction of obeying oneself as the basis of freedom. Rousseau's General Will is in many ways equivalent to the will of Hobbes' Absolute Sovereign in that it is absolute and sovereign and that which infallibly determines the common good, yet it attempts to combine subordination with freedom and self-government, since in theory each citizen obeys only himself, even though he is not acting for his private interest. Just as for Hobbes the acts of the Sovereign are by definition the acts of the citizens, so for Rousseau, who also did not distinguish between society and state, the General Will is the true will of the citizens, so that "whoever refuses to obey the General Will shall be compelled to do so by the whole body. This means nothing less than that he will be forced to be free," that is, forced to obey himself by following the General Will which alone can direct the State to the common good. It directs the absolute power of the body politic over each of its members even as it "binds or favors all the citizens equally." Furthermore, although the General Will is always right the people themselves do not always know what it is that they will, which necessitates a public authority to discern it accurately. Such an authority, given the power to interpret an infallible but mysterious will, would have to be a dictator.[10] It is Morley's argument that modern democracy is an outgrowth of the insidious notion of the General Will, which denies the central importance for freedom of individual self-government.

It should be noted that in his *Discourse on the Origin of Inequality* Rousseau assumed that although human nature in its natural state is benign and therefore does not need self-government, it is easily corrupted by property, by the claim of a particular will to something as "mine." At the beginning of *The Social Contract* Rousseau famously states that "man is born free; and everywhere he is in chains. One thinks himself the master of others, and still remains a greater slave than they. How did this change come about? I do not know. What can make it legitimate? That question I think I can answer." The chains are the restraints of society into which we have fallen from the Arcadian state of nature. It is the General Will that legitimates the chains of society and the State because the General Will enables the individual citizen to enjoy the freedom of autonomy by blindly obeying the State.

What does all of this mean to Morley? He begins, in *Freedom and Federalism*, with the tension between order and freedom, a tension that exists because human beings are not entirely good. The promise of the General Will is that in the collective human beings are infallibly good, because they obey themselves as they are in their true nature.

The political drawback of the "mystical" infallible General Will is that it necessarily involves tyranny, and Morley traces the sorry history of such dictatorial governments from the Jacobins in the French Revolution to the Communist states of the twentieth century. Therefore, the General Will, which represents the ideal of self-government in the form of the "omnipotent government," the State, is, Morley says, "in theory thoroughly democratic" but also "fundamentally, and in practice ruthlessly, opposed to that faith in the potential of the individual on which the government of the United States is founded."[11] The theoretical recognition of the individual fails to translate into a respect for individual personality and rights. Instead, everyone is absorbed into the state collective.

Morley concluded that the American form of government was, in fact, designed to be a "living refutation" of the General Will.[12] It was certainly founded on some different assumptions, namely, that human nature is not entirely good, that human beings are, however, capable of self-government, and that human flourishing requires the maximum amount of freedom in society's arena of voluntary association, balanced with the minimum necessary amount of order imposed by the coercive power of the State. The Founding Fathers, who were well acquainted with ancient history, as well as with human nature, very deliberately did not design the United States government to be a democracy. As Morley observes, the Constitution "sets up roadblocks calculated to frustrate the will of the majority."[13] While they were sufficiently impressed by the irrational tendencies of human beings for Hamilton to declare that a mob in which every individual was a Socrates would still be a mob, they also believed in the human capacity for self-government, given sufficient motivation and education in virtue. The Framers wanted a strong enough national government to protect and preserve the country but a weak enough government to allow for the greatest possible freedom for states, localities, and individuals. Power was divided in every possible way and the federal government was intended to be small and relatively remote from the lives of the citizens, compared to state and local governments, in order to ensure the maximum amount of freedom for all and to respect the rights of individuals and minorities. In *The Federalist Papers* Madison warned against the dangers of "faction," by which he meant any group, including the majority, which sought to promote its own interests at the expense of the common good. Accordingly, Morley analyzes in detail the structure of the government that was set up, with a particular emphasis on its federal character since one of the major components of the checks- and-balances system is the tension between states and central government.

However, Morley saw that it did not take long for the modern trend toward democracy, rooted in great part in Rousseau, to begin to exert its effects through the emphasis on equality. There were, for example, American admirers of the Jacobins in the French Revolution, and the Republican Party of Jefferson took its name from the defenders of the French Republic. By the 1830s Alexis de Tocqueville had no difficulty in discerning the beginnings of a trend toward democratic dictatorship in America, because of the excessive regard for the majority opinion, which was assuming virtual omnipotence, an "ever increasing despotism of the majority," unlimited power being "in itself a bad and dangerous thing." In Tocqueville's opinion, "the main evil of the present democratic institutions of the United States does not arise, as is often asserted in Europe, from their weakness, but from their irresistible strength. I am not so much alarmed at the excessive liberty which reigns in that country as at the inadequate securities which one finds there against tyranny."[14]

The kind of despotism that Tocqueville foresaw developing in a democratic nation would, he thought, probably be more extensive and milder than that of the Roman Empire and "would degrade men without tormenting them." His description of the "immense and tutelary power" that would paternalistically control people's lives in such a despotism bears an uncanny resemblance to Dostoevsky's Grand Inquisitor's happy society in which human beings are reduced to the status of children whose main responsibility is to rejoice, while, in Tocqueville's words, the government willingly labors "to spare them all the care of thinking and all the trouble of living."[15]

Morley recounts the story of the beginning of the United States in *Freedom and Federalism,* and then focuses on the Fourteenth and Sixteenth Amendments as subtly but significantly undermining the federal structure of the government to control the states and the citizens. Morley observes in this the replacement of American federalism with Rousseau's General Will, with Thaddeus Stevens, whom Morley characterizes as "a personification of the General Will,"[16] playing a significant role in undermining federalism during Reconstruction, a process that would accelerate steadily in the twentieth century through Wilson's progressivism and FDR's New Deal and that puts the American political psyche at odds with itself. Although the American political system "is clearly and positively anti-socialist," nonetheless the germs of socialism have been incubating in American society to the point where the population is now almost evenly split in some polls on the fundamental question of the type of society America should be.

It was with the covert growth of totalitarianism in America in his own time, despite the original constitutional dispersal of power in the federal system of government, that Morley was most concerned. He saw the Fourteenth Amendment as a dangerous revision of the Fifth, because while the latter states that no person shall "be deprived of life, liberty, or property, without due process of law," the Fourteenth Amendment modifies this to say "nor shall any State deprive any person of life, liberty, or property, without due process of law." This effectively casts the federal government as the defender of the citizens against the state governments, thereby disrupting the division of power in the original Constitution. Also, the Sixteenth Amendment increases the concentration of power in the federal government over the citizens by granting it the power to tax the incomes of the citizens. Morley believed that these amendments compelled the Supreme Court to offer Constitutional interpretations that contained elements of "totalitarian democracy," which then had to be absorbed and confined within bounds generally consistent with original content."[17]

Another of the historical factors hostile to federalism, in Morley's analysis, has been war, because the successful prosecution of a war requires the concentration of power. This began with the War of 1812 and then increased substantially with the Civil War and the wars of the twentieth century, with each major war increasing the national power and reducing the federal principle. War also requires higher taxes for national defense, which "cut down the financial resources of the States and make it all but impossible for most people to provide for their own security. Then more centralized taxation is imposed to return to the States and people, under controls, a part of what has been taken from them!"[18] Morley believed that war and the extension of American power around the world served mainly to diminish the freedom of American citizens. He was critical of the Allies' "Unconditional Surrender" policy in World War II as lacking in good sense and as imposing on the victors the burden of administering postwar Germany, but primarily as undermining American liberty by requiring a kind of "unconditional surrender" of the citizens during wartime to their own government. "Complete subordination of the individual to the State is a heavy price to pay for victory in a society based on the principle that government is made for man, not man for government."[19]

As evidenced by his resignation from *Human Events*, Morley was also a critic of the Cold War. He regarded military response to the Soviet threat as yet another prolongation and extension of centralized government power as a way of keeping the economy stimulated and thought that the struggle against Communism should involve primarily "mind and spirit" rather than "conscripted bodies." In 1957 Morley published an essay "American Republic or American Empire" in which he defended the thesis that "we seem to have reached the stage, in our national evolution, where we have a vested interest in preparation for war" because "our economy apparently needs the constant stimulus of a threat of large-scale war."[20] Spending enormous sums on defense prevents depressions by constantly stimulating the economy. In fact, he believed that to cease preparation for war would have disastrous effects on the economy. Although the problems would eventually correct themselves, Morley believed that Americans lacked the patience for enduring even temporary economic setbacks. "They have been led to expect continuous prosperity and they would probably rebel if it came to a sudden, if only temporary, end."[21] This has created a fundamental contradiction in American political life between our federal, non-centralized institutions, and our "imperial," power-centralizing policies. In this case "democracy" seems to offer the solution that the people as a whole really want whatever the central planners choose, according to the General Will. However, while foreign policies, particularly those of powerful empires, often require subtleties and complexities, public opinion tends to be simplistic. So public opinion must be manipulated by an Orwellian use of language if America is to be a superpower (even though the Constitution was not designed for a superpower), because "world leadership requires centralization of power in the capital of the nation that seeks dominance." Somewhat pessimistically, Morley suggests the possibility that "the era of our Federal Republic is drawing to its close,"[22] which would unfortunately mean the end of our freedom. The irony that Morley sees is that the very freedom that enabled America's rise to world leadership is undermined by that rise.

The Power in the People, published four years before *Freedom and Federalism,* derives its title from William Penn, who wrote in 1676 that "... we lay a foundation for after ages to understand their liberty as men and Christians, that they may not be brought into bondage but by their own consent; for we put the power in the people...." In this book, which complements *Freedom and Federalism,* Morley focuses not on the division of power in the government but on the founding of American freedom in the conviction that the individual is fully capable of self-government, and therefore power must be dispersed as much as possible among the individual citizens who generate public order from the internal order of their own souls. As Morley put it, "the exercise of self-discipline is the very center and well-spring of the liberal creed." The power in the people is precisely that of self-government that minimizes the need for State power, and the self-government is necessarily under the authority of God. Indeed, the two are antithetical, for, as Benjamin Franklin observed, "Man will ultimately be governed by God or by tyrants."

Morley himself considered liberty "a human birthright" that was grounded in Christian belief and moral integrity, and he understood the dangers of the growth of tyranny in secularism and moral decay. He believed that there is a necessary moral and even spiritual dimension of free enterprise, as "service to the Creator," which means it is certainly not simply about greed. Liberty, which he often, but not always, distinguishes from freedom as having a more moral and spiritual meaning, is the political outgrowth of individual self-government. This self-government is so essential to the understanding of what America is that Morley considered social legislation a symptom of retrogression rather than progress because it means that the State is encroaching on self-government.

In a 1963 essay "Political Conditions for a Free Society" Morley elaborated on the specifically Christian foundation of political freedom. He thought that both Christ and St. Paul were the sources of an understanding of freedom as "an attainable political objective."[23] and that Paul's "complete conviction as to the divinity of Christ" meant that Christ's commands always override those of Caesar and therefore Christ bestows a liberty beyond the domain of the political, a liberty that is based on self-discipline, under Church guidance. "It may readily be argued that Christian belief is the *sine qua non* for political freedom when it is held with personal conviction and not as a mere colorless inheritance."[24]

One could also read Morley's thesis as an adaptation of Plato's argument that the degree of order in a political system derives from its presence in the souls of the citizens. Plato assumed that only a very small minority were capable of the self-government necessary for them to take part in public governance, but the founders of the American system of government believed that almost all human beings are capable, with the proper spiritual and moral education, of governing themselves, thus obviating the need for a strong political authority. With the rise of Rousseauian democracy and secularism, and the decline of both Christian self-discipline and of public understanding of how a truly free country is governed, the awareness of living under the authority of God has also significantly declined. The void of authority will be filled by the State which insidiously assumes more and more of the responsibilities that used to be a matter of personal maturity. The loss of this maturity is evident in the increasing susceptibility to demagoguery. As Morley notes in *The Power in the People*, "the ease with which the accomplished demagogue can practice deception is due not so much to the lure of his oratory as to the shocking lack of any critical faculty among the electorate," a lack that has obviously worsened in the sixty years since Morley wrote this. The result has been a public tolerance of increasing State power, and diminishing liberty, that has produced a situation that Morley considered "evil in itself," and an evil more serious in America than in other countries because "here this malignant growth has jeopardized the only political experiment that was ever consciously directed to the end of securing the blessings of liberty for the people as a whole." And the more power that is concentrated in the State the more "public service" attracts the most ambitious, power-hungry, and unscrupulous politicians (or the more the enormous power seduces politicians into becoming ambitious and unscrupulous).

Perhaps in 1949 Morley's warnings of developing totalitarianism would have seemed incredible to a people who had just defeated the Nazis and Fascists and were already in the throes of a Cold War with the Communists, yet another form of totalitarianism. It would have seemed impossible to most Americans that the United States was not simply inhabited or even infiltrated by a certain number of Communists but was in its very political psyche infected with the same plague. Morley understood that America was immersed in its own internal struggle between freedom and enslavement for the sake of security. It is arguable that this struggle has now reached a crisis point such that within the next few years the United States will either reanimate the spirit of liberty or will succumb to the relentless forces of demagoguery, dictatorship, and collectivism.

In the light of contemporary events much of Morley's critique of American politics seems prescient and illuminating. His isolationist foreign policy views seem more debatable, but this is probably because of the dilemma in which the United States has found itself for the past century. While in principle it would have been far better for the freedom of American citizens had the United States not been drawn into the World Wars of the twentieth century and not been compelled to lead the free world in the forty-year Cold War, these were in practice not viable options, particularly the Second World War and the Cold War. How could it have been in the interest of the United States to allow aggressive totalitarian ideologies to conquer and enslave the rest of the world? There could not be a *modus vivendi* with either Nazi Germany or the Soviet Union because they were evil and expansionist by nature. American isolationism would have left a power vacuum in the rest of the world that Communism would have rushed to fill. It was, unfortunately, events beyond America's shores and control that forced it to offer as much resistance as possible to evil. To the extent to which the growth of centralized government has been the consequence of war it has been the apparently unavoidable price that America has had to pay for protecting itself against totalitarian ideologies. Our current "war on terror" is a similarly unavoidable necessity of confronting and defending ourselves against an evil not of our making. It has, of course, increased the centralization of power in order to protect American soil against terrorists, but isolationism is not an option.

However, *The Power in the People* is a book about the vital importance and enormous difficulties of preserving freedom in a world in which liberty is easily undermined. It was Morley's passionate conviction that the price of freedom is indeed eternal vigilance, and that, for all its historic greatness, America has not been quite vigilant enough.

Michael Henry
St. John's University

Notes

1   This and other biographical information is taken from Morley's memoirs, *For the Record,* published in 1979 by Regnery/Gateway, Inc., in South Bend, Indiana. This provides a detailed account of his life and career up until the early 1950s.

2   Ibid., 271.

3   Ibid, 324.

4   Ibid., 353.

5   Felix Morley, "Conservatism Takes Shape: *Human Events,*" in *Conservatism in America Since 1930: A Reader*, ed. By Gregory L. Schneider (New York: New York University Press, 2003), 46-47.

6   Ibid., 45.

7   Felix Morley, review of *Fugitive Essays: Selected Writings of Frank Chodorov.* The review appeared originally in *Reason*, July 1981. The citation here is to its availability on the website http://www.cooperativeindividualism.org/morley-felix_on-frank-chodorov.html.

8   Joseph R. Stromberg, "Felix Morley: An Old-Fashioned Republican Critic of Statism and Interventionism," in Journal of Libertarian Studies, Vol. 2, No. 3, 275. Morley also discusses Rousseau's General Will in his essay "Individuality and the General Will" in *Essays on Individuality*, ed. By Felix Morley (Philadelphia: University of Pennsylvania Press, 1958), 82-102.

9   Felix Morley, *The Power in the People* (Los Angeles: Nash Publishing, 1949), 70.

10   A European contemporary of Morley, Aurel Kolnai, also discusses the political problem that democracy contains the seeds of the "totalitarian aberration" because the sovereignty of the people is too easily transformed into the "omnipotence of the National Will." From the anti-democratic side we find the fundamentally dictatorial idea of the General Will in the writings of the Nazi apologist Wilhelm Stapel, whom Kolnai quotes: "Opposition is tantamount to Treason. Opposition has no longer any moral justification.... The people do not know what they want: they have only instinct. But the Leader knows

what the people want: that is what makes him a Leader." Quoted in Aurel Kolnai, *The War Against the West* (New York, The Viking Press, 1938), 129 and 162.

11   Felix Morley, *Freedom and Federalism* (Indianapolis: Liberty Press, 1959), 33.

12   Ibid., 38.

13   Ibid., 18.

14   Alexis de Tocqueville, *Democracy in America* (New York: Alfred A. Knopf (Everyman's Library), 1994), Vol. I, 260.

15   Vol. II, 317-318.

16   *Freedom and Federalism,* 79.

17   Ibid., 99, 101.

18   Ibid., 143-144.

19   Quoted in Stromberg, 270.

20   Felix Morley, "American Republic or American Empire," in *Modern Age,* Summer 1957, 20.

21   Ibid., 23.

22   Ibid., 30-31.

23   Felix Morley, "Political Conditions for a Free Society," in *The Necessary Conditions for a Free Society,* ed. By Felix Morley (Princeton: D. Van Nostrand Company. Inc., 1963), 5.

24   Ibid., 6.

Foreword to the Third Edition

BY HERBERT HOOVER

This new edition of *The Power in the People* is reprinted without a single change of statement or emphasis from the original copy, as first put into type two years ago. That is good evidence of the enduring value of this book. Having been one who urged Dr. Morley to write I have some spiritual interest in it.

There is comfort for us all in a study of the American political tradition that stands up with such permanence during a period of growing anxiety and doubt. In the welter of topical publications in the political field, as poured from the presses since VJ Day, there are very few that have successfully resisted the test of time and the rapidly shifting crises. For this achievement something more than an appeal to current emotionalism is necessary.

Dr. Morley's original and stimulating examination of "the blessings of liberty" possesses qualities as vital as they are unusual. It has, as a primary asset, an ease and clarity of expression that has won unstinted praise from the reviewers.

The famous Literary Supplement of the *London Times* called *The Power in the People* a "beautifully written" book, performing an "invaluable service." That is in part due to the skillful compression by which the author confines the exposition of his thought to less than 300 pages. The manuscript, he tells me, was nearly twice as long in the original draft.

But there is much more than solicitude for the reader's time in this book. There is a scholarship no less profound because it is gracefully worn. There is a faith in the ideas and ideals of the American Republic that is not less eloquent because of the care with which the sources of our institutions are traced to their historical origins. This book is not ephemeral because the matters of which it treats are "not of an age, but for all time."

Historical background alone, however, would not have made *The Power in the People* what it is. The author has subordinated erudition to the journalistic skill that has won him respect in the newspaper and radio world as well as in academic surroundings. It is the facility with which the gifts of the reporter and the researcher are blended that gives this book distinction. Its unusual accomplishment is to reveal the deep significance of current events against the backdrop of a living and influential past.

Two years ago Dr. Morley advised us "to abandon the fond illusion that the better we understand Soviet Russia, the easier it will be to establish amicable relations between the two countries." He asserted that: "The effort to destroy Christianity has stimulated reconsideration of the truths for which Christ stood." He concluded that: "We shall never make the world safe for democracy. But we can keep and continuously strengthen the power in the people, here at home. Only thus will the light of this Republic continue to shine before mankind, as a beacon unique in history."

Reading *The Power in the People* again, two years after its publication, I am again impressed both by its insight and its foresight. Only a thorough student of American institutions could have anticipated current controversies so accurately; only a highly trained reporter could have clarified their significance so helpfully.

Dr. Morley reminds us that while our social and political institutions are all designed to promote diffusion of power, our latter-day policies are creating a rapidly increasing concentration of power. And I might add that modern wars inevitably result in concentration of power and a loss of power by the people.

It is not surprising that *The Power in the People* continues in demand, and that this new edition is called for two years after original publication. Whether or not it was so designed, this is a book that is destined for longevity.

I possibly do not agree with a small part of all it says. And some readers will disagree with passages that seem profoundly true to me. But time has already demonstrated that there is much in this study which withstands and outlasts all criticism. I do not believe that this new edition will be the last appearance of *The Power in the People.*

New York
January, 1951.

Preface

This book, written a quarter of a century ago, is now reprinted without change from the original edition.

That does not imply unusual prescience on the part of the author, nor any lack of contemporary value in the matters discussed herein. *The Power in the People* is concerned with the noble aspirations on which the United States were established. What is on record there is imperishable. But the story is now even more cogent than it was during the myopic period that followed the shattering close of World War II.

This new, though unrevised, edition appears as the country prepares to celebrate the bi-centennial of its independence. Much attention will then be paid to the enormous material progress which has developed a strip of undeveloped colonies into the most powerful of nation-states. It may be hoped that the question of our spiritual advancement will also receive consideration. Progress there is far more dubious.

For all our military might, and boastfulness, Americans feel neither happy nor secure today. The symptoms of this unease are too numerous to catalog, too obvious to specify. Combined they constitute a national case of schizophrenia, of split personality that tragically divides a great people, not only in handling but even in the defining of their problems.

We have in unprecedented measure personal, family, racial, sexual, sociological, economic, financial and international tensions. But underlying all this ferment is a fundamental political cleavage which no political party has as yet confronted squarely.

Our historic institutions were devised for a course of action which contemporary policies largely contradict.

Our Federal Republic was established on the then novel principle of separated and balanced powers. Both in the state and federal governments the executive, legislative and judicial controls were carefully divided from each other, as also in the relations of the local and central units. Today our policies, at home and abroad, insistently call for more and more concentration and centralization of power. Small wonder that from this clash, between the character of our institutions and the conduct of our affairs, comes schizophrenia!

When institutions and policies are in direct conflict, one or the other must give way. So far it is our institutions that have surrendered most. This is apparent in every band of the social and political spectrum—from the present plight of small, independent colleges to the difficulties of the Congress in endeavoring to terminate an undeclared, unpopular, unsuccessful executive war.

Above any detail, however, is the national restiveness among a people who realize that in some surreptitious way the power assured them by the Constitution has been usurped. They pay taxes, as never before, but the vital representation without which taxation is tyranny seems to be lost. Americans who were citizens have become subjects again, as was the case before 1776.

Republics are not noted for longevity. Two centuries is well beyond the average age of the many that have come and gone since the Romans failed. So at our scheduled bi-centennial, flag-waving and parades will not be enough. Much more is needed.

What is required from us to maintain our Republic is the theme of this book. A wider understanding of those requirements is more imperative now than when it was first printed.

FELIX MORLEY
GIBSON ISLAND, MARYLAND
AUGUST, 1972

Introduction

This Republic was not created by accident. The "New Order" proclaimed on the Great Seal of the United States did not come into effect automatically. It cannot be sustained automatically. Perpetuation of the American way depends upon general interest in the deeper aspects of what is an essentially co-operative enterprise.

While there are many admirable studies on the development, the institutions, and the political theory of our country, of late there have been surprisingly few attempts to examine the actual significance of this federal union in the long panorama of history. That is what this book seeks to do.

The thought that has been woven into the American pattern of life is not particularly abstruse. It has aspects of sublimity, but that which is sublime is not difficult to appreciate. Indifference is always the chief impediment to understanding. Always the best way to combat indifference is to arouse interest, which becomes vital and permanent if focused on underlying principles. But first these principles must be examined and identified.

Though familiarity does not necessarily breed contempt, it certainly tends to dull the edge of curiosity. So it is natural that foreign observers have long been more interested than Americans in analyzing the differences that distinguish our Republic from any other political experiment of this or earlier times. It has not, however, been the concern of foreigners to point out that if we fail to recognize and value our advantages for ourselves, they will tend to disappear. The more excellent the type of government, the more subject it is to deterioration. The perpetuation of this Republic can no longer be taken for granted by its citizens.

De Tocqueville, writing in 1832, admitted that "in America I saw more than America." And the same transcendent quality impressed itself on Bryce, who said in 1888 that his endeavor was to trace "what is peculiar" in America "to its fundamental ideas." As both these observers realized, the fundamental ideas of America are decisively different from those that have controlled in Europe.

Anyone who is really interested in the role of the United States in world history will probably familiarize himself with de Tocqueville's *Democracy in America* and with Bryce's *The American Commonwealth*. But neither of these enduring books, nor any contemporary study in the field of politics, is primarily directed to an examination of the thought whereby the United States has evolved to its present position of majesty. The current tendency of American political analysis is descriptive rather than speculative. This is deplorable for a people who owe so much to the political application of abstract ideas.

Since the days of de Tocqueville and Bryce, and especially since the debacle of European civilization, the necessity of examining the validity of American political philosophy, as such, has become increasingly apparent. The advance of Communism has brought "ideological warfare" into common parlance. But a war of ideas cannot be won on quicksands of intellectual confusion. Our verbal difficulties—with such key words as "liberty" and "democracy"—are illustrative of an appalling lack of certainty in the thought that words are designed to express.

Many of our blunders and much of our apprehension traces to this confusion. Its elimination requires a conscious and sustained effort to separate the basic from the superficial. There is no longer any need to defend the desirability of any honest endeavor to clarify and simplify. But to outline this objective is the easiest part of our undertaking.

A study in American political philosophy must necessarily chart its course between Scylla and Charybdis. On the one hand, the shallow shoreline of descriptive detail, no matter how interesting or illustrative, must be avoided. On the other hand, the exploration of deep water soon involves us in concealed hazards where the presumptuous pilot is the least reliable.

But we know that the passage is there and the spirit of adventure alone would call us to attempt its intricacies. The navigation of the fifteenth century was primitive and faulty; yet it discovered America. Now America is ready for rediscovery—by Americans. If the voyage charted by this book encourages more skillful navigators to more thorough exploration, it will have served its purpose.

The journey that we shall undertake may seem at times to wander a little, in time and space. If so, it is always with the objective of seeing more clearly what lies ahead. The American tradition cannot be carried forward without appreciation of whence it came, and how it grew. The tradition is strong because its roots run deep and wide. We shall try to trace them. We seek to know the soil that provides our sustenance.

The men who established this Republic thought continually of "posterity." The dream of building a Commonwealth more gracious than any which had gone before was ever in their minds, and was reflected in their acts. The constant aim, as one of them wrote, was to "lay a foundation for after ages to understand their liberty as men and Christians." For this purpose, said William Penn, "we put the power in the people."

To put the power in the people implies faith. It implies that the component individuals are, for the most part, already endowed with self-control. This Republic is grounded in the belief that the individual can govern himself. On the validity of that belief it will stand—or fall.

As our title implies, we seek to examine this dual power—that which the people possess as individuals and that which has been entrusted to them as citizens of this Republic. That endeavor is not the less desirable because, in this age of disintegration, it demands a continuous effort to integrate.

We seek to find whether there is really unity and meaning in the American way of life. We ask whether our generation, in its turn, is thoughtful for posterity, which in time will ask what we have done with the heritage provisionally entrusted to us.

The Power in the People

Chapter 1

The Purpose of the Republic

The many advantages of American citizenship are repeatedly and often stridently proclaimed. Yet the most fundamental of all these assets—the one that underlies and supports every right we possess or claim—is easily overlooked. This Republic is distinctive in history for one supreme reason. Its government assumes, and is designed to strengthen, a moral code of honorable individual conduct.

Phrases indicating the rich content of our political inheritance have lost much of their inner significance. "The American way of life" more often than not refers to material circumstance. So does "the American standard of living." A way of life and a standard of living are not matters of perquisites, but of conduct. The implications embrace the deepest thoughts, the finest emotions, the highest aspirations of which man in his capacity as citizen is capable. Indifference to these overtones of itself suggests a corruption of republican virtue.

The American contribution to human progress has been outstanding. And it all traces back to a successful blending of the individual desire for advancement with a practical system of representative government. In this political achievement we find the basis of the unrivaled productive accomplishment that is an important characteristic, but certainly not the central purpose, of this Republic. Only a relatively small number of Americans would assert that there are no spiritual values in our governmental system. But those who continuously endeavor to keep such values bright are scarcely more numerous. The majority, in all probability the great majority, of contemporary Americans are indifferent to their heritage.

This apathy toward the original American ideal is more serious than outright opposition, which may indeed helpfully stimulate revaluation. Indifference has no such redeeming feature. Its manifestation is a shallow discontent, which can be as pronounced in a spoiled nation as in a spoiled child. Having no objective, this discontent finds no satisfactory outlet. What the feverish quest for acquisition and diversion does accomplish is to dull those analytical and critical faculties that our system of government demands from its citizens. The result is an increasing separation of popular desire and constitutional purpose. Beyond a certain point the two will become irreconcilable. Americans of this generation are uneasily aware that they have reached the parting of the ways.

It is a matter of elementary common sense for us to be familiar with the plan of the political mansion that we inhabit. Remodeling and extensions are always in order. But modernization should be in harmony with the original design and must not press too heavily on the foundations that support the whole. We are life tenants; not owners. Others will dwell in the United States when we are gone. The Republic requires of its citizens not only a sense of responsibility for the future, but also some appreciation of the past. And though our governmental system makes us as free to abuse as we are to use, it does not follow that discrimination between use and abuse is unimportant.

To avoid the injury to structure that becomes destruction, a deeper and more general political understanding has become a national necessity. This does not involve laborious inquiry into the mechanical detail of government. It is enough to sense the beauty and symmetry of an inspiring design. True appreciation, however, does require some exploration in the difficult terrain of abstract ideas. For this type of thinking the vocational education of our schools and colleges gives all too little training. On the other hand, native intelligence, even without academic support, has from the outset shown itself quick to understand the purpose of the Republic.

II

Some national governments, like that of Russia, have either inherited or acquired unlimited power over their subjects. Other governments, like that of Great Britain, have developed so as to respond to the will of a parliamentary majority, no matter where that may lead. The American system does not fall into either of these classifications. It was designed to prevent usurpation of absolute power by any individual; by any group; or by the spokesmen of the people to whom, as a whole, so much was given.

The United States, correctly designated, is neither a dictatorship nor a complete political democracy, but a federal republic created to make it easier for every resident to advance himself, in the sense of moving from lower to higher standards. Clearly, such a system depends for its perpetuation on continuous and vital faith in the capacity of the individual for self-advancement. That faith, in turn, demands "the assurance that every man shall be protected in doing what he believes his duty against the influence of authority and majorities, custom and opinion." [1]

The authors of the Constitution had no uncertainty as to the nature of their handiwork. Clarifying the underlying political theory, James Madison wrote in *The Federalist* (No. 39):

> It is evident that no other form [than the "strictly republican"] would be reconcilable with the genius of the people of America; with the fundamental principles of the Revolution; or with that honorable determination which animates every votary of freedom, to rest all our political experiments on the capacity of mankind for self-government.

From the very beginning of our history as a nation, thoughtful men have recognized that the permanence of the Republic—admittedly a "political experiment"—would be determined by this capacity of the individual to govern, or control, himself. The founders could do no more than embody a political philosophy

---

[1] Lord Acton, Essay on *The History of Freedom in Antiquity.*

in an organic law, then start the Republic on its way. They could not determine the character of the posterity that would take over.

The word "republic," however, is one of many political terms that we must learn to use more precisely, if there is to be any meeting of minds on the ideas that such words were designed to convey. Long before the autocrats of the present Russian regime described the Soviet Union as a federation of republics, Madison had commented on "the extreme inaccuracy with which the term has been used in political disquisitions." So, in the issue of *The Federalist* quoted above, "the master-builder of the Constitution" reasoned that a republic has:

> . . . a government which derives all its powers directly or indirectly from the great body of the people, and is administered by persons holding their offices during pleasure, for a limited period, or during good behaviour. It is *essential* to such a government that it be derived from the great body of the Society, not from an inconsiderable proportion, or a favored class of it . . . It is *sufficient* for such a government that the persons administering it be appointed, either directly or indirectly, by the people; and that they hold their appointments by either of the tenures just specified . . .

A republic, therefore, must have a truly representative government. If the fact were not so frequently ignored, it would seem superfluous to point out that the success of all representative government necessarily depends on the quality of the active electorate. When the machinery of selection is honestly operated, by the action of competitive political parties, the elected officers will almost automatically be representative of those who choose them, and the appointed officials not much less so. It follows that representative government, as distinct from that of a dictatorship, is very unlikely to demonstrate qualities, for good or evil, which are not influential among the majority of the active electorate.

This reasoning, rather than any demonstrable desire to protect class privileges, supported the early constitutional limitations on the franchise and explains the American decision to restrain the democratic tendency in representative government. As its name continues to remind us, only the House of Representatives was at the outset made directly representative of the people. Until ratification of the Seventeenth Amendment, in 1913, the Senate was chosen by indirect election, as still holds for the President and Vice-President—the Senate by the state legislatures, and the chief executive and his deputy by the Electoral College.

We know, from the detailed reports kept by Madison of the debates in the Federal Convention, that there was then no resolute opposition to popular election of what was called "the first branch of the National Legislature." On the other hand, few of the delegates believed that it would be safe to have the second chamber thus chosen. The prevailing opinion was voiced by Edmund Randolph of Virginia when he observed, during the first week of the proceedings in Philadelphia, that "the general object" of the convention that wrote the Constitution was:

> . . . to provide a cure for the evils under which the United States labored; that in tracing these evils to their origin, every man had found it in the turbulence and follies of democracy; that some check therefore was to be sought for, against this tendency of our [state] governments; and that a good Senate seemed most likely to answer the purpose.[2]

III

In a notable speech to the convention, the following week, Madison summarized his idea of the developing purpose of the American political system. According to his own report, he "considered an election of one branch, at least, of the Legislature by the people immediately, as a clear principle of free government." But among the objectives of the system in formulation was "the necessity of providing more effectually for the security of private rights, and the steady dispensation of justice." The new "national government" must on the one hand be able to sustain "republican liberty" against "the abuses of it practiced in some of the states." On the other hand, this new government must be strong enough to preserve "the rights of the minority," continuously jeopardized "in all cases where a majority are united by a common interest or passion."

[2] Madison *Debates*, May 31, 1787.

This last observation rephrases Plato's classic warning that unrestricted democracy must degenerate into dictatorship, and incidentally anticipates the manner in which Hitler was later to accomplish the transition in Germany, through the agency of a single disciplined and fanatical party. Because of the perpetual difficulty in reconciling majority and minority rights, Madison argued that there is only one defense "against the inconveniences of democracy, consistent with the democratic form of government." That is "to frame a republican system on such a scale, and in such a form, as will control all the evils which have been experienced." [3]

Madison chose his words with an accuracy and delicacy in which modern political discussion is shockingly deficient. An elastic federal republic, democratic in form but carefully safeguarded against the "inconveniences" of democracy, was what he sought, and what actually was established for the United States. Only the Pennsylvania delegation, under the leadership of James Wilson, finally voted for the direct election of Senators. Only the New Jersey delegation—with Maryland divided—finally voted against election "by the people" of what therefore properly came to be called the House of Representatives.

While clearly antagonistic to unbridled democracy, the contemporaneously secret debates of the Philadelphia Convention also reveal complete confidence in the common sense and practical wisdom of the American people as then constituted. "These are," exclaimed Charles Pinckney of South Carolina, "as active, intelligent and susceptible of good government as any people in the world." The necessary political action was to "suit our Government to the people it is to direct." This in turn demanded adherence to and trust in the representative principle. Every political system, said Pinckney, "must be suited to the habits and genius of the people it is to govern, and must grow out of them." Then, as to objective, using Milton's fine phrase about "the blessings of liberty," Pinckney contended:

[3] *Ibid.*, June 6, 1787.

Our true situation appears to me to be this,—a new extensive country, containing within itself the materials for forming a government capable of extending to its citizens all the blessings of civil and religious liberty,—capable of making them happy at home. This is the great end of republican establishments. We mistake the object of our Government, if we hope or wish that it is to make us respectable abroad. Conquest or superiority among other Powers is not, or ought not ever to be, the object of republican systems. If they are sufficiently active and energetic to rescue us from contempt, and preserve our domestic happiness and security, it is all we can expect from them,—it is more than almost any other government ensures to its citizens.[4]

The representative system, which John Stuart Mill later called "the ideal type of a perfect government," was therefore chosen for the United States, with due realization that:

Every kind and degree of evil of which mankind are susceptible, may be inflicted on them by their government; and none of the good which social existence is capable of, can be any further realized than as the constitution of the government is compatible with, and allows scope for, its attainment.[5]

The meticulous care that was taken to control the government of the Republic, by checks and balance and division of powers, is common knowledge. But what seems to have been forgotten, and should therefore be emphasized, is the part that a distinctive philosophy played in the design of this complicated political machinery. Underlying the whole plan, in Madison's memorable words, is "that honorable determination . . . to rest all our political experiments on the capacity of mankind for self-government." Of recent years it has been increasingly assumed that Americans are no longer capable of governing themselves. In view of conditions that have everywhere followed the destruction of self-government, a restoration of this faith would seem to be not only honorable, but actually essential for survival.

[4] *Ibid.*, June 25, 1787.
[5] *Representative Government*, Ch. 2.

IV

If people do not possess the capacity to govern themselves, they are, inevitably, governed by others. The same is true of a people who have had that capacity, and lost it. The only possible alternative to self-government is external government.

But domestic discords tend to multiply if a political system designed to encourage people to govern themselves is increasingly distorted in order to subject them to remote administrative dictation. A century ago conflicting interpretations of the Constitution were shaping up toward a civil war. Although continuing conflicts of interpretation may be expected, they will be confined within reasonable bounds if there is more general effort to understand and clarify the purpose of the Republic.

There are only three ways in which an enduring discord between government and governed can be resolved: (1) a fundamental change in the form of government; (2) a positive affirmation of the principles underlying the original form; or (3) a modification of the original form in the direction of popular desire. The last, or compromise, method is the one that has been practised under our representative system, as evidenced by the immortality of Mr. Dooley's conclusion that "the Supreme Court follows the election returns."

Political reformers, however, are often curiously unaware of the fact that their efforts, in the aggregate, do literally reform the governmental system. So, when constitutional change is not accompanied by public awareness of its implications, the seeming modification of original purpose actually operates to bring an unrecognized change of political form. Although this metamorphosis may temporarily go unnoticed, its very insidiousness will serve to sharpen the eventual issue: Is the Republic approaching the end of its life span, or can we reanimate and restore the political philosophy from which its original vitality was derived?

Not every American will as yet admit that the issue is upon us in this stark form. Some are of the opinion that domestic discord is serious only when business is stagnant. It should be added that a political system leaves much to be desired if it operates smoothly only in periods of material prosperity. Others argue that if the men whom we elect and appoint to high office were "statesmen" rather than "politicians," the business of government would be well conducted and discord would be reduced. But this is to confuse cause and effect and to ignore the very nature of representative government, which naturally conforms to the prevailing morality of the electorate. Any lack of integrity in American political leadership traces directly to apathy, or worse, in American public opinion and in the agencies that inform it. To maintain otherwise is in effect to repudiate the representative theory and to approve the bitter verdict of Alexander Pope:

> For forms of government let fools contest;
> Whate'er is best administer'd is best.

It is, therefore, important to realize, and to confront, the disagreeable fact that many keen political thinkers have from the beginning been pessimistic about the permanence of the American form of government. Benjamin Franklin, in moving the signing of the Constitution, at the close of the historic Philadelphia Convention, asserted almost in Pope's words that "there is no form of government but what may be a blessing to the people if well administered," and went on to predict that the federal union "is likely to be well administered for a course of years and can only end in despotism, as other forms have done before it, when the people shall become so corrupt as to need despotic government, being incapable of any other." [6] This ominous anticipation confirms the conclusion to which one is forced by theoretical reasoning. Either popular faith in the republican form of government must be recovered, or that form will continue to be changed until it no longer has any vital relationship with that laid down for posterity in 1787.

A certain inflexibility is inherent in the government of any nation controlled by a written constitution, even though that adopted for the United States has demonstrated elasticity that bears tribute alike to the genius of its authors and to the political capacity of the generations which have operated the inherited

[6] Madison, *op. cit.*, September 17, 1787.

mechanism. There is, however, a limit to intelligent adaptation and there is reason to think that we have already reached, or exceeded, that limit. In consequence, it has become an imperative duty of citizenship carefully to review the reasons why faith in the original purpose of our political system is still justified.

When this is done, objectively and comprehensively, it will be found that there is strong argument for sustaining, as opposed to destroying, the original design of the Republic. Increased social discord is not attributable to the principles that underlie our system of government. On the contrary, subversive activity has made headway primarily because of general failure to understand, appreciate, and observe those principles—as valid today as they were in the eighteenth century; as valid now as they have always been and ever will be.

V

Political form, a subject that necessarily engrossed the framers of the Constitution, receives close attention from Oswald Spengler in his opinionated but nevertheless extraordinarily prescient study on *The Decline of the West*. For a people, as for an athlete, this German philosopher maintained, the matter of form is all important. "The form abstracted from the life-stream of a people is the condition of that people with respect to its wrestle in and with history." [7] Thus Spengler, writing at the close of World War I, paraphrased the remark of Charles Pinckney, already quoted, at the Philadelphia Convention of 1787: "a system must be suited to the habits and genius of the people it is to govern, and must grow out of them."

But the contrasting use of the words "form" (*Gestalt*) and "system" is to be noted. To the eighteenth century American lawyer, assisting at the birth of a nation, the important matter was to adapt governmental procedures to the nature of the gov-

[7] *Op. cit.*, Vol. II, Ch. XI. The reasoning derives from de Montesquieu, who asserted (*The Spirit of Laws*, Book I, Ch. III) that a nation's laws "should be so appropriate to the people for whom they are made, that it would be very exceptional if those of one nation prove suitable for another."

erned, emphasizing representation as the device whereby a changing public opinion would be allowed to modify, but not destroy, the political system as established. To the twentieth century German scholar, gloomily anticipating the collapse of European civilization, procedural system was far less important than underlying form:

> No real constitution, when taken by itself and brought down to paper as a system, is complete. The unwritten, the indescribable, the usual, the felt, the self-evident, so outweigh everything else that— though theorists never see it—the description of a State or its constitutional archives cannot give us even the silhouette of that which underlies the living actuality of a State as its essential form; an existence-unit of history is spoilt when we seriously subject its movement to the constraint of a written constitution.[8]

Though Spengler was no Nazi, and indeed relied on the preservation of German cultural form to avert the rise of what he called Caesarism,[9] the above excerpt indicates why his work was useful to Hitler. For National Socialism to triumph in Germany, it was necessary to shatter the "constraint" of the Weimar Constitution. Spengler had dignified this course in advance, by saying that the organic law of the German Republic failed even to reflect "the living actuality" of Germany.

As Spengler assisted Hitler, so Hegel (1770-1831) had paved the way for Spengler. It was Hegel's mystical conception of the State "as the divine upon earth" that led to Spengler's disastrous conclusion that "a people is *as* State" and to his assertion that "World-history is, and always will be, State-history." Nevertheless Spengler ungrudgingly admitted one instance in which the political State was for a long time subordinated to the cultural Estate. "In England," he observed, "the Declaration of Rights [1689] in reality put an end to the State. . . . On the other hand,

[8] *Ibid.*

[9] "By the term 'Caesarism' I mean that kind of government which, irrespective of any constitutional formulation that it may have, is in its inward self a return to thorough formlessness." Spengler quotes Caesar's own assertion when he crossed the Rubicon: "*Nihil esse rem publicam, appelationem modo sine corpore ac specie.*" (It is nothing to be a republic, a term now without substance or distinction.)

the word 'Society' established itself as the expression of the fact
that the nation was 'in form' under the Class- and not under the
State-regime." [10]

Consideration of the nature of the State, and its relationship to
Society, will be a very important part of our study. But at the
moment it is sufficient to point out that for the American people
a part of what Spengler calls "form" is preservation of their
unique political system. And it must be realized that this system
stands out in history not because of its mechanical features, but
fundamentally because the Constitution codified the thinking of a
Society which was in general opposed to artificial privilege or monopoly of any kind, especially those that the State seeks to sanctify.
That opposition continues resolute, as we shall see, because it is
grounded in eternal verities of a religious nature.

The founders certainly believed, and frequently asserted, that
the primary purpose of government is to secure private property.
Gouverneur Morris, of Pennsylvania, told the convention that
"property was the main object of Society." He argued that: "The
savage state was more favorable to liberty than the civilized . . .
it was only renounced for the sake of property which could only
be secured by the restraints of regular government." [11] But the
general intent to make the new nation republican and classless,
and to insure that the acquisition of property would be open to
the individual industry of all, was shown in many ways. We
recall at this point the provision in Article I of the Constitution
that: "No Title of Nobility shall be granted by the United States,"
and the corollary, in the First Amendment, that: "Congress shall
make no law respecting an establishment of religion." The American people simply did not want to be directed by Lords Spiritual
and Lords Temporal. They would build their nation on religious
conviction, out of sovereign States, but they would not subject
their Society to sovereign Estates.

Thus, in a manner that many Europeans have found it difficult
to understand, the *system* of the American Constitution emanated
from, became a part of, and remains interwoven with, the *"form"*

[10] *Ibid.*
[11] Madison, *op. cit.*, July 5, 1787.

of the American people. The popular reverence for this organic law has puzzled foreign observers, and a customary explanation abroad is that Americans are more legalistic than other peoples. As good a case could be made for the argument that Americans are less law-abiding than most. What may seem at first glance to be a formalistic attitude is more often than not an individual expression of adherence to the original republican purpose. A part of that purpose was to strengthen national form by constitutional law, and simultaneously to adapt the organic law to pre-established national form.

VI

Since the two are interwoven, the American *system* of government cannot be profoundly modified without destroying the traditional *form* of the American people. Conversely, if popular form deteriorates, as a result of such factors as alien influences, internal corruption, or imperialistic expansion, it will become impossible to maintain more than the shell, if that, of constitutional government.

Luxurious living and manifestations of imperial power may easily coincide with a fatal inner decay, as is realized by all who have considered the decline and fall of the Roman Republic. Nor is the story of Rome in any way exceptional. After examining all the recorded instances in which the expansion of governmental undertakings immediately preceded internal collapse, Arnold Toynbee reaches a general conclusion which should be sobering to those who think that no objective is any longer too grandiose for centralized planning:

> Whatever the human faculty, or the sphere of its exercise, may be, the presumption that because a faculty has proved equal to the accomplishment of a limited task within its proper field it may therefore be counted upon to produce some inordinate effect in a different set of circumstances is never anything but an intellectual and a moral aberration and never leads to anything but certain disaster.[12]

[12] *A Study of History*, Vol. IV, p. 504.

The outstanding faculty of the American people, as individuals, has been self-reliance. As a Society we have been distinctive for an equalitarian belief that has done much to surmount the stubborn barriers of class and race and creed. As a State our most notable contribution, paradoxical though it may sound, has been the intentional and determined limitation of the power of political authority.

The individual characteristics are in large measure a heritage from the pioneer period when, wholly aside from intrinsic desirability, self-reliance and voluntary co-operation were both essential for survival. The seemingly arbitrary restraint of political authority is an imposed characteristic, to the extent that it is decreed by the Constitution rather than continuously and insistently demanded by public opinion. But these limitations would not have been written into the organic law unless, at the time of the formation of the Republic, they had been consistent with, and in general approved by, the popular will.

When the American people have been self-reliant, mutually helpful and considerate, determined in their mistrust of political authority, this nation has been "in form"; its tradition alive; its contribution to civilization outstanding. Confusion has arisen as form has been neglected. The restoration will require, for all of us, at least as arduous an effort, and as rigorous self-discipline, as the athlete consciously applies to himself in order to remedy physical deterioration.

Our effort will require, in particular, a clearer general understanding of the nature of the State, and a more realistic appreciation of what political government, which is the State in action, can and cannot accomplish.

VII

The American political system and the American political purpose are inseparable. Therefore, it is wholly appropriate that the purpose should be succinctly set forth, within the compass of a single sentence, in the Preamble of the Constitution. Gladstone may have been somewhat rhetorical when he pronounced this document, as a whole, "the most wonderful work ever struck off at a given time by the brain and purpose of man." But the fifty words of the Preamble certainly merit comparison, for compact political thought, with any expression, of any period, in any language:

> WE THE PEOPLE of the United States, in Order to form a more perfect Union, establish Justice, insure domestic Tranquility, provide for the common defense, promote the general Welfare, and secure the Blessings of Liberty to ourselves and our Posterity, do ordain and establish this CONSTITUTION for the United States of America.

The immediate background of this remarkable statement of purpose should be better known.

On August 6, 1787, just ten weeks after the Philadelphia Convention had settled to its labors, the first completed draft of the Constitution was reported back from the Committee of Detail, composed of Oliver Ellsworth (Connecticut), Nathaniel Gorham (Massachusetts), Edmund Randolph (Virginia), John Rutledge (South Carolina), and James Wilson (Pennsylvania). Under the chairmanship of Rutledge this committee had decided that the Constitution should have a preamble. But it concluded that this should be brief and precise, "since we are not working on the natural rights of men not yet gathered into Society, but upon those rights, modified by Society, and interwoven with what we call the rights of States." [13]

Consequently, the Preamble as reported back to the convention from the Committee of Detail was merely a bald statement that: "We the people of the States of [naming the thirteen] do ordain, declare and establish the following Constitution for the Government of Ourselves and our Posterity."

This preamble embodied the great decision to establish a national government by social contract, but did not attempt to define the purpose of the new government. It was approved without any opposition on August 7, 1787, though more than a month was then spent by the convention in scrutinizing the draft Constitu-

[13] The original of these notes is in the handwriting of Randolph, with revisions by Rutledge. See *The Records of the Federal Convention*, Max Farrand, editor, 1937 edition, Vol. II, pp. 137-38.

tion line by line. The thoroughness of the examination is indicated
by the fact that Madison's notes for this period alone fill exactly
300 printed pages.

On Monday, September 10, the revised draft was referred to a
committee that, on the preceding Saturday, had been "appointed
by ballot, to revise the style of, and arrange, the articles which
had been agreed to by the House." [14] The elected members of
this Committee of Style and Arrangement were Alexander Hamilton (New York), William Samuel Johnson (Connecticut), James
Madison (Virginia), Gouverneur Morris (Pennsylvania), and
Rufus King (Massachusetts). Dr. Johnson, later president of
Columbia College and, at 60, the oldest of the group, served as
its chairman.

These five men, between their appointment on September 8
and the presentation of the revised draft on September 12, recast
the imperfect style and illogical arrangement of the approved
articles and in addition wrote the Preamble in its present form.
Never, in the political field, has so great a responsibility been
fulfilled more satisfactorily. The Preamble, however, could not
have been written so compactly unless the people to whom it was
submitted had been alert, as Americans were then, to the importance of political ideas.

We know that the major credit for the redrafting goes to
Gouverneur Morris.[15] We know from the result that this redrafting completely altered the previous intent to avoid a statement of
philosophic purpose in the Preamble. We must infer, in the absence of source material on this point, that the whole Committee
on Style and Arrangement approved this important decision. Certainly the Constitutional Convention as a whole regarded this
development of the Preamble as a change for the better. It eliminated one superfluous word in the committee draft,[16] which was

[14] Madison, *op. cit.*, September 8.
[15] Cf. Farrand, *op. cit.*, Vol. III, pp. 170, 420, 499.
[16] This had employed the infinitive form "to establish justice." The word
"to" was eliminated, giving consistency to the phrasing of the sequence of objectives.

then adopted, as printed above, with the signing of the Constitution on September 17, the date still honored as Constitution Day.

The Preamble has received inadequate attention in the many comprehensive and searching studies made of the Constitution of the United States. Presumably that is because, being an introductory statement, the preamble to a constitution has only moral force. The subsequent articles lay down the definite rules of government, while the usual function of the initial statement is to announce the purpose, and indicate the political philosophy, of the organic law that follows.

Precisely for that reason this book is primarily concerned with the Preamble and only incidentally with specific articles and amendments of the Constitution. As to the latter, both in formulation and operation, there have been and still are profound differences of opinion among the American people. The statement of republican purpose, as contrasted with the means whereby this end is sought, has always received a significant unanimity of support. For instance, the Preamble was almost the only part of the original Constitution that the authors of *The Federalist* (Hamilton, Jay, and Madison) did not feel called upon to defend.

VIII

The magnitude of the challenge now confronting the American people makes it the more deplorable that there is available so little commentary on the purpose, as distinct from the mechanics, of their system of government. Conflict of counsel and confusion of policy are the certain results whenever the underlying purpose of any political system is obscured. For such conflict and confusion there is in our case the less excuse, since the Preamble to the Constitution summarizes the purpose of the Republic in a single compact sentence.

In spite of this remarkable condensation, however, no less than six separate objectives are set forth for the American system of government. These are: "[1] to form a more perfect Union, [2] establish Justice, [3] insure domestic Tranquility, [4] provide for the common defense, [5] promote the general Welfare and

[6] secure the Blessings of Liberty to ourselves and our Posterity."

The lack of detailed records makes it impossible to prove that
the last of these six general objectives was regarded as the most
important. But that conclusion is implicit in the arrangement.
The first five are not merely less elusive than the last, but are also
logically antecedent to it. Moreover, there is a difference in nature between the culminating objective and those that are preliminary. All these preliminary advantages can be paternalistically
provided *for* the people. But the "Blessings of Liberty," however
defined, can be realized only as they are consolidated *by* the people. And they depend for their realization, as the other aims do
not, on the character *of* the people. Political authority can theoretically "secure," but obviously cannot even begin to create, the
blessings that spring from an aspiration as necessarily individualistic as liberty.

Furthermore, only one of the six intentions listed in the Preamble in any way requires the complicated system of representative government laid down for the Republic. None of the first
five necessitates the specific articles that follow the Preamble; nor
the amendments that have followed the articles. Indeed, much of
the body of the Constitution definitely hampers the intent of the
Preamble, excepting only that final and paramount purpose to
"secure the Blessings of Liberty."

A centralized dictatorship, benevolent or otherwise, could have
established a more definitive union than that which after three
quarters of a century experienced a tragic civil war over the issue
of its perpetuation. Similarly, our system of government was not
needed to establish at least a measure of justice; nor to preserve
domestic peace; nor to create a military establishment; nor to
promote the general welfare. All these aims have been attained,
in greater or lesser degree, by governments operating under very
different organic laws, or even by governments without any written constitution at all.

It was with good reason believed, however, that the blessings
of liberty could be secured only by a definite division of powers
between the federal government and the states, and among the

executive, legislative, and judicial branches in both national and state government. This dual separation is, of course, designed not to increase the authority of government over the individual, but to protect the people from the abuse of authority entrusted to the State. The Constitution of the United States sets specific limits to the power of government so that the latter may *not* repress the individual characteristic of liberty.

In one of *The Federalist* papers (No. 37) Madison makes an observation that comes home with particular cogency to every worker in the field of political science. He reminds us that:

> The use of words is to express ideas. Perspicuity, therefore, requires not only that the ideas should be distinctly formed, but that they should be expressed by words distinctly and exclusively appropriate to them. But no language is so copious as to supply words and phrases for every complex idea, or so correct as not to include many equivocally denoting different ideas. Hence it must happen that however accurately objects may be discriminated in themselves, and however accurately the discrimination may be considered, the definition of them may be rendered inaccurate by the inaccuracy of the terms in which it is delivered.

Among the many reasons for reverencing the memory of James Madison is his unswerving insistence on using the most exact words available in the English language to convey the thought of those—himself *primus inter pares*—who established the Republic. And Madison was a member of the committee that wrote the Preamble to the Constitution; which states that its culminating objective is to "secure the Blessings of Liberty."

The definition of "liberty" requires separate treatment. But the verb "secure" is important also. Webster's *Dictionary of Discriminated Synonyms* is helpful:

> One *secures* that which may get lost, or which may escape, or which may permit invasion or intrusion if allowed to remain loose or to work loose; the word usually implies care or protection as the end of the action.

Before inquiring closely into the nature of "the blessings of liberty," we can agree that they are something "which may get lost."

IX

It was in the issue of the New York *Daily Advertiser* of January 11, 1788, that Madison commented on the tendency of all languages to include words "equivocally denoting different ideas." Three quarters of a century later Abraham Lincoln grappled with the same problem. "The world has never had a good definition of the word 'liberty,' " he said in Baltimore, "and the American people, just now, are much in want of one."

The date was April 18, 1864. The massacre of scores of Negro soldiers, following the storming of Fort Pillow by Confederate troops under Major General Nathan Bedford Forrest, had just occurred. Throughout the entire North the hotheads, and the armchair warriors, lusted for revenge. There was "great hope" that the President "would call for a war to exterminate the ruling class of the South, take their lands and property, and make their names a byword and a hissing among nations." [17]

But Lincoln, in an election year, not even certain of renomination, used the occasion to tell his listeners of the importance of understanding more precisely what liberty means:

> We all declare for liberty; but in using the same word we do not all mean the same thing. With some the word liberty may mean for each man to do as he pleases with himself, and the product of his labor; while with others the same word may mean for some men to do as they please with other men, and the product of other men's labor. Here are two, not only different, but incompatible things, called by the same name, liberty. And it follows that each of the things is, by the respective parties, called by two different and incompatible names—liberty and tyranny.

More than 2000 years earlier Plato had reasoned that this is no paradox; that in the political field thesis and antithesis may form an unhappy synthesis. "Thus liberty, getting out of all order and reason, passes into the harshest and bitterest form of slavery." [18]

If what is liberty to one can be construed as tyranny by another,

---

[17] Carl Sandburg, *Abraham Lincoln, The War Years*, Vol. III, p. 41.
[18] *Republic*, Book VIII.

as Lincoln asserted and as is confirmed by the tragic era following World War II, then there is urgent necessity for careful definition. Otherwise we may awaken to find that a government established to secure the blessings of liberty has actually produced the damnation of tyranny.

Indeed, that unexpected and generally undesired outcome is wholly probable whenever democratic processes place representative government in the hands of men willing to exploit ignorance in order to further the centralization of power. The danger is the greater because there may be no insincerity whatsoever in popular failure to mark the line of demarcation between liberty and tyranny. The common inability to correlate cause and effect, the common indifference to what history has to teach, the common assumption that one man's opinion is automatically as good as another's, are together sufficient to explain why people seeking liberty none the less often support measures leading in exactly the opposite direction.

The cause of liberty, for this very reason, is menaced by intelligent critics as well as by unintelligent advocates. None would call John Ruskin an ignorant man, but he could speak of "that treacherous phantom which men call liberty." [19] We tend to forget that many doctrines of National Socialism, in so far as this is definable as the authoritarian, dictatorial rule of an "elite" that mistrusts liberty, have a most respectable English-speaking background. "All this of liberty and equality, electoral suffrages, independence and so forth, we will take, therefore, to be a temporary phenomenon, by no means a final one." This is not Hitler ranting in 1940; it is Carlyle lecturing in 1840.[20]

An attempt to clarify what we mean by "liberty" does not deprive us of the emotional values surrounding this noun. It does not necessarily rule out, as ambiguous or deceptive, the apostrophic invocations of liberty with which poets of every land and age have stirred the blood. On the contrary, the opening lines of Byron's famous sonnet may helpfully be recalled for their distinc-

[19] *Seven Lamps of Architecture*, Ch. VII.
[20] *Heroes and Hero Worship; The Hero as Priest.*

tion between the spiritual aspiration of liberty and the physical condition of freedom:

> Eternal Spirit of the chainless Mind,
> Brightest in dungeons, Liberty, thou art!

Yet the words "liberty" and "freedom" have long been used almost interchangeably. Byron does so, in the poem just quoted. So does Lovelace, in *To Althea from Prison*. Dictionaries sanction this practice by listing each of the two nouns as a synonym for the other. The choice between them would often seem to depend primarily on metrical consideration—on whether the cadence of a phrase is brought out more happily by the three-syllable Latin derivative, or by the blunt, modernized form of the Old English "fréodom." Nevertheless, there is a definite distinction between the ideas that the two nouns represent. And the distinction is certainly important for a people who maintain that a major purpose of their system of government is to "secure the blessings of liberty."

"Freedom" is pre-eminently a noun descriptive of status or condition. The suffix "dom" is the same as that found in "kingdom," "officialdom," or "Christendom." But whereas the kingdom is the realm of the king, and officialdom the realm controlled by officials, freedom is obviously the realm where rulership and restraint are minimized. Ability to reason is not implied in the term "freedom," as it is in the case of "liberty." The former noun, therefore, may be used to describe a condition appropriate to the lower animals, where "liberty" would clearly be an extravagant term. Even oysters may be said to have freedom. But they will never have liberty.

That is because the oyster does not possess the power to discriminate, which is one of the two essential ingredients of liberty. Only as we ascend the biological scale, to consider species that have developed the ability to select, does the word "liberty" become at all appropriate. And the higher we ascend in this scale, the more evident is an important distinction that can be made clear only by distinguishing between liberty and freedom. We speak of giving a caged bird its "freedom," or of setting it "at liberty."

The use of the preposition in the one case, and not in the other, is significant. For "at liberty" means that the bird must now decide whither it shall fly, whereas it will have freedom even if it merely flutters from the open cage to the ground and cowers there.

While the Prisoner of Chillon was not free, it could still be said by the poet that he enjoyed liberty, as the "eternal spirit of the chainless mind." Conversely, men can be free to come and go, as the domesticated animals are free, but still be spiritually subordinated to some form of power that provides their material wants. And the spirit of liberty, involving individual choice, can gradually be stamped out for men, not only by denial of the power of individual choice, but also by ill-directed choice. So the cultivation of selective standards is seen to be the second essential ingredient of liberty.

Mere freedom of choice undoubtedly places its possessor "at liberty." But to reach the essence of liberty, and certainly to secure its blessings in co-operative living, choice must be exercised in conformity with moral principles. There must be a sense of personal responsibility, of self-restraint, and therefore of self-government. As Lincoln fully realized, liberty does not mean "for each man to do as he pleases with himself" nor for "some men to do as they please with other men." That can happen, and often does happen, in a state of freedom. But freedom to indulge oneself, or to persecute others, is not liberty, which is inextricably associated with a responsibility to other men. When that sense of personal responsibility is missing, there is no liberty, even though a condition of animal freedom, devoid of any moral element, may temporarily remain.

The men who wrote the Constitution of the United States had few conveniences at their disposal. But in two respects, at least, their thinking was greatly superior to that which passes as currency today. They were at home in the field of abstract ideas upon which, much more than upon the production of material wealth, the continuation of the American way of life depends. And they were thoroughly familiar with those eternal truths that alone give a sense of conviction and significance to human existence.

When the founders spoke of the blessings of liberty, they did

not discount the value of freedom. But it is apparent to any
student of the period that they generally used the word "liberty"
to convey a sense of individual responsibility which the alternative
noun "freedom" does not imply. The blessings of freedom may
be of very questionable value. Those of liberty, properly understood, are priceless.

X

There is a stern incompatibility between a political system
based on principle and a political direction guided by opportunism.
In recent years this incompatibility has become all too apparent
in the United States. The problem thus posed can be resolved
either by eliminating principles from our governmental system, or
by adhering to principles in our governmental practice. These are
the inescapable alternatives. Precisely because the issue can be
thus sharply defined, it is imperative also to sharpen our political
thinking by clarifying the words, and thereby elucidating the
ideas, that are involved.

Just two years after the Constitutional Convention, when the
amendments composing the Bill of Rights were still pending before the first session of the First Congress, representative bishops,
clergy, and laity of the Protestant Episcopal Church also met in
convention in Philadelphia. Their purpose was to determine, and
make effective for American usage, the changes in the *Book of
Common Prayer* rendered appropriate by the achievement of
political independence. The changes, we are told in the preface
to the altered form, were confined to those that "local circumstances require." But the opening sentence of the preface, as ratified by this religious convention on October 16, 1789, and as now
printed at the beginning of the Prayer Book of the Protestant
Episcopal Church, merits general attention:

> It is a most invaluable part of that blessed "liberty wherewith Christ
> hath made us free," that in his worship different forms and usages may
> without offence be allowed, provided the substance of the Faith be
> kept entire; . . .

The quotation from Galatians 5:1 makes a clear distinction between the attained, but not necessarily permanent, condition of freedom and the individually attainable and then indestructible concept of liberty. That the condition of freedom can be maintained only by the divinely implanted urge for liberty was fully understood when the Republic was launched. Its primary purpose was to make sure that in the United States this urge should not be contravened by arbitrary government.

The blessings of liberty, which political government may safeguard or destroy but can never itself provide, are therefore intimately connected with personal belief in, and practice of, Christian doctrine. As Paul told the Corinthians also: "Where the Spirit of the Lord is, there is liberty."

Chapter 2

The Nature of the Republic

In his introduction to *The American Commonwealth,* James Bryce observed that "explanations drawn from a form of government, being easy and obvious, ought to be cautiously employed." This English student of our political institutions was well aware that such explanations should be particularly cautious with reference to the United States.

For this caution there are two reasons, one general and one particular. Nobody will contend that a written constitution can ever perfectly mirror the fluctuating spirit of the people whom it governs. And, in the case of the United States, there is the further fact that the governmental system is not so much positive as intentionally negative.

While this suspicion of temporal authority reflects a deep-rooted American characteristic, it also makes a study of our legal institutions inadequate for understanding the nature of the Republic. Many Americans, let alone foreigners, are surprised to find that the words "no" and "not," for the most part employed in restraint of governmental power, occur 49 times in the seven original articles of our Constitution. This negative approach to a positive objective also pervades the first ten amendments, composing the Bill of Rights, which culminate in two sweeping and ever memorable limitations on political authority:

The enumeration in the Constitution, of certain rights, shall not be construed to deny or disparage others retained by the people. (Amendment IX)

The powers not delegated to the United States by the Constitution, nor prohibited by it to the States, are reserved to the States respectively, or to the people. (Amendment X)

To "secure the blessings of liberty" the founders of the Republic deemed it as necessary to restrain as to establish political authority. In American political thought, as distinct from that of the European continent, the State until recently was always regarded as a severely limited and artificial instrumentality. A form of government thus conceived is unlikely to repress the individual creative urge that impels men toward various forms of personal accomplishment.

Indeed it is impossible to read even the bare text of the Constitution at all carefully without realizing that the American Republic was specifically designed to safeguard individual enterprise *against* the State. The men who wrote this organic law were all convinced that natural impulsion would serve better than external government in the planting, the harvesting, and even in the equitable—which does not mean automatically equal—distribution of the fruits of labor.

Agricultural terminology is appropriate because the eighteenth century American lived close to the soil, or close to the sea or forest when husbandry took the form of fishing or hunting. At the time of the Constitutional Convention the country contained a fair number of small manufacturers and artisans. There was a sprinkling of substantial merchants and bankers and a rather high proportion of lawyers and ministers, as well as other professional men. But even Philadelphia, then the largest city, in 1787 had a population of less than 40,000. Whatever his calling, no American of that period was wholly aloof from the land. The pleasures and the penalties of the great metropolitan ganglia of today were alike unknown.

Nevertheless, it would be a serious mistake to conclude that the founders envisaged an indefinite continuation of the small rural economy they knew at first hand. In addition to an understanding of history that was, in many cases, profound, these men possessed the imagination to visualize something of the complicated sociological future of their country.

As early as 1751 Franklin had anticipated that the American population "will in another century be more than the people of England." [1] And Madison, who in 1787 foresaw serious difficulties arising "from the connection between the great capitalists in manufactures and commerce, and the numbers employed by them," later estimated that the population of the United States might reach 192,000,000 by 1930. With these calculations before him he wrote: "To the effect of these changes, intellectual, moral and social, the institutions and laws of the country must be adapted, and it will require for the task all the wisdom of the wisest patriots." [2]

II

If the group that wrote the Constitution had not included a number of men with extraordinary foresight, the Republic would not have lasted, let alone prospered, as has been the case. But they were not mere theorists. Active leadership in their respective communities had also made these men hard-headed politicians. The unparalleled opportunity to establish a wholly new political system was seized, without ignoring the overshadowing problem of the day. There was nothing academic about this immediate dilemma. Under the Articles of Confederation the former colonies, having achieved their independence, were rapidly drifting into a condition approaching anarchy. Yet everything in the American tradition made centralized government repulsive to a large proportion of the population.

In the present period of governmental hypertrophy we tend to forget that those who made the American Revolution were by no means unanimous in wanting to establish another Nation-State. One of the newly independent colonies—Rhode Island—refused

---

[1] Carl Van Doren, *Benjamin Franklin*, p. 217.
[2] *The Madison Papers*, Allston Mygatt edition, Vol. III, Appendix 4.

to send delegates to Philadelphia even to discuss the subject of federal union. When the Constitution was finally hammered out, a strong minority of the delegates refused to sign, for the most part because they opposed the projected centralization of political power. In Virginia alone the opposition counted such outstanding men as George Mason, Edmund Randolph, and Patrick Henry, the last of whom had refused on principle to accept appointment to his state delegation. In New York, from which no delegate other than Alexander Hamilton would sign, the opposition was even stronger. We owe *The Federalist* essays, essentially a brilliant campaign document, to Hamilton's very reasonable fear that his own state would reject the Constitution.

Contemporary tension is reflected in the narrow margins by which the "Big Four" finally ratified the Constitution in the state conventions elected by popular vote to settle that single burning issue. Pennsylvania assented on December 12, 1787, by 46 to 23; Massachusetts on February 6, 1788, by 187 to 168; Virginia not until June 26, 1788—when nine states had acted favorably and the Constitution was therefore already in force for them—by 89 to 79. New York approved still later (July 26, 1788), by the even closer margin of 30 to 27.

Eighteenth century Americans, valuing individual liberty above all else, simply would not construct a Nation-State without simultaneously making it part of the record that concentrated political power is, and continuously should be, suspect by those whom it subjects. In consequence, with the need for central government and the determination to preserve local government sharply at variance, it was foreordained that the Constitution would contain elements of compromise.

Evidence of this is apparent in the text, as in the provision giving every state equal representation in the Senate to offset representation proportionate to population in the House. Contemporary attacks on this and other instances of expediency were numerous and vociferous. They were effectively answered by Alexander Hamilton, who had himself wanted a much stronger central government, in the closing number (85) of *The Federalist*. There Hamilton appositely quoted David Hume, whose death in 1776 had spared him the charge of partisanship as to the philosophic merits of the American Constitution:

> To balance a large State or Society, whether monarchical or republican, on general laws, is a work of so great difficulty, that no human genius, however comprehensive, is able, by the mere dint of reason and reflection, to effect it. The judgements of many must unite in the work; experience must guide their labor; time must bring it to perfection, and the feeling of inconveniences must correct the mistakes which they *inevitably* [Hamilton's emphasis] fall into in their first trials and experiments.

To determine the true nature of the American Republic one must therefore look deeper than the written Constitution, of which Washington wrote almost apologetically that "it is liable to as few exceptions as could reasonably have been expected." "Individuals entering into society," he said defensively, "must give up a share of liberty to preserve the rest." [3]

Nevertheless, the Constitution represents an unprecedented and unparalleled effort to integrate a system of government with an individualistic code of personal conduct. This explains the deep-rooted and continuing determination that in the United States political action shall not be allowed to regiment the individual. Most Americans are confused rather than convinced when smartly told that "rugged individualism" produces "ragged individuals." The observation is clever. But it seeks to puncture more than commercial platitudes. To attack the principles underlying free enterprise is to impugn the traditional morality of the American people.

It is, however, a fundamental of American political theory that the clash of opinion between individuals and groups and parties should be vehement and continuous. As long as the American people differ with each other there is no danger to the Republic, for its philosophy assumes that they will so differ and its structure encourages them to altercation. Difference of opinion becomes discord and the security of the Republic is threatened, not when

[3] Max Farrand (Ed.), *The Records of the Federal Convention*, Vol. II, pp. 666-7.

there is cleavage among the governed, but when it develops over the issue of personal liberty, between those who do the governing and any sizable or otherwise significant minority of those who are governed. It was to avert this ever present danger that the Constitution was drawn to balance and restrain the powers of government, giving political substance to the assertion, in the Declaration of Independence, that governments derive "their just powers from the consent of the governed." And this means the acquiescence of the great body of the governed—not merely the consent of a bare majority.

David Hume, in the passage cited, suggested that time might achieve a condition of "perfection" for a government balanced on general laws. Clearly that will never be the case with the American Republic, so long as its citizens differ pronouncedly one from another in their ambitions, interests, and mentality. Perfection implies achievement and the Republic, for all the definition of its organic law, is designed not as an achievement, but for achieving. The nature of the Republic is as much dynamic as static. The individual citizens who give it substance are not regarded as mechanical robots, properly subject to "universal training." They are dignified as human beings whose claim to the expression of personality must never be arbitrarily denied by external government.

A *form* of government thus tailored to individualism can never attain perfection, because the human integer, which in the aggregate gives representative government its quality, is adversely affected by the failings of mortality. On the other hand it may reasonably be asserted that our governmental *system*, as such, does actually approach perfection, in so far as it is wholly competent to represent the quality of its citizens.

The operators, not the machinery, form the subject of concern. The human element holds the seed of life, and alternatively the germ of death, for the Republic.

III

We shall not understand the nature of our Republic if we fail
to realize that its organic law was the product of concession. Indeed the record of the Philadelphia Convention is throughout one
of adjustment of conflicting viewpoints.

At one extreme, in the deliberations from which a new Nation-
State emerged, was the position of Alexander Hamilton. He
thought that the President of the United States should hold office
for life, with similar tenure for members of a Senate to be composed entirely of landowners. The British Crown, without the
hereditary feature, and the House of Lords, deprived of patents
of nobility, were model institutions in Hamilton's mind. His
draft for the federal Constitution provided that: "The Senate
shall exclusively possess the power of declaring war," in addition
to that share of the treaty-making power actually concentrated in
the upper chamber. Hamilton also strongly favored centralization
of power at the expense of the states and would have had all the
state governors, endowed with a comprehensive veto, appointed
by the national government as its agents.[4]

At the other extreme were the adherents of Thomas Jefferson,
serving as Minister Plenipotentiary in France at the time of the
Philadelphia Convention. The decadence of the French court, as
the monarchy drew to its turbulent end, made Jefferson the more
anxious to prevent centralized government in the United States.
Indeed it was largely because of the abuses of personal political
power that he defined prerevolutionary France as "the worst-
governed country on earth," and the government of Great Britain
under George III as "the most flagitious which has existed since
the days of Philip of Macedon."[5] Therefore, it is not surprising
that Jefferson advised from Paris, on August 4, 1787, "to make
the states one as to everything connected with foreign nations, and
several as to everything purely domestic."[6]

[4] The text of Hamilton's draft constitution is printed as Appendix V of *The
Madison Papers.* Hamilton's elaboration and defense of these views is minuted
in the *Notes* for June 18, 1787.

[5] Albert Jay Nock, *Jefferson,* p. 105.

[6] Quoted by Gilbert Chinard, in *Thomas Jefferson,* p. 197.

The Constitution as adopted was for diametrically opposite reasons a disappointment both to Hamilton and to Jefferson. But the former swallowed his doubts to produce the brilliant advocacy of *The Federalist*. And Jefferson, not to be outdone in co-operation, magnanimously advertised these essays as "the best commentary on the principles of government ever written," frankly admitting that they had "rectified" him "on several points." [7] The stature of its initial leadership helped to make judicious conciliation a part of the nature of the Republic.

Adjustment of conflicting opinions by reasonable modification is, moreover, implicit in the Constitution. If the United States were really a political democracy, as is so often loosely asserted, then this factor of conciliation would not be vital to successful government. The will of the majority would habitually override the will of the minority, to the extent that the representative process permitted formulation of this majority will. But the American system of government, in spite of suggestions to the contrary which demonstrate confusion in our political thought, is not that of an unbridled democracy. What we have is a representative republic and, in the language of *The Federalist*:

> It is of great importance in a republic not only to guard the Society against the oppression of its rulers, but to guard one part of the Society against the injustice of the other part. Different interests necessarily exist in different classes of citizens. If a majority be united by a common interest, the rights of the minority will be insecure. . . . Justice is the end of government. It is the end of civil Society. It ever has been and ever will be pursued until it be obtained, or until liberty be lost in the pursuit. In a Society under the forms of which the stronger faction can readily unite and oppress the weaker, anarchy may as truly be said to reign as in a state of nature, where the weaker individual is not secured against the violence of the stronger . . .[8]

Concessions to the minority are not necessary in a democracy. Concessions to the majority are not necessary in a tyranny. But in a republic, designed to prevent and not to induce tyranny, con-

---

[7] *Ibid.*, p. 200.

[8] No. 51: the authorship is attributed to Hamilton or Madison. The reasoning throughout seems more characteristic of the latter.

cessions by both majorities and minorities are as oil to the machinery of government. The majority must not dominate in an oppressive manner and the minority must not insist upon its guaranteed rights in a way that will perpetually frustrate the majority. The spirit of conciliation, in short, is an essential part of the nature of the Republic.

There is, of course, a point at which conciliation may begin to undermine principle, becoming compromise of a nature intolerable to honorable men. In the honest opinion of many on both sides that point was reached, and exceeded, in the issues of constitutional interpretation that led to the Civil War. Of course political concessions may and do impinge on principle. But an equally frequent victim of encroachment is self-interest, which likes to masquerade as principle.

There is no insurmountable difficulty in this matter when the individual himself conscientiously draws the boundary between honorable concession and dishonorable compromise. Conscience teaches us to distinguish the surrender of personal prerogative from the sacrifice of impersonal principles. In American politics, certainly, the art of conciliation, even to the degree of "logrolling," has always been regarded as a proper practice. It could not be otherwise, since our system of government demands concession and would break down without that element.

IV

The manner in which the Bill of Rights was adopted provides a good illustration of the important role played by concession from the earliest days of the Republic. In order to obtain quickly what would now be called a "viable," or workable, national government, those who most strongly emphasized the blessings of liberty were nevertheless willing to submit the Constitution to the people without a catalogue of specific individual guarantees. Those who argued that such specification was "not only unnecessary in the proposed Constitution, but would even be dangerous"[9] were nevertheless willing to modify that opinion.

[9] Hamilton, *The Federalist*, No. 84.

This willingness was certainly not diminished by the many criticisms of the Constitution raised in most of the state conventions of ratification. It is significant that the first ten amendments, as eventually adopted, were modeled on those drafted by the minority in the Pennsylvania convention, for its demands contained the entire substance of our present Bill of Rights.[10]

North Carolina and Rhode Island had not ratified, and were therefore still outside the Union, when Madison on June 8, 1789, in the first session of the First Congress, moved the consideration of constitutional amendments which together would comprise a bill of rights. Reviewing the many criticisms directed against the Constitution as adopted, he gave his opinion that:

> . . . the great mass of the people who opposed it, disliked it because it did not contain effectual provision against the encroachments on particular rights, and [for] those safeguards which they have been long accustomed to have interposed between them and the magistrate who exercised the sovereign power . . .[11]

In the same speech Madison declared that he himself did not consider a formal bill of rights essential for the protection of the individual against governmental authority. On the other hand, he could see no valid objection to emphasizing in this manner that "the great object in view is to limit and qualify the powers of government, by excepting out of the grant of power those cases in which the government ought not to act, or to act only in a particular mode." These exceptions, he noted, are directed "sometimes against the abuse of the executive power, sometimes against the legislative, and, in some cases, against the community itself; or, in other words, against the majority in favor of the minority." [12]

It is these constitutional limitations on the will of the majority that insure, for as long as the first ten amendments to the Constitution stand, that the United States shall *not* be a political democ-

---

[10] McMaster and Stone, *Pennsylvania and the Federal Constitution,* 1888 edition, pp. 321-3; see also James Brown Scott, *The United States of America,* p. 327.

[11] *Congressional Register,* Vol. I, p. 426.

[12] *Ibid.,* pp. 430-31.

racy, if that signifies a system of government under which the will of the majority is in every circumstance supreme. And even if the American Republic should be thus corrupted, it could still be heralded that here was one government which in certain specified fundamentals actually met the challenging requirement of John Stuart Mill:

> If all mankind minus one, were of one opinion, and only one person were of the contrary opinion, mankind would be no more justified in silencing that one person, than he, if he had the power, would be justified in silencing mankind.[13]

A doctrine as truly liberal as this could never be agreeable to all men, and least of all to those who have fantastically confused liberalism with the suppression of opinion distasteful to them. Fortunately, there was little self-righteous political thinking in the formation of the American system of government. Those most influential in that achievement were truly political philosophers, able to rise above personal prejudice in their effort to bring governmental practice into conformity with moral principles. Though Hamilton and Jefferson, as an outstanding illustration, disagreed sharply on the desirable means, they were nevertheless in full accord in their desire to "secure the blessings of liberty."

That objective requires restraint on the power of the State. As to the degree of the restraint there was, and is, room for wide difference of opinion. But adjustment of individual viewpoints on methods may reasonably be expected when there is firm agreement as to the objective sought. The men who wrote the Constitution counted heavily on good will to make their aspirations for the new form of government effective. So this conciliatory spirit came to be embedded in the nature of the Republic.

The practical importance of this may be emphasized by considering the sad frustration of a wholly different political system in which the desirability of conciliation was covertly denied. The Charter of the United Nations, which established a veto power for privileged Members, is a case in point, for none who really

---

[13] *Essay on Liberty*, Ch. 2.

wish to further agreement will stipulate an insurmountable veto power in matters of operation. Partly because of this emphasis on the veto a constantly frustrated commission of the United Nations took nearly three years even to draft an international bill of rights, without binding force on any Member government.

The very first Congress of the United States, on the other hand, could move decisively toward the establishment of constitutional guarantees in this field. On September 25, 1789, just two years after the writing of the original Constitution had been completed, twelve amendments designed as a bill of rights were approved by Congress. The ten most significant were ratified by the states and were, on March 1, 1792, certified by the Secretary of State as an integral part of the Constitution. Only visionaries ever expected any such development in the case of the United Nations, because its nature, apparent to the discerning as early as the Dumbarton Oaks draft charter, was opposed to conciliation.

The conciliatory spirit that was so important in producing the Bill of Rights continues to be one of the great sources of strength in the American way of life. The diversity and variety of human personality renders it essential that any system of government cherishing the individual should make allowance for many conflicting viewpoints and should not impede their voluntary adjustment. The only workable alternative to a governmental system that encourages agreement is one that encourages repression. And the latter, no matter how fair its initial pretense, is in nature, and will therefore eventually become in action, a system of tyranny, whether the tyrant be an individual, an estate, a bureaucracy, or a mob.

Just as the form of the American Republic is directed against monopoly of any kind—social, religious, political, or economic— so, as a corollary, its nature demands an individual willingness to respect the opinions of others, and an aptitude for voluntary adjustment of individual viewpoints. In a democracy such adjustment may be demanded. In a republic, up to the point where moral principles are endangered, it is expected.

V

It is the nature of the Republic to encourage the harmonizing of conflicting viewpoints. But opportunistic compromise is not in the nature of a system of government based on moral principles. At any given moment right and wrong cannot be safely compromised. But neither, politically speaking, can right and wrong always be surely recognized.

So it is often difficult for even the most conscientious individual to decide whether he should concede or stand firm on a particular political issue. In the operation of representative government the decision would be practically impossible, were it not for the device of the party system. By their adherence to varying—perhaps opposing—principles, political parties enable the citizen to bring the moral element into politics. The party is one means through which the individual can project his standard of living outside his immediate circle, thereby influencing the life of the nation as a whole. "In America," Bryce concluded, "the government counts for less than in Europe, the parties count for more."

While the history of political parties in the United States has an English background, to be examined later, we must accept Bryce's verdict that the American party system really "begins with the Constitutional Convention of 1787." In *The American Commonwealth* Bryce warned his fellow countrymen against trying to find any basic similarities between English and American political parties, noting that the latter "are pure home growths, developed by the circumstances of the nation." He concluded that the origin of American party division is found in the clash of "the centrifugal and centripetal tendencies," so dramatically personified in the antagonism between Jefferson and Hamilton. "In a sort of general way," observes this English observer cautiously, "one may say that while one party [the followers of Jefferson] claimed to be the apostles of Liberty, the other [the Federalists] represented the principle of Order." [14]

In other words, the distinctive attribute of American political parties is that from the very outset—and at the outset more pro-

---

[14] *The American Commonwealth*, Third Edition, Vol. II, pp. 5 and 6.

nouncedly than in later years—they have reflected differences of principle and have therefore been fundamentally philosophic in character. This important characteristic, much less pronounced in European party history, runs through the whole skein of American political organization. The names have changed; the major parties have even largely reversed their traditions, so that each has come to uphold principles it formerly opposed. But the connection with political principles, though often honored in the breach by party leaders, has never been wholly forgotten. Always one of the two major parties has laid primary emphasis on individual *liberty*; always the other has favored extension of governmental *authority*.

This division has been a matter of disagreement on means rather than of fundamental antagonism in regard to ends. While Hamilton is alleged to have called the public "a great beast," it cannot be maintained that he was hostile to the cause of individual liberty. While Jefferson is quoted as having said that "the tree of liberty is watered in the blood of revolution," he was actually as anxious to stabilize Society as were any of his contemporaries. The point is that political parties in the United States have generally stood for something deeper and more significant than privilege for a landed, a monied, or a proletarian class. On the other hand, no American political leader has ever successfully maintained that his party is identified with Good and the opposition with Evil. American thought is too wholesome and common sense to permit that hypocrisy.

Because liberty is impotent without order, and because order is stultifying without liberty, there is always room for adjustment between the viewpoints of political leaders who enlist under one or the other of these two banners. Nevertheless, an opposition between the two schools of thought is eternal and inevitable because, in Bryce's words, "it springs from differences in the intellect and feelings of men which one finds in all countries and at all epochs."

None can precisely identify the factors that lead some to a pessimistic, others to an optimistic, judgment on the subject of human nature. But the facts that can be cited by the pessimist and the faith that sustains the optimist are equally real. Moreover, the pessimist is seldom devoid of a form of faith and the optimist seldom at a loss for pertinent facts, to sustain their contrasting attitudes.

This duality is latent in every individual. We admit it by saying that people have "moods" and are at different times inclined or disinclined in a particular direction. Because of this duality no balanced intelligence can praise liberty without some mental reservations in behalf of authority, nor advocate authoritarianism without considering its depressing effect on liberty. To quote Viscount Bryce once more:

> Every sensible man feels in himself the struggle between these two tendencies, and is on his guard not to yield wholly to either, because the one degenerates into tyranny, the other into an anarchy out of which tyranny will eventually spring. The wisest statesman is he who best holds the balance between them.[15]

VI

The alternation in human nature, and in the physical conditions of the surrounding universe, is a central problem of philosophy; just as the particular enduring conflict between Good and Evil is a central problem of religion.

If we examine the fragments of early Greek thought still extant, we find Heraclitus emphasizng the characteristic of ceaseless change: "You cannot step twice into the same river, for other and yet other waters are ever flowing on." But how, retorted contemporary Parmenides, "can a thing both be and not be"? Not change but its opposite, immutability, was to Parmenides the fundamental law.

So when Empedocles set out to reconcile the dynamic and the static viewpoints, he was forced, by the weight of evidence on both sides, to the conception of a twofold rhythm, a continuous tidal ebb and flow in the affairs of men. "In one movement a unity builds itself up out of a plurality into sole existence; in another

---

[15] *Ibid.*, p. 19.

movement it disintegrates, to make a plurality out of a unity. . . . This perpetual alternation never ceases."

As Arnold Toynbee points out, in his examination of the origins of civilizations,[16] the discovery of rhythm and the process of thesis, antithesis, and synthesis are not to be attributed exclusively to Hellenic reflection. Sinic philosophers quite independently depicted the alternating forces of Yin and Yang, representing shadow and sunlight, water and fire, rest and motion, or other interlocking opposites. It is not the province of this study to consider the universality, nor the grandeur, of the conception of eternal pulsation. But we do note that it has been discerned by a long series of profound thinkers, in every age and civilization, down to the contemporary English writer who reminds us that: "Life is a constant process of focus and expansion. This is the systole and diastole of Time itself, the alternating current that drives the Universe." [17]

Further excursion into the field of metaphysics would only emphasize what is too much ignored by contemporary Americans— that their Republic is far more than an administrative mechanism. The authors of the Constitution were eminently practical men. But to consider this political achievement critically is to see that they realized the distinction we have drawn between the *condition* of freedom and the *urge* of liberty; that they realized the impossibility of maintaining freedom unless those who are "at liberty" are able to exercise self-restraint; that their consequent objective was a political system permitting a happy balance and conciliation between the dynamic and the static. In short, the problem to which they resolutely addressed themselves was how to integrate a liberty of divine origin with an order of human manufacture.

This integration demands constant adjustment of individual prejudice. And for the continuous political operation of the conciliatory process it was also necessary to evolve the extraconstitutional machinery of party government. It is no accident that from the beginning one of our major political parties has tended to em-

---

[16] *A Study of History*, Vol. I, Section II B.
[17] Gerald Heard, *The Ascent of Humanity*, p. 260.

phasize what man can do by governing himself; the other, what can be done for man by governing him.

By the same token it is no accident that in the United States the popular instinct has sensed that the two-party system is in accordance with "the systole and diastole of Time itself," and therefore operates with a success the more striking by comparison with the disasters attendant upon the multiplicity of parties characteristic of European governments.

VII

In retrospect one can see clearly that the American system of government implied and demanded two organized parties—an administration and an opposition—for successful operation.

The supreme need for agreement, without which the Republic could never have been launched, prevented its founders from realizing the necessity of party organization. They had passed through an ordeal in which the most heroic effort by well-disposed men had barely succeeded in forming the federal union. They quailed at the thought of partisanship that would inevitably seek to promote, rather than to resolve, the natural divisions in public opinion.

This explains why we find Madison writing (*The Federalist*, No. 37) of "the pestilential influence of party animosities"; and why Washington, in his Farewell Address, took occasion to warn "in the most solemn manner against the baneful effects of the spirit of party."

It seems curious that men of such sagacity did not appreciate the full political implications of the respresentative system they had established. It seems curious, in view of the rise of the single dictatorial party in our day, that they did not visualize the importance of political division as an additional safeguard against concentrated tyranny. It seems curious, finally, that men who could so clearly see the importance of balanced powers did not conclude that two opposing parties were necessary to keep those powers balanced. But one could give many illustrations of the ease with which the presence of an immediate evil obscures political perspicacity. The very present danger to the men who wrote the Constitution was what they frequently referred to as "faction," by which they seem to have meant what today we would call "pressure groups." That the self-interest of disciplined, nationally organized parties would, by open competition with each other, prove in the public interest was simply not anticipated.

For this lack of foresight there were reasons other than the immediate necessity of securing more unity among the scarcely united states. This union had to take form as a nation before national parties could in turn arise. Washington in particular, Madison not much less so, felt and was above domestic political rivalries. The first President in the field, the fourth President in the forum, had given all they possessed to harmonizing and conciliating for the general American welfare. It was impossible, because it would have seemed degrading, for these men to step down from national to party leadership.

Psychologically, moreover, both Washington and Madison were of the judicial rather than the opinionated type, of which Hamilton and Jefferson were in their opposite ways representative. Again, it would have demanded superhuman vitality for men who had spent so much of their controversial ability in the struggle for independence to take sides with equal fervor in comparatively uninspiring domestic antagonisms. Even Hamilton and Jefferson were party men in the field of political thought rather than in that of political action. So it is not really surprising that the revolutionary generation had passed away before party division, in the modern sense of the word, began to crystallize—just prior to and during the Administration of John Quincy Adams.

Nevertheless, this division was from the beginning inherent in the American form of government. For all his dislike of "the spirit of party" Washington could see, in the passage already noted, that: "This spirit, unfortunately, is inseparable from our nature, having its root in the strongest passions of the human mind." What he did not see is that, if intelligently controlled, the passionate spirit of party will operate constructively. Nor did he realize that both partisanship and conciliation, the tendency to divide as much as the willingness to unite, are alike a part of the nature of the Republic.

The fact that the authors of the Constitution did not foresee the rise of party government is not surprising. In many respects they builded better than they knew. And what they created was not a dead structure, lacking the opportunity of development and growth. It was, on the contrary, a vital political system, attuned to the nature of man, with all the possibility of improvement pertaining to the nature of man.

VIII

Partisanship, on the one hand, and a conciliatory attitude, on the other, are not the only qualities inherent in the nature of the Republic, and therefore necessary to the character of its citizens, if this idealistic form of government is to be maintained. The existence and development of tolerance is also implied, and in an active rather than a passive sense.

The virtue of tolerance is of course averse to the spirit of partisanship—as it is allied to that of conciliation. The tolerant man will discount the excessive claims that rigid party division encourages and will simultaneously seek to emphasize that which is common in conflicting viewpoints, rather than that which is irreconcilable. Tolerance may therefore be called the balance wheel between divisive and unifying forces. It is, of course, a fundamental characteristic of the Christian religion. The New, as contrasted with the Old, Testament is rich in such admonitions as: "He that is without sin among you, let him first cast a stone . . ."

The Constitution places much reliance on the virtue of tolerance, not merely in defending specific individual rights against encroachment by the State or by the majority, but even more in the fundamental intent to "secure the blessings of liberty." To attain this end for one individual without limiting it for others is a problem far easier to state than to solve. A prerequisite of solution is obviously a tolerant attitude toward viewpoints other than one's own. To tolerate means to endure something actually disagreeable: a virtue always difficult to achieve. Too often, tolerance is regarded as nothing more than a somewhat contemptuous indifference toward an unwelcome opinion. To be the active characteristic that is required by our system of government, toleration must have a positive content. It must at least admit the possibility of values in what may seem at first glance valueless.

In the *Essay on Liberty*, John Stuart Mill has made a universal case for what he well defines as "the duty of toleration." But the general logic of his reasoning has a particular applicability for Americans. Among a heterogeneous people, basing their claim to political independence on the assumption of a fundamental human equality, hostile to artificial privilege, opposed to preferential position for any church or estate, and committed by circumstance to the protection of minority interests—for such a people tolerance is actually more than a virtue, and more than a duty. It is a clear necessity.

Although this conclusion is intellectually obvious, it is by no means always emotionally acceptable. And difficulty here is exacerbated by the ease with which individual revulsion against intolerance may produce a different, but no less objectionable, form of the same characteristic. This inverted intolerance is often particularly apparent in racial issues, as in the admission of Negro students to private educational institutions that must (and should) place limits on their student load and are therefore sometimes prone to make race one criterion of limitation. In this issue it is not infrequently argued that Negroes should be admitted *as* Negroes, which is of course no less intolerant than exclusion for the same reason. Similarly, legislation like the pleasantly titled Fair Employment Practices Act would make the federal government as intolerant toward local customs as those customs are, undoubtedly, intolerant of more than lip service to equalitarian principles.

The continuous definition and application of tolerance is one of many responsibilities that were transmitted to posterity, along with more clear-cut objectives, by the founders of the Republic. Their work made it essential for all Americans to be tolerant, actively tolerant, if we wish to preserve our inherited form of government. The principles laid down are subject to contradictory interpretation, and in specific issues the guideposts are frequently obscure. But to be thus "at liberty" is of itself evidence that the Republic is not unduly restrained or mortified by the dead hand of the past. Our political institutions are designed to focus and clarify, rather than to solve the countless problems of citizenship. That is well, because these problems are inseparable from—are indeed an index of—life and growth.

IX

The quality of democracy—using the word to describe a personal attitude rather than a political system—is also a part of the nature of the Republic. A generally democratic attitude, sharply different from that which prevailed in seventeenth and eighteenth century Europe, was indeed a well-developed American characteristic long before there was any concerted effort for political independence.

Democracy, as an equalitarian approach in all aspects of human relationships, results naturally from faith in the fundamental decency of human beings. Those with democratic instincts believe that individual conduct is of greater significance to mankind than is intellectual power, physical beauty, muscular strength, or any other personal attribute or inherited advantage. "Kind hearts are more than coronets, and simple faith than Norman blood." As is true of tolerance—to which the virtue of democracy is closely allied—the equalitarian attitude has been enormously strengthened by the teachings of the Christian religion.

This fact is so generally recognized as scarcely to need emphasis. "By this shall all men know that ye are my disciples, if ye have love one to another." [18] But the encouragement that Christianity gives to the democratic attitude is many-sided; by no means dependent upon the insistence on human fraternity. There is the constant glorification of the humble: "Blessed be ye poor; for yours is the kingdom of God." [19] There is the parallel condemnation of material accumulation: "Verily I say unto you, that a rich man shall hardly enter into the kingdom of heaven." [20]

[18] John 13:35.
[19] Luke 6:20.
[20] Matthew 19:23.

There is the scorn of earthly power: "For what is a man advantaged, if he gain the whole world and lose himself . . .?" [21] Finally there is the enduring challenge to official arrogance, chronicled by Mark and Matthew in practically identical words: "Render to Caesar the things that are Caesar's, and to God the things that are God's."

These texts, and many others of similar import, were as guiding lights to the resolute men and women who came to America not merely to worship as they wished, but even more to live, so far as humanly possible, in the manner that Christ ordained. And the conditions of living in the New World, where the co-operative attitude was as important as individual reliability, in turn strengthened democratic influences among a sincerely Christian people. Since Tom Paine can scarcely be charged with any excess of religious fervor, his evidence on this point is the more important:

> As America was the only spot in the political world where the principles of universal reformation could begin, so also was it the best in the natural world. An assemblage of circumstances conspired, not only to give birth, but to add gigantic maturity to its principles. . . . The wants which necessarily accompany the cultivation of a wilderness, produced among them [the colonists] a state of Society, which countries, long harassed by the quarrels and intrigues of governments, had neglected to cherish. In such a situation Man becomes what he ought. He sees his species, not with the inhuman idea of a natural enemy, but as kindred; and the example shows to the artificial world, that Man must go back to Nature for information. [22]

Faith in the underlying worth of men, as such, was unquestionably an important element in the demand for political separation from class-conscious England. With the achievement of independence, and the withdrawal of the royal representatives, the democratic passion flared high. It certainly played a substantial role in delaying the establishment of a national government. "The radical leaders of the Revolution," in the words of Charles A. Beard, "had not thrown off British agencies of economic coercion for the mere purpose of substituting another centralized sys-

[21] Luke 9:25.
[22] *The Rights of Man*, Part II, Introduction.

tem of legislative, executive, and judicial control." [23] In 1786 the Massachusetts insurrection known as Shays' Rebellion gave proof that democratic sentiments and Christian forbearance are not necessarily allied.

The oft-repeated assertion that the framers of the Constitution were anxious to check any further development of democratic "turbulence" is sustained by the records of the Convention. Intimations that they were primarily interested in their personal property rights are much more difficult to substantiate. Professor Beard has written scathingly that: "More than half the delegates in attendance were either investors or speculators in the public securities which were to be buoyed up by the new Constitution." [24] Albert Jay Nock raised the percentage. "The Constitution," he asserts, "had been drafted . . . by men representing special economic interests. Four-fifths of them were public creditors. . . ." [25]

Actually, this only amounts to saying that most of the framers of the Constitution had supported the cause of independence to the extent of buying the War Savings Bonds of their day. That is a curious basis for impugning the quality of patriotism. There would seem to be at least as much reason for questioning the motives of those who had failed to make this investment—or speculation, as at the time it certainly was. Moreover, only a few years earlier, the hopelessly inflated American dollar had suffered a forty-to-one devaluation, ordered by Congress on March 18, 1780. This expropriation, of 97½ per cent, was at the expense of every "public creditor," in proportion to his holding.[26]

Much criticism of the "conservatism" of the Constitutional Convention is equally far-fetched. Of the delegates, Mr. Nock has charged that: "Not one of them represented the interest of production." How that can be said of men like Washington, Franklin, and Madison, unless no intellectual worker is to be considered a producer, is incomprehensible. But criticisms of this

[23] Charles and Mary Beard, *The Rise of American Civilization*, Vol. I, p. 302.
[24] *Ibid.*, p. 311.
[25] *Op. cit.*, p. 176.
[26] The effects of this inflation and the abortive efforts to combat it by governmental price-fixing are well summarized by Irving Brant, in his biography of *James Madison*, Vol. I, Ch. 17.

character, from scholars as generally liberal in their thinking as Professor Beard and Mr. Nock, have done much to establish the belief that in its constitutional origin our government is tainted by a narrow self-interest.

This unsustainable argument has helped to obscure one of the most interesting and important characteristics of the Republic. It is designed to provide a people who are instinctively democratic with a government calculated to safeguard them from the excesses of democracy as a political system. Every adherent of Christianity must believe in democracy as a way of life. But every student of history knows that democracy, as a method of government, is affected with an instability that swings easily into tyranny. How to provide a democratic people with a stable republican government was the problem that confronted the founders at Philadelphia. The formula they found is not above criticism. But it has worked.

X

So the nature of the Republic is seen to require among its citizens the possession, exercise, and co-ordination of a number of seemingly conflicting qualities. These we have identified as partisanship balanced by the spirit of conciliation; as adherence to principle coupled with a tolerance sufficiently active to avert bigotry; as faith in democracy tempered by the critical faculty which teaches us that, if developed into a political system, democracy becomes a snare and a delusion, fatal to all the objectives that it seeks.

Many a writer has described the mechanical balance in our governmental system. But singularly few have emphasized that this balance cannot be maintained unless the system is supported by a sense of citizenship that is itself well balanced. No representative system can operate successfully if there is deterioration in the quality of the people whom it represents. If form ceases to animate system, the latter will cease to be malleable and will imperceptibly become brittle and breakable. That change is threatened for the United States.

When Madison said that we "rest all our political experiments on the capacity of mankind for self-government," he spoke with precision. Every American citizen, as an individual, carries on his shoulders a full share of responsibility for the perpetuation of the Republic. To meet this responsibility he must constantly strive to develop the important qualities that are demanded by the nature of our political system. And the good citizen must further develop the powers of discrimination and moral courage— so that he will know when to emphasize one necessary quality above another and will possess the determination to do this in the face of a mass opinion that will always tend to condemn divergence from the momentarily popular pattern of thought. A people which has chosen the difficult road of Christianity, and built its government on that teaching, cannot be individually half-hearted in allegiance.

Self-government is the very heart and core of the American way of life. This is demonstrable in many ways, but perhaps most effectively by the fact that legal sovereignty cannot be located in any organ of the United States government. In Great Britain the majority in Parliament is clearly the absolute sovereign, "since every Act of Parliament is binding on every Court throughout the British dominions, and no rule, whether of morality or of law, which contravenes an Act of Parliament, binds any Court throughout the realm." [27] Similarly, legal sovereignty in Soviet Russia clearly vests in the Council of Ministers, of which the ruling dictator is chairman. The Constitution of the Union of Soviet Socialist Republics says (Article 67): "Decisions and orders of the Council of Ministers of the U.S.S.R. are binding throughout the territory of the U.S.S.R." [28]

But, as many a lawyer and political theorist has pointed out, the American system of government makes it impossible to attribute a final authority to any official or organ of government. "Theoretically, therefore, the conception of sovereignty cannot apply to the United States since nowhere in its structure is it pos-

[27] A. V. Dicey, *The Law of the Constitution* (of Great Britain), Eighth edition (1915), p. 425.

[28] Official translation, published by the Washington Embassy of the U.S.S.R., December, 1947, p. 20.

sible to locate legally supreme and unlimited power." [29] To put this very important point in the clear summarization of a great Russian jurist:

> . . . it would be rather difficult to say where sovereignty, in the sense of habitual predominance, resides in . . . the United States of America. Not in Congress, because its enactments may be overruled by the Supreme Court as being contrary to the Constitution. Not in the Supreme Court, because its decisions are judicial and not governmental. Not in the people at large, because it is not a juridical, but a social and historical entity. Not in the Conventions for the reform of the Constitution, because they operate only on very exceptional occasions and are fettered in making their decisions by very restrictive rules as to majorities: and a sovereign trammelled in this way would be a contradiction in terms. *The truth seems to be that the basis of law is provided not by one-sided command, but by agreement.* (Emphasis supplied.) [30]

This careful legal examination by Professor Vinogradoff brings us to the same conclusion reached by a more political analysis earlier in this chapter. Under a government in which legal sovereignty cannot be located, responsibility for reaching reasonable agreement is carried directly to the individual citizen. His disposition to agree is no mere convenience of social life; it is the actual basis of our constitutional law. To find what the Quakers so well describe as "the sense of the Meeting"—the formula whereby a conscientious group may "go forward with unity"—is an imperative and permanent quest for all Americans, not merely a part of the Discipline for members of that small sect, which has been influential beyond its numbers in American history.

The Christian virtues take shape as particular qualities. Each must be developed by the individual. They can never be inculcated by royal decree or sumptuary legislation. Legal sovereignty cannot be located in any organ of American government precisely because this Republic assumes that the individual, under divine guidance, is sovereign. It follows that the patriotic American,

[29] Huntington Cairns, *Law and the Social Sciences*, p. 226.
[30] Paul Vinogradoff, *Common-Sense in Law* (Home University Library Edition), pp. 34-35.

though law-abiding, will always be prepared to repudiate attempted extensions of the limited and contingent authority of the State. The Republic, based on individual willingness to resist governmental coercion of any kind, will endure as long as the essentially rebellious spirit of liberty remains alive in the hearts of its citizens.

Chapter 3

The Heritage of the Republic

The American people are not mindful of history. In consequence, they neither appreciate their own institutions at true value, nor understand why other peoples have a very different outlook on political problems. The result is unnecessary friction, both in the handling of domestic affairs and in matters of foreign policy.

This deficiency of American interest in historical background is inherited. Whatever the nostalgia of the early emigrants, as their frail ships carried them away from Europe, there was little opportunity for dwelling in the past once they had crossed the Atlantic. Beyond the beachheads stretched a wild, seemingly limitless, and none too hospitable continent. The colonists looked forward to the subjection of the land, not backward to recollect the subjection of men in the more cultivated countries from which they came.

But these pioneers brought with them more than high courage and crude tools. The seventeenth century, which saw their plantations expand and multiply and take root, was a remarkable period in many ways and many places. Nowhere was it more remarkable than in England, where the great majority of the first Americans, other than aborigines, were born and reared. From England these adventurers brought ideas that were eventually to flower in the Republic.

The Puritan Revolution of the seventeenth century is one of the great phenomena of history. It was simultaneously a refor-

mation and a renaissance. There was in it an almost apostolic
Christian fervor. There was a combination of resolute thought
and poetic sensitivity that found its most noble expression in the
writings of John Milton. There was an experimental spirit which
led on to the developments of modern science. And along with
other characteristics there was the mysticism of the Quakers, the
ardent democratic faith of the Levellers, and more than a trace of
idealistic Socialism in the doctrines of the Diggers.

Restriction of the royal authority was not the fundamental objective of the Puritan Revolution. That reform was only a necessary step toward the desired political end. The real goal was
the development of individual liberty. The essentially religious
search for this end, and the confusion and cross-purposes attendant
on that search, are revealed in the abundant literature of the period. But nowhere is the underlying philosophy summarized
more clearly than in the various polemical essays of Milton. The
passage that gave rise to our phrase "the blessings of liberty" is
illustrative of the political thought carried from England by the
early American colonists:

> Let us consider whether or no the Gospel, that heavenly promulga-
> tion, as it were, of Christian liberty, reduce us to a condition of slavery
> to kings and tyrants . . . It is evident that our Saviour's principles
> concerning government were not agreeable to the humour of princes.
> . . . Our liberty is not Caesar's. It is a blessing we have received
> from God Himself. It is what we are born to. To lay this down at
> Caesar's feet, which we derive not from him, which we are not be-
> holden to him for, were an unworthy action, and a degrading of our
> very nature. . . . Being therefore peculiarly God's own, that is, truly
> free, we are consequently to be subjected to Him alone, and cannot,
> without the greatest sacrilege imaginable, be reduced into a condition
> of slavery to any man, especially to a wicked, unjust, cruel tyrant.
> . . . Absolute lordship and Christianity are inconsistent.[1]

Milton was secretary to Oliver Cromwell, then Lord Protector,
when he developed this argument. It was not a sermon, but an
earnest attempt to lay down a practical theory of government.
This essay, and many others which flowed from the poet's pen,

---

[1] *Pro Populo Anglicano Defensio* (1651).

give a clear outline of what the Puritan Commonwealth was seeking to achieve. The function of the State should be severely limited. It is the province of political government to preserve peace and order, but the only purpose of this policing is to facilitate the condition of freedom, in which condition the blessings of liberty may be developed by individual effort. The outward law is actually a mark of bondage—a sign of that servitude from which man is liberated by obedience to the inner law "under the influence of the Holy Spirit." [2]

Milton realized—or certainly came to realize—that intelligence alone is inadequate to emancipate mankind from the bondage of government. The factor of human weakness outweighs the strength of human reason, unless the latter has spiritual aid. That is the moral of *Paradise Lost,* especially in the poignant passage where Eve's self-control is overcome by the flattery of the Serpent. She eats of the forbidden fruit because the reasoning power in which "our credulous Mother" puts her trust is not strong enough to keep her from sin. Eve argues that God's discipline is limited to arbitrary prohibitions, such as not attempting to defy the force of gravity. In every ordinary case, Eve asserts, reason alone will serve as adequate guide to conduct. The unhappy sequel shows that Milton means it as casuistry when Eve protests that, generally, "our Reason is our Law":

> But of this Tree we may not taste nor touch;
> God so commanded, and left that Command
> Sole Daughter of his voice; the rest, we live
> Law to our selves, our Reason is our Law.

As a political force, the Puritan Revolution had collapsed when Milton wrote *Paradise Lost,* as was the case when Bunyan wrote *The Pilgrim's Progress.* The many reasons for Puritan inability to form an effective earthly government concern us only incidentally. But we are necessarily concerned with the force of the ideas, and the effect of the changes, brought by this tremendous English uprising of the mid-seventeenth century, and of the sec-

[2] *De Doctrina Christiana.* See also A. S. P. Woodhouse, *Puritanism and Liberty,* Introduction *passim.*

ond, less violent, attempt in 1688. These two risings were seemingly unsuccessful. But they produced the seeds that found
favorable soil, and flowered, in America.

The purpose and nature of the Republic cannot be fully understood—it will falsely seem to be a mechanical and matter-of-
course achievement—unless we appreciate the Puritan aspirations,
the problems that proved too much for even the greatest of seventeenth century Englishmen, the lessons of a failure that nevertheless assisted the formation of a government actually adequate
to secure the blessings of liberty.

II

To the directors of the London Company, recruiting adventurers for the precarious settlement of Jamestown, Captain John
Smith sent wholesome advice in regard to the type of immigrants
needed by colonial Virginia. "Nothing," he wrote, "is to be expected thence but by labor." [3]

A few years later the Pilgrims, raising funds to finance the
Mayflower expedition, agreed that, like Jacob, they would work
for seven years of bondage in order to lay "some good foundation . . . for propagating and advancing the gospel of the kingdom
of Christ in those remote parts of the world." [4]

In April, 1681, immediately after Charles II had signed the
Charter of Pennsylvania, William Penn wrote confidentially of
his plan of government. "For the matters of liberty and privilege," he told a small group of Friends, "I purpose that which
is extraordinary, and to leave myself and successors no power of
doeing mischief; that the will of one man may not hinder the
good of an whole country." [5]

These illustrations, chosen almost at random from the wealth
of available documentary evidence, serve to remind us of the
purposes that animated many of the first American settlers. From
Massachusetts to the Carolinas the original immigrants came to

[3] Quoted by Charles and Mary Beard, *The Rise of American Civilization*,
Vol. I, p. 39.
[4] See Reuben J. Thwaites, *The Colonies*, pp. 116-17.
[5] Quoted by W. W. Comfort in *William Penn*, p. 141.

build a new society, based upon individual exertion, freedom of religious worship, and abolition of privilege. It was their design and accomplishment to cut themselves loose from the dominations of both State and Church as practiced in the Old World.

The part played by the urge of religious liberty in the early colonial settlements is well known. But the religious element should be considered as an integral part of the political philosophy that the colonists were seeking to establish long before the Revolution of 1776. Nonconformity in the ordained procedure of divine worship was only one aspect of the struggle of seventeenth century individualism against the authoritarian principles of the Stuarts.

The rise of England as a Great Power coincided with the reign of Elizabeth (1558-1603). Emphasis on the achievement of that brilliant reign has tended to minimize the ruthless assertion of State supremacy over Society that was then, as always, necessary for centralized aggrandizement of material power. Naturally, bureaucracy being then in its infancy, the concentration of power was focused in the personal control of the monarch. And to justify this absolutism the theory of the divine right of kings was promulgated. Because of the union of Church and State in England, under Henry VIII, the doctrine of divine right received important theological as well as political support. It was soon reduced to a syllogism of which the major premise was that *resistance to divine authority is unlawful.* Then came the fallacious minor premise that *the king derives his authority from God.* This leads to the logical conclusion that *resistance to the king is never lawful.* But the syllogism collapses before the argument that all men, commoners as well as kings, derive what authority they possess from God.

The threat of Spanish invasion and the wise leadership of Elizabeth combined to keep the divine right issue from coming to a head during the last half of the sixteenth century, the more so because Parliament was then an undeveloped as well as an unrepresentative institution. But when the great queen died, in 1603, and was succeeded by the stubborn and intractable James I, the struggle that was to have so much meaning for America flared out. As religion was the chief motive power of the age, the conflict became most acute in the religious field.

While Protestant nonconformists suffered, the regimentation imposed on them was less severe than on the Romanists, who were with good reason suspected of plotting against the State. The long series of Acts of Supremacy and Uniformity can be reviewed in any thorough account of the late Tudor and early Stuart periods. Here we need mention only those sponsored by James I from 1606 to 1610, which banned recusants from public office, debarred them from the legal and medical professions, authorized the search of their homes for Popish books and relics, offered bribes to any who would disclose the names of those refusing to attend Anglican service, and extended the death penalty for conversion to Romanism, already imposed on the agent, to the convert himself.[6]

Of this legislation, reminiscent of that developed by the Nazis against the Jews, Professor Prothero has written: "However eager in the cause of persecution the government might have been, the inherent difficulty of putting into action a coercive and inquisitorial system of such minuteness and universality would have rendered it practically impossible to carry out the law."[7]

In other words, the coercive will of the seventeenth century authoritarian State was not implemented by adequate administrative machinery. But the clear intent of the monarch to persecute, at a time when England was free from any threat of foreign invasion, stirred the English people, acting independently and through Parliament, to resistance. That resistance was stimulated when James I, in 1616, in a statement to the judiciary on his prerogative, laid down the edict that all "which concerns the mystery of the King's power is not lawful to be disputed" and "it is presumption and high contempt in a subject to dispute what a King can do, or say that a King cannot do this or that."[8]

[6] The text of these drastic Acts "for the better discovering and repressing of Popish Recusants" is printed in G. W. Prothero's *Select Statutes of the Reigns of Elizabeth and James I*, pp. 256-68.

[7] *Ibid.*, Intro., p. 52.

[8] Text of this address on "Prerogative and the Judges," is given in Prothero, *op. cit.*, pp. 399-400.

III

All this, of course, was background for the civil war that led to the execution of the son and successor of James I. Equally, it was background for the founding of the American colonies by Englishmen, both Protestant and Catholic, who regarded freedom with rigorous privation in the New World as preferable to submission with relative security at home. Life in England when the American colonies were being launched was far from miserable, in material advantages, for the least privileged groups. "Upon the whole, as compared with other periods of our history," concludes an English historian who has specialized on the Stuart epoch, "this was an age when the poor were well treated by the public action of the community." [9]

What seventeenth century Englishmen sought in America was not so much material advantage as the religious and political freedom which did not then obtain in England. A part of the evidence is that during the period of the Commonwealth and Protectorate, when parliamentary government seemed to have triumphed, there was a pronounced movement from the colonies back to the Mother Country. "In the twenty years of Puritan supremacy at home, as many persons perhaps had returned from New to Old England as had gone out from Old to New." [10]

But care should be taken not to exaggerate the picture. Aside from the "gentlemen, goldsmiths and libertines" who gave Smith so much trouble at Jamestown there were, in all the colonies, those who had come unwillingly. For these the prevalent talk of freedom was bitterly ironic. Convicts were included among the many indentured "servants" and the first shipment of Negro slaves became involuntary Virginians a year before the Pilgrims landed on Plymouth Rock.

The spirit of intolerance, furthermore, was a stowaway on the *Mayflower* and other early immigrant ships. In Massachusetts those who had suffered persecution soon showed themselves adept in persecuting others. Virginia closed her territory both to Puri-

[9] George Macaulay Trevelyan, *England Under the Stuarts*, p. 29.
[10] *Ibid.*, p. 357.

tans from New England and to Papists from Maryland. The latter colony for years experienced more civil strife than the average, which was high. Any attempt to paint Americans, at any period from 1606 to 1776, as a Utopian band of happy brothers would be absurd. From the beginning, strife and contention were in the air. After the bloody suppression of Bacon's Rebellion (1676) by Governor Berkeley of Virginia, King Charles II commented: "That old fool has hanged more men in that naked country than I have done for the murder of my father."

On the whole, however, the colonial conflicts contributed to progress along a definite line of political evolution. When Roger Williams was exiled from Massachusetts for "divers new and dangerous opinions" (1636) he fled to Narragansett Bay and there established Providence Plantation. When the theoretical constitution that John Locke helped to write for the Carolinas failed miserably, the settlers there slowly worked out a system of government to suit themselves. Throughout the colonies, at different times in different places, there were periods of near anarchy. But the rich response of the new land to labor, and the independent spirit of most of the settlers, together provided the desired opportunity for founding a type of civilization unknown in Europe. Everywhere the dominant emphasis was on self-government rather than on imposed government; on the development of Society, not on the aggrandizement of the State.

Behind this new political development there was conscious political theory, continuously discussed in town and village meetings, continuously taught in unadorned churches and primitive frontier schools. It was the theory quaintly expressed in 1682 by William Penn in his first "Frame of Government" for Pennsylvania:

> Governments, like clocks, go from the motion men give them, and as governments are made and moved by men, so by them they are ruined too. Wherefore governments rather depend upon men, than men upon governments . . . for liberty without obedience is confusion, and obedience without liberty is slavery. To carry this evenness is partly owing to the constitution, and partly to the magistracy; where either of these fail, government will be subject to convulsions . . .

where both meet, the government is like to endure. Which I humbly pray and hope God will please to make the lot of this of Pennsylvania. Amen.

To support and secure a new civilization, a new State was in process of gestation. The grand design was emancipation, not regimentation. People were to be citizens, not subjects. For the divine rights of kings the colonial leaders substituted a new, a revolutionary, and a highly idealistic political doctrine: the divine right of men. The word brought hope to the discouraged English revolutionists. And throughout all Western Europe, in communities shattered by the Thirty Years' War to an extent comparable with the wreckage of World War II, the story of God's country spread.

Travel was difficult but settlers with the initiative to make the effort were welcomed. Soon the steady stream of emigrants from Britain was strengthened by rivulets of like-minded men and women from the long Rhine valley, from Scandinavia, and from France. America, clearly, was destined to be much more than a group of English colonies. And its social judgments would in general be based on the character, not on the heredity, of the individuals who merged themselves in the current setting toward the "New World."

IV

The Civil War in England became inevitable, considering the personal character and absolutist political creed of Charles I, with the passage by Parliament of The Grand Remonstrance, on November 22, 1641.[11]

As Charles with some reason protested, this lengthy indictment of his rule was printed and broadcast before presentation to him, on December 1. Its central point was an open threat (Sect. 197) to refuse appropriations unless the king would agree to the confirmation of his "Councillors, Ambassadors and other Ministers" by Parliament. Charles retorted sharply that "it is the undoubted right of the Crown of England to call such persons to our secret

[11] For text of the remonstrance and the royal reply, see *Constitutional Documents of the Puritan Revolution*, edited by Samuel Rawson Gardiner, pp. 202-36.

counsels, to public employment and our particular service as we shall think fit."

On January 3, 1642, the king brought impeachment proceedings in the House of Lords against the five members of the House of Commons (Pym, Hampden, Hazlerigg, Holles and Strode) who were the principal authors of The Grand Remonstrance. For this highhanded action there was no constitutional authority, as the Lords pointed out. Thus thwarted, Charles, the next day, moved personally, with an armed bodyguard, to arrest the Puritan leaders on the floor of the House. Forewarned of the coming outrage on the Commons, Pym and his associates had gone into hiding. Surrounded by his swordsmen the king stalked to the Speaker's desk; surveyed the rows of silent, standing members; lamely announced "the birds are flown"; and walked out again. Now there could be no healing of the breach. Within a week the king had fled from London, not to return until, seven years later, men gathered at Whitehall to watch fulfillment of Cromwell's grim promise: "We will cut off his head, with the crown upon it."

Unlike the French Revolution, the epic seventeenth century struggle in England was not primarily a war between classes, for many of the gentry sided with Parliament while some merchants, artisans, and laborers, as well as great landowners, voluntarily followed the banner of the king. Unlike our own Civil War, that in England, more than two hundred years earlier, was not a regional conflict, for while the Parliamentary cause predominated in the south and the east a great part of the country was evenly balanced between the adherents of both sides. Unlike the Thirty Years' War in Europe, the end of which was contemporaneous with the English struggle, the latter was not deeply embittered by religious fanaticism. Though the Catholics for the most part sided with the king, both parties were predominantly Protestant. And a Christian attitude of mercy and forgiveness to the defeated royalists was as much emphasized as military efficiency had been in the building of Cromwell's "New Model" army.

To a greater extent, perhaps, than any other military conflict in modern history the English Civil War was one of abstract political ideas, thereby arousing "a nobler speculative enthusiasm among the chiefs and their followers, but less readiness to fight among the masses of the population, than in other contests that have torn great nations." [12] It was the peculiar character of this conflict, as much as its coincidence with the period when American institutions were being formed, which made its trans-Atlantic influence so great. The American heritage was molded not only by the physical conditions of the frontier, but also by the mental stimulus of England's Civil War. Were local evidence of this fact lacking, one could infer it from the considered opinion of English historians on the importance of the struggle between king and Parliament. In the words of Trevelyan:

> The First Civil War is the decisive event in English history. The defeat of the King's armies alone enabled Puritanism to survive in England and Parliamentary institutions to triumph.
>
> For if Charles had won, those who could keep alive resistance to Anglican and royal absolutism must have sailed for America. The men who formed the strength of the anti-monarchical and the Puritan part of the community, were always contemplating emigration. England sent enough of these elements to found a new world; but if the war had gone differently, she would have sent out enough to ruin herself. The most adventurous merchants, the most skilled artisans, the Lords and gentlemen who took counsel for the liberties of their country, the ploughmen who saw visions, the tinkers who dreamed dreams, were perpetually thinking of New England. Thither twenty thousand Puritans had already carried their skill and industry, their silver and gold, their strivings and hopes. The Roundhead armies were raised by men of the merchant class, and were led by landed gentlemen of the type of Cromwell, who were not, like the Cavaliers, deeply attached to the soil . . . Such men would have emigrated rather than live under the military despotism of an Anglican King. Thus defeat in the field would have ruined forever the cause of Parliament, and would have driven the Puritans out of England. Freedom in politics and religion would never have been evolved by the balance of parties, for one party would have left the land. Without its leadership, the mass of Englishmen, indifferent as they showed themselves to the result of the Civil War, would never again have risen in revolt against

[12] Trevelyan, *op. cit.*, p. 229.

a royal Church and a royal State. The current of European thought and practice, running hard towards despotism, would have caught England into the stream.[13]

For England, however, the conflict was not as immediately decisive, in a political sense, as the above conclusion, taken from its context, would seem to indicate. "Brave Oliver" found it far easier to unseat the doctrine of divine right than to evolve a workable system of constitutional government to replace it.

V

The problem of holding an even balance between the potential anarchy of a free Society and the potential tyranny of an empowered State is both the most difficult and the most important in the sphere of politics. Cromwell's effort to solve it, through his "Instrument of Government," was thoughtful and intelligent. This constitution for a British Republic was never formally adopted. But from the end of 1653 until the death of the "Lord Protector" on September 3, 1658, Great Britain—and incidentally the American colonies—were governed under its terms. Moreover, the influence of this "Instrument of Government" on the eventual Constitution of the United States was so pronounced as to cause surprise that it is largely ignored by studies of the American political system.[14]

The death of Oliver Cromwell ended the political power, though not the influence, of the Puritan Revolution. The attempted rule of his son Richard ("Tumbledown Dick") lasted only a few months. Exhausted by years of disorder, the English people as a whole welcomed the arbitrary action of General Monk. He occupied London and organized the election of a "Free Parliament," which in turn voted for the restoration of the Stuart monarchy, in accordance with the terms of the Declaration of Breda. On May 25, 1660, eighteen and a half years after The Grand Remonstrance to his father, Charles II returned from exile

[13] *Ibid.*, pp. 225-6.
[14] For the text of the "Instrument of Government," see Gardiner, *op. cit.*, pp. 405-17.

to land on Dover beach. England's republican revolution was at an end. But every end is also a beginning—in this instance, of the American Republic.

Across the broad Atlantic, in the scattered settlements of New England and Virginia-Maryland, the ebb and flow of the struggle in the mother country aroused partisanship, which doubtless would have been even more keen if communications had not been so primitive. Fortunately the Dutch and Swedish settlements, in New Netherland and along the Delaware respectively, helped to separate the strongly Puritan colonies of New England from predominantly Royalist Virginia. The feuding in the then raw colony of Maryland, where Lord Baltimore had established the first settlement in 1633, indicated what might have happened if northern Roundheads and southern Cavaliers had been closer together on the long seaboard. That latent political antagonism was destined to play a part in our own Civil War.

Coming when it did, however, the first English revolution was more instrumental in developing American self-government than in dividing the colonies into antagonistic camps. One significant political result was the formation of the New England federation, joining the embryonic governments of Massachusetts Bay, Plymouth, Connecticut, and New Haven in "a firm and perpetual league of friendship and amity for offence and defence," under the name of the United Colonies of New England. In these early articles of confederation there was no reference to either king or Parliament. "Freed from the supervision of the English government, the colonists began to think of themselves as beyond the mother country's control, trading wherever they pleased and conducting their affairs much in the manner of independent States." [15]

This phenomenon was as apparent in Virginia as in New England, even though the population of the oldest colony was doubled, largely as a result of Cavalier immigration, during the disestablishment of the monarchy. The colonists were deeply interested in England's political changes, but there is ample evidence to show that this interest was intellectual rather than

[15] John C. Miller, *Origins of the American Revolution*, p. 30.

emotional. If the clash of ideas seemed more important than the clash of arms to Englishmen at home, this was much more the case for their cousins who were growing up as Americans. As such they were forced to give primary attention to the problem of the form of government that could most satisfactorily knit together, protect, and strengthen the social life which they had come to the New World to develop.

Indifference to the patriotic, though not the political, aspect of the war in England was strengthened by the large number of colonists for whom the English flag had no nationalistic appeal. This applied to the Dutch, the Swedes, the Germans who pressed into Pennsylvania, the French Huguenots trickling into the southern colonies, and also many of the Scottish and Irish settlers. To all of these, America was far more important for itself than as a part of England's Empire. To many of the agricultural population, whether or not Charles kept his head seemed less important than the continued good health of the family cow. But few were indifferent to the underlying question of whether the Parliament would eventually establish representative government. The more intelligent colonists could see the impact of this issue on themselves, on their children, and on the country that had become their home.

The Puritan Revolution in England, as we have seen, was inconclusive. A century after the execution of Charles I another English king, of the House of Hanover, was again asserting the royal prerogative, almost as stridently as had the Stuart monarchs. It took a second revolution, in England, and a third, originating in America, firmly to establish not only the independence of the United States but more particularly the Puritan ideal of a controlled and representative government. We cannot say that the American Revolution would not have taken place if the two in England had been averted. But we do know that the English revolutions, over the lessons of which men in this country reflected long and deeply, provided a political philosophy for the American rising, and largely determined the character of the new State which rose from the upheaval.

Two Englishmen in particular, both of whom will always rank

high in the world's roster of outstanding political thinkers, clarified the issue.

VI

The first of these two, in point of time, was Thomas Hobbes, who was born in the year of the Spanish Armada and whose long life (1588-1679) lasted for nearly two decades after the restoration of the Stuart monarchy. Therefore his calm and scientific scrutiny encompassed the whole tumultuous series of events that revolved around the scope and limitation of governmental authority. That Hobbes was well aware of the magnitude, as well as the difficulty, of this fundamental issue is shown in the judicial tone of all his political writing, especially in the foreword to *Leviathan,* where he summed it up:

> Beset with those that contend, on one side for too great liberty, and on the other side for too much authority, 'tis hard to pass between the points of both unwounded.

No chain of political thought can be wholly immunized from the circumstances that envelop the thinker. The condition of England when Hobbes, in Paris, was writing *Leviathan* went far to justify his basic assumption. This was "that during the time men live without a common power to keep them all in awe, they are in that condition which is called war; and such a war as is of every man against every man." Under such circumstances, Hobbes concluded in a famous passage, the life of man is "solitary, poor, nasty, brutish and short." [16]

This assumption of human depravity in the absence of some overriding temporal power led Hobbes to even-handed condemnation of the Jesuits, the Puritans, and the Quakers. All of these placed spiritual authority above that of the political State and were, therefore, in one way or another, "sowers of anarchy." Perhaps the worst of all were the Quakers, who, under the leadership of George Fox, were contemporaneously insisting on the importance of individual conscience and developing the doctrine of the "inner light" as the final guide of personal conduct. Of these be-

---

[16] *Leviathan,* Ch. XIII.

lievers in revelation, Hobbes said with scathing accuracy that "every boy or wench thought he spoke with God Almighty."

Because Hobbes served as mathematical tutor to Charles II, before the Restoration, and because he presented a copy of *Leviathan*, written on vellum, to that exiled prince when the book was completed, in 1651, some have attacked his political philosophy as opportunist. None who has examined the brilliant reasoning of *Leviathan* is likely to accept this criticism. The case that Hobbes built up for centralized authority, free from popular interference, would have been useful to Charles I, had it appeared before his execution. It was certainly useful to Charles II, to George III, and could have been useful to Lenin. But Hobbes was no believer in divine right or any other form of mysticism, pure or applied. His argument was that individual self-interest, called laissez faire a little later, must lead to governmental tyranny. His conclusions were ably reasoned, on eminently practical considerations.

The position to which they led can best be summarized in Hobbes' own classification "Of Those Things that Weaken, or Tend to the Dissolution of a Commonwealth," which is the title of Chapter XXIX of *Leviathan*. There the "doctrines repugnant to civil society" are listed as:

1) that a man to obtain a kingdom, is sometimes content with less power, than to the peace and defence of the commonwealth is necessarily required;
2) that every private man is judge of good and evil actions;
3) that whatsoever a man does against his conscience is sin;
4) that he that hath the sovereign power is subject to the civil laws;
5) that every private man has an absolute propriety in his goods; such as excludeth the right of the sovereign;
6) that the sovereign power may be divided.

Since these six "diseases" of a commonwealth were, in effect, the fundamental articles of political faith of the American colonists, it is easy to appreciate the effect of *Leviathan* on the dawning political consciousness of the New World. The proportion of Americans who read this book contemporaneously was probably about the same as the proportion that today can claim to have waded through the far more turgid pages of Karl Marx. But the effect of the parallel philosophies was in each case similar. For one who approvingly followed the argument for complete individual subordination to centralized planning there were ten who felt it to be irrational as well as wrong. And, fortunately, the man to give the case against Hobbes effective presentation was at hand, in the person of John Locke.

VII

The admitted purpose of Locke's essays on civil government was to justify the second, bloodless, English revolution of 1688. The Stuart Restoration had applied Hobbes' arguments for undivided sovereignty not wisely but too well. There is painful modernity in some of the excesses that were committed. To prove that Cromwell was really dead, his decayed body was exhumed and hanged at Tyburn, the motive being the same as in the public exhibition of Goering's corpse at Nuremberg, after that Nazi leader escaped the gallows by suicide.

Such sadistic actions, however, were of less political consequence than the infamous "Clarendon Code," designed to eliminate all opposition to the monarchy, and well illustrated by the "Five Mile Act" of 1665. This act prohibited any clergyman or schoolmaster from coming within five miles of an incorporated town until he had sworn that he would not "at any time endeavor any alteration of government, either in Church or State." The grim irony of this and similar repressive statutes was their coincidence with the secret plotting of Charles II, both with the Vatican and with Louis XIV of France, "to alter the doctrines of the Church of England into those held by the Church of Rome." [17]

Nevertheless, in spite of all the excesses, abuses, deception, and outright terrorism of his reign, the political skill and shrewd opportunism of Charles, coupled with popular aversion to another civil war, kept this king on the throne until his death in 1685.

---

[17] Trevelyan, *op. cit.*, p. 366.

Charles II was then succeeded by his brother, James II, last of the
Stuart monarchs, who reigned only three years.

Ushered in by peasant revolt in the west of England, the liquidation of which sent many admirable political exiles to the American colonies,[18] this short reign ended ingloriously when William
of Orange accepted the secret invitation to take the throne extended to him by a number of leading lords and clergy, headed
by John Churchill. In February, 1689, William and Mary were
jointly established in office by a duly elected constitutional convention—legitimacy being attributed to the choice both because
Mary was the daughter of James II, and because William's
mother was the daughter of Charles I. The immediate passage
of a bill of rights, containing many provisions later incorporated
into the Constitution of the United States, confirmed the liberty
of the subject and the authority of Parliament as against the
dictatorship of the Crown.

It was this Revolution of 1688 for which John Locke, the son
of one of Cromwell's officers, provided the necessary philosophical
basis. His youth, like Hobbes' middle age, was passed amid the
vast upheaval of the Civil War and there was much, as in their
mathematical leanings and their mutual admiration for Descartes,
which these great political thinkers shared in common. Of the
two, however, Locke was the more active in public life, for some
time combining his practice as a physician with service as secretary
to the Council of Trade and Foreign Plantations, where he
learned much concerning the developing American colonies.
Locke's part in writing the "Fundamental Constitutions for the
Government of Carolina" has been mentioned. He also contributed to the political education of William Penn, whose viewpoint
he shared in matters other than religious toleration.

Two sentences in his first *Letter on Toleration* go far toward
summarizing Locke's political philosophy, and help to clarify the
vital distinction between Society and State that Hobbes had so
completely missed:

[18] Monmouth's Rebellion is the subject of several historical novels: *Lorna
Doone*, by R. D. Blackmore; *Micah Clarke*, by Sir Arthur Conan Doyle; *Captain
Blood*, by Rafael Sabatini.

The whole trust, power, and authority of the magistrate [19] is vested in him for no other purpose but to be made use of for the good, preservation and peace of men in that Society over which he is set, and therefore that this alone is and ought to be the standard and measure according to which he ought to square and proportion his laws, model and frame his government. For, if men could live peaceably and quietly together, without uniting under certain laws, and growing into a commonwealth, there would be no need at all of magistrates or politics, which were only made to preserve men in this world from the fraud and violence of one another; so that what was the end of erecting of government ought alone to be the measure of its proceeding.

Locke, at this point, did not take direct issue with the assertion of Hobbes that the life of man, in a state of nature, is "solitary, poor, nasty, brutish and short." But he did reiterate and revive the Puritan belief that the aim of civil government is not to control man, but to help him to control himself. Hobbes, on the other hand, had developed an argument encouraging the conclusion that governmental coercion is not only essential, but even desirable because of the allegedly depraved nature of man. There is certainly no sympathy in Hobbes for Hamlet's contemporary protest against:

"The insolence of office, and the spurns
That patient merit of the unworthy takes" [20]

It is in the second treatise *Of Civil Government* (1690) that Locke really engages with Hobbes, pointing out that even in a state of nature man cannot be called a really vicious animal. Agreement, tacit or expressed, to enter into a social contract, itself proves men to be reasonable. One obvious purpose in the formation of any State is to protect that private property which begins with a man's own person—"this nobody has any right to but himself"—and extends to that with which "he hath mixed his labour." Life, liberty and the means for the pursuit of happiness are less

[19] The title is used in the broad sense of any executive officer of civil government.
[20] Act III, Sc. 1, ll.73-74.

tangible forms of individual property, to preserve which men form a commonwealth. As Professor Orton points out: "What Locke is defending is property as the extension of personality." [21]

VIII

Hobbes' contrasting theory was that in creating the State men became its subjects, placing the sovereign power outside and above themselves. This argument Locke denied. Those who bear allegiance to a State are not its subjects but its citizens. They have surrendered only such natural rights as must be surrendered for the better protection and development of their personalities.

In consequence, the law-making power is of the first importance in every commonwealth and must be subject to certain principles: (1) It cannot be "absolutely arbitrary over the lives and fortunes of the people," since all civil government is in the nature of a trust. (2) There cannot be government by decree, but only "by promulgated standing laws and known authorized judges." Otherwise the "peace, quiet and property" of men "will still be at the same uncertainty as it was in the state of Nature." (3) Government "cannot take from any man any part of his property without his own consent." This consent may be granted by duly-elected representatives, but even so taxation must not be confiscatory. Since men created the State to preserve private property, the State cannot be utilized to dissipate private property, for this would be "too gross an absurdity for any man to own [admit]." (4) "The legislative cannot transfer the power of making laws to any other hands, for it being but a delegated power from the people, they who have it cannot pass it over to others." Locke would have been appalled by the growth of what we call administrative law.

For Hobbes' argument that the evil nature of man makes dictatorship inevitable, Locke had a challenging retort:

> Absolute monarchs are but men; and if government is to be the remedy of those evils which necessarily follow from men being judges

[21] William Aylott Orton, The Liberal Tradition, p. 110.

in their own cases, and the state of Nature is therefore not to be endured, I desire to know what kind of government that is, and how much better it is than the state of Nature, where one man commanding a multitude has the liberty to be judge in his own case, and may do to all his subjects whatever he pleases without the least question or control of those who execute his pleasure? [22]

The philosophical structure designed by Locke fitted perfectly into the political necessities of the American colonists. The colonists were not disturbed by charges that the idea of social contract arising from the state of nature is pure fiction, for The Mayflower Compact and other communal agreements to subdue the wilderness were actually a part of their heritage. In Locke's distinction between Society and State the colonists found the philosophical justification of all their efforts to create a way of life preferable to that which they had left behind in various European principalities. The attack on absolutism vindicated their criticisms of royal authority without seeming to have relevance to dictatorial practice in their own glass houses. The gathering cry of "no taxation without representation" of course sprang directly from Locke's denunciation of such procedure. And his defense of the right of rebellion against tyranny, intended to defend the English Revolution of 1688, could be applied with devastating effect to the successors of William and Mary on the British throne.

John Locke died a little over a year before Benjamin Franklin was born. The latter tells, in his *Autobiography*, of reading Locke's *Essay Concerning Human Understanding* "when about sixteen years of age." That would have been some twenty years before the birth of Thomas Jefferson. Shortly before his death the principal author of the Declaration of Independence replied with customary dignity to accusations that this great document was "a commonplace compilation," containing "no new ideas." Said Jefferson of the Declaration: "Richard H. Lee charged it as copied from Locke's treatise on Government . . . I only know that I turned to neither book nor pamphlet while writing it. I did not consider it as any part of my charge to invent new ideas altogether

[22] *Second Treatise of Civil Government*, Ch. II, par. 13.

and to offer no sentiment which had never been expressed before." [23]

By 1776, in other words, the ideas of John Locke had become an intrinsic part of the body of American political thought.

IX

The Puritan Revolution in England did more than undermine the theory of State supremacy. To it we also owe establishment of the two-party system, a political device remarkable for its mechanical simplicity and efficiency, and possessing the even greater merit of guiding the deepest and most passionate human emotions into an orderly contest between those who are entrusted with, and those who aspire to, the exercise of political power.

Much of the credit for the origination of party government must go to that amiable, even though misanthropic, mathematician, Thomas Hobbes, whose reaction to the famous Forty-Seventh Theorem of Euclid was: "By God, is it possible?" [24] It was the great contribution of Hobbes to apply mathematical precision to political problems—to develop the careful work of Aristotle in laying the foundations of political *science*. Our Democrats and our Republicans alike can trace their party affiliation, whether inherited, reasoned or accidental, to Hobbes' observation, already quoted, that the golden mean between the advocacy of liberty and the advocacy of authority is difficult to locate.

Hobbes, influenced by contemporary anarchy, aligned himself on the side of authority. Locke, sickened by Stuart absolutism and eager to defend the peaceful solution offered by the accession of William of Orange, thereupon worked out an alternative philosophy of liberty.

Of course the division in political thinking did not originate with these two Englishmen, influential though their respective

[23] Gilbert Chinard, *Thomas Jefferson*, p. 71. See also Dumas Malone, *Jefferson the Virginian*, Ch. XVI and Miller, *op. cit.*, Ch. VIII.

[24] The square on the hypotenuse is equal to the sum of the squares on the two other sides. A pleasant biographical sketch of Hobbes is found in *The Story of the Political Philosophers*, by George Catlin.

reasoning and speculation proved to be. The cleavage between those who regard individual liberty as of transcendent importance and those who conclude that the individual must conform to political discipline for the sake of the "general welfare" can be traced back to Socrates and Plato, who may be called protagonists of the respective schools. So, for those who are careful not to minimize the importance of Oriental civilization, are Lao-tze and K'ung Fu-tze (Confucius). Clearly there is the pulsating rhythm of Yin and Yang, of thesis and antithesis, of statics and dynamics, behind these contrasting schools of thought.[25]

But Hobbes and Locke were unique, and remain vital to us, because their philosophical speculation was adapted to and was adopted by a politically minded people grappling with a pervading and difficult political issue—the rivalry of Crown and Parliament. Today we speak of Executive and Legislature. They are essentially the same well-seasoned rivals, under other names.

X

Actual party division in England originated during the tyrannical reign of Charles II. While all were weary of the seemingly futile blood letting of the Civil War, the underlying issue between the prerogative of the king and that of Parliament remained unsolved. It had not been settled by the arbitrament of arms; so Englishmen concentrated on solution through political procedures.

Anthony Ashley Cooper, later first Earl of Shaftesbury, who gave two of his names to the rivers that join at Charleston, South Carolina, was the friend and patron of John Locke. Though a skeptic and politician to his fingertips Cooper was also a true liberal, proving himself time and again as advocate of civil liberty and religious toleration for all Protestants, and as unswerving opponent of absolutism in Church or State. Like many another courageous leader of these troubled years, the Earl of Shaftesbury

---

[25] For a thorough inquiry into the evidence of these "integrations" and "differentiations" see Toynbee, *A Study of History*, esp. Vol. I, Part II, "The Genesis of Civilizations."

spent time in the Tower of London for his views. He therefore
had more than academic interest, as a leader in Parliament, in two
measures before the Parliament of 1679. One of these—the
Habeas Corpus Act—enforcing speedy trial for political prisoners,
became law. The other—the Exclusion Bill—designed to prevent
the accession of James II to the throne, failed when Charles II
dissolved Parliament to prevent its passage.[26]

The issue and the passions aroused were closely akin to those
that a generation earlier had led to armed hostilities. But the
packed and unrepresentative parliaments of Charles II contained
many more courtiers, and fewer stubborn Puritans, than Charles I
had confronted. In consequence, Shaftesbury's group chose the
pacific course of petition. All over England, among the humble
as well as the exalted, the agents of the liberal parliamentary
leaders collected signatures for the demand that Parliament be
permitted to reassemble. For the first time the yeomen, the small
merchants, and the master craftsmen were asked—even entreated
—to express themselves personally on an issue of government. By
thousands they responded, and peaceful politics suddenly became
the business of the average man.

Alarmed by the multitude of the "Petitioners," the Court leaders busied themselves with securing the names of those willing to
express abhorrence of Shaftesbury's methods. This also brought
politics down to the level of the common man, who has perhaps
more right to claim the seventeenth than the twentieth century
as his own. Whether "Petitioner" or "Abhorrer," his opinion
was asked and use of his undistinguished name was requested in
connection with affairs of State. The development was unprecedented in England. And it provided the practical basis of party
organization at the very time when, by natural coincidence, its
theoretical significance was being thought out.

The year 1680 saw the cumbersome appellations of Petitioner
and Abhorrer change to Whig and Tory. For this, though for
no other reason, it is fitting to recall the name of Titus Oates, the
prototype of the informers who flourished in Nazi Germany, who

[26] For text of these measures, see *Select Statutes and Documents, 1660-1832*,
edited by C. Grant Robertson, pp. 92-104.

serve the N.K.V.D. in Communist Russia and who may always
be expected to appear in the service of the State whenever the
latter sets out to persecute some element in Society.

The feverish political excitement of the reign of Charles II
concentrated on the question of whether his brother James, known
to be a Catholic and strongly suspected of being in league with
Louis XIV of France, would be the next king. This was the background that inspired the anti-Catholic legislation of the period,
and the atmosphere was made to order for a clever scoundrel like
Oates. The stories, of the Popish Plot that he concocted, and of
the wretched reign of terror resulting from it, do not concern us
here. But it was at this time that Oates would loudly denounce
as a "Tory"—the Irish name (tōruidhe) for those who murdered
Protestant settlers in that country—any dignitary who questioned
the authenticity of his plot. The quick retort of the Catholic leaders, close to the throne and hoping to be more so, was to label
their traducers with the appellation of bandits of another stamp
—that of the Scottish whiggamors, or mare drivers, who were
guilty of horse stealing and worse along the English border.

Thus, in an exchange of biting epithets, came the christening of
the Tory and Whig parties, the former standing for supremacy
and absolutism on the part of the Crown, the latter for the subordination of the king to Parliament. At the outset the Whigs
were dominant, partly because the fear of Catholic restoration
aligned the entire Anglican Church as well as the London mobs
on their side, partly because of the greater organizing ability of
men like Shaftesbury and his fellow members of the famous Green
Ribbon Club—the Union League of its day.

Indeed it was not until the "divine right" issue and the "Protestant Succession" had been simultaneously settled, by the "Glorious
Revolution" of 1688, that the Tories became powerful. The more
moderate Statism of Viscount Bolingbroke, who sought the "forti-
fication of Toryism," replaced the *Leviathan* of Hobbes as their
text. To Bolingbroke's *Letters on the Spirit of Patriotism*—as
Locke to Hobbes half a century earlier—Edmund Burke soon
responded with his *Vindication of a Natural Society*, arguing

ironically that only when the State disciplines Society do we find
a situation where it holds:

> . . . that those who labour most enjoy the fewest things and that
> those who labour not at all have the greatest number of enjoyments.
> A condition of things, this, strange and ridiculous beyond expression.

Burke wrote those words in 1756, only twenty years before the
American colonies declared their independence. By then the
name of Tory, on this side of the Atlantic, was applied to all who
advocated submission to British authority; the Whigs were those
who denied the British Parliament a right to tax the colonies. The
application of the names had changed, as it had changed in England. But the essential division, between those who placed the
State first and those who placed Society first, still held, and on
this issue the English-speaking people of America were preparing
a third political revolution. It was the logical climax of the two
preceding ones in England.

By this time, also, the international picture had come to favor
American separation. In 1680, the year when Tories and Whigs
were first so classified, Louis XIV had annexed the entire Missis-
sippi Valley. While encircled by French territory, to the north
and west, the seaboard colonists were understandably loath to
break the English connection. But in 1763 France was forced to
cede Canada to England. Thereupon France ceased to be a potential conqueror of the colonies, becoming instead a potential ally.
This new strategic situation brought almost immediate flowering
of the political thought that for generations had been preparing
the birth of the American Republic.

Chapter 4

Strength and Weakness

Throughout our national history the critics of Alexander Hamilton have shown a bitterness comparable to the devotion of his admirers. But the worst enemy of the principal author of *The Federalist* could never characterize him as a demagogue. So all Americans can still respond unreservedly to that unusually reverential passage in which, after denouncing the "arrogant pretensions of the Europeans," Hamilton concluded that: "It belongs to us to vindicate the honor of the human race." [1]

Conviction that the destiny of America would prove of supreme importance to all mankind is strongly marked throughout the early days of the Republic. To identify this conviction in Hamilton, who had little faith in democracy, is to emphasize its general prevalence in the first generation of American citizens. They were alert to the wisdom of Washington's advice not to "entangle our peace and prosperity in the toils of European ambition, rivalship, interest, humour or caprice." Nevertheless, those who read the Farewell Address in 1796 were equally responsive to the first President's admonition "to give to mankind the magnanimous and too novel example of a people always guided by an exalted justice and benevolence."

This late eighteenth century prose, with its beautiful cadence, was not merely rhetorical. Americans then believed that they had

[1] *The Federalist*, No. 11.

something exceptional to offer to mankind. We know that they were well aware of the significance of their potential contribution; that they were deeply eager for its fulfillment. These early Americans were familiar with the long European record of frustration, a part of which we have recalled in the preceding chapter. After a difficult and often desperate struggle they had achieved political independence. Now the material, the cultural, and the spiritual opportunity of that victory lay before them.

II

In the earning of their daily bread the citizens of the new Republic found themselves freed from all the numerous and hampering restrictions of British mercantilism.

This policy, which today would be called *autarky*, or economic nationalism, had helped to instigate the Revolution, both by artificial channeling of foreign commerce and by prohibitions on the development of domestic manufactures. Opposition to the various economic controls imposed by the British Parliament was more than a matter of political theory on the part of the colonists. Many were in the position of the ruined Pennsylvania ironmaster who, in 1771, was given a post in the Philadelphia customhouse. Restrictions placed by the British government on that colonial industry had driven him bankrupt. This, explained Governor John Penn, in making the appointment, "has been the case with most people who of late years have engaged in that sort of business." [2]

Immediately after Britain acknowledged American independence, William Pitt sought to push through a hostile Parliament legislation that would have repealed the Navigation Acts and established unconditional free trade between the two countries. Conceived in the magnanimous spirit of true statesmanship, this proposal might well have achieved Pitt's purpose of healing the wounds of war and making a good customer and firm friend of the infant but robust Republic. The refusal of Parliament to go along had momentous consequences.

[2] Quoted by John C. Miller, in *Origins of the American Revolution*, p. 22.

The immediate effect was to confine all commerce between Great Britain and the West Indies, largely in American hands during the colonial period, to British ships. On top of this economic blow, the English sought to monopolize all the direct trade with the former colonies for their own shipping. This was possible only as long as each of the thirteen states, virtually independent nations under the Articles of Confederation, could be handled separately. Thus loss of the carrying trade combined with the inflation and dislocation of the Revolutionary War to develop a very serious economic situation from Massachusetts to Georgia. Sheer necessity played its part in the convening of the Federal Convention, and in the subsequent adoption of a constitution in which Sections 8, 9, and 10 of Article I vest in the federal government alone the right of levying customs duties, which "shall be uniform throughout the United States."

In this manner was established the enormous and unrestricted market available to American producers of every type. Co-operative accumulation of wealth was to be expected—given the natural resources of the country; the energy, intelligence, and independent spirit of its citizens; the circumstances that focused their thinking on their own affairs; the definite limits placed on governmental interference. There was no miracle in the rapid American development of such well-distributed prosperity as the world had never before seen or even imagined.

The generation that achieved American independence was, however, more certain of the cultural than of the material opportunities of the new nation. Prior to the industrial revolution, indeed, none could foresee the productive possibilities of mechanical development. Even Alexander Hamilton, at least as farsighted as most of his contemporaries, predicted—in the issue of *The Federalist* quoted above—that Americans would remain "for the most part exclusively addicted to agriculture." But it was a civilization of "village Hampdens," rather than that of an aristocracy with a proletarian basis, that was anticipated.

III

The southern colonies, of course, might have given a very different direction to American development. There the institution of slavery rooted quickly and for some decades threatened to produce a Society so different from that of the North as to make permanent incorporation in a single State, even a federation, impossible.

The system of primogeniture and that of entail—for slaves as well as for land—had threatened to establish a measure of feudalism in one part of the New World. During its period of establishment the Anglican Church in Virginia reproduced, in miniature, all of England's semipolitical religious intolerance. The legend of southern aristocracy, however, is more fictional than factual. Painstaking research has revealed that actually only three Virginia families "derived from English houses of historic note." The southern settlers, aside from slaves, were the same sort of minor gentry, yeomen, small merchants, and indentured servants that had emigrated to New England and the Middle Colonies. "But those who climbed upward into the possession of great plantations quickly assumed the cultural guise of the English aristocracy in that flexible fashion so characteristic of all mankind." [3]

It was Thomas Jefferson, the son of a hard-working, back-country farmer, who really turned Virginia, and with it the intellectual direction of the entire South, into the destined stream of American cultural development. His leadership, of course, was strongly supported. James Madison, George Mason, George Wythe, and others labored in the sessions of the Legislature to such effect that Jefferson could tell Franklin, in August, 1777, that Virginians had moved from monarchical to republican forms "with as much ease as would have attended their throwing off an old and putting on a new suit of clothes." [4]

It should be emphasized that all of these men, and many of the successive southern leaders, were as strongly critical of slavery as

[3] Charles and Mary Beard, *The Rise of American Civilization*, Vol. I, p. 128.
[4] Quoted in James Parton, *Life of Thomas Jefferson*, p. 219 (sixth edition). See also Dumas Malone, *Jefferson the Virginian*, pp. 252-7.

any northern abolitionist. George Mason, at the Constitutional Convention in 1787, even argued that his own and other southern states should not be admitted to the Union until the practice had been outlawed. The issue was not whether slavery was socially desirable, but when and how the inherited cancer should be eradicated. Not the pressure for emancipation, but the dictation of centralized government, caused the South to resort to arms in 1861. Its battle was not alien to, but was basically in behalf of, the American tradition. Defense of states' rights was no more an indorsement of slavery, at the time of the Civil War, than opposition to a federal antilynching law was an indorsement of mob murder three generations later.

So from New England to Georgia, in spite of climatic, economic, and political differences, there was, as the colonies grew to maturity, an underlying and binding cultural unity. It was appreciated by Edmund Burke in his great though fruitless speech on "Conciliation with America." It was demonstrated by General Grant in his magnanimity to the fallen foe at Appomattox. It is again apparent now that so many Americans, recognizing the falseness of the gods they have been urged to worship, are endeavoring to restore tarnished values by an effort of mind and will. For such enduring faith, making itself evident in every period of protracted crisis, there should be some fundamental explanation. And there is.

The basis of America's cultural unity is not material prosperity, which came so rapidly and was so inadequately digested as to bring much of the corruption anticipated by Benjamin Franklin. Whenever we seek for the real sources of American strength we find them, in the last analysis, resting on the belief that the individual is at least potentially important, and that he fulfills himself through voluntary co-operation in a free society. This belief implies an instinctive hostility to the State—an agency created to discipline Society and with a consequent tendency to assume the direction of all social functions.

Freedom is a condition, dependent upon the continuous exertion of the relatively few who really reflect on the nature of liberty. There are those, as Milton pointed out, who will never have "the love of genuine liberty which a good man only loves and knows how to obtain." Men who do not emphasize the connection between freedom and conduct—"however much they may brawl about liberty, they are slaves both at home and abroad, but without perceiving it . . ." [5]

For those who incline toward slavery, a master is always forthcoming, and the State can equitably exert the necessary discipline through law. But it is beyond the power of the State—no matter how benevolent, no matter how authoritarian—to insure the condition of freedom that is maintained only by the individual love of liberty. Freedom is, indeed, the very opposite of Status which, in any place, at any time, must operate to limit and define, rather than to enlarge and dignify, the role of man as something more than a reasoning animal. And from a fundamentally religious belief in the spirit of liberty springs the American hostility to Status and to the State as the agency most competent to bind Status on mankind.

The seventeenth century, when the foundations of American civilization were being laid, was in many ways a period similar to our own. Then, as now, "two irreconcilable philosophies of life engaged in mortal combat." [6] Amid the confusion and contention of the times, the issue stands out clearly. Shall Man be subject to the authoritarian State or shall he restrain State powers to the minimum necessary for an orderly Society? In seventeenth century England the issue focused on the power of the established Church as an arm of the State. Today, when men are less religious, it is a question of whether all social life—including the spiritual—shall be subordinated to State control.

The early Americans made their choice. The great majority of them could approve the words of William Penn when he said, of Pennsylvania: "I went thither to lay the foundation of a free colony for all mankind." Almost a century later, speaking in the House of Commons on March 22, 1775, Edmund Burke told a

[5] *Defensio Secunda* (an address to Cromwell urging him to rely on the leaders of the Independents).

[6] George F. Willison, *Saints and Strangers*, p. 8. A careful, readable study of the Pilgrims and the ideas and ideals for which they stood.

hostile audience that: "In this character of the Americans, a love of freedom is the predominating feature which marks and distinguishes the whole. . . . This fierce spirit of liberty is stronger in the English colonies probably than in any other people of the earth." [7]

Though the English State in 1775 was very powerful—relatively as much so as our own today—it could not tame the "fierce spirit" of the colonists. Yet that spirit has been tamed, and greatly. The complex causes for the softening process must be examined.

The method of this examination is of great importance. Let us consider the prejudice in the medical profession against the doctor who relies on his own diagnosis in the case of those who are near and dear to him. This prejudice, when a serious ailment is involved, does not question the physician's skill. It merely argues that professional talent may under some circumstances be affected adversely by personal emotions. Therefore, when disease strikes hard in the doctor's household, an independent medical opinion is customarily sought by him.

For similar reasons we shall now turn to a remarkable social and political diagnosis of America by a discriminating foreigner. It is not merely the skill of his analysis that makes this particular examination so valuable to us. Equally important is the time at which it was made. The Republic was then firmly established. Its great strength was beginning to mature. But the symptoms of fundamental weakness in the organism had also reached the point at which they could be, and were, identified. The weakness then discernible to a brilliant diagnostician is now apparent to every thoughtful man.

IV

A ship from Havre sailed in to Newport, Rhode Island, on May 9, 1831. It landed a young Frenchman, still short of his twenty-sixth birthday and proud of the Norman lineage respon-

[7] *Conciliation with America*. His resolution to that end was lost by a vote of 270 to 78.

sible for his resounding name: Alexis Charles Henri Clerel de Tocqueville. With him was another young magistrate in the service of the French government, Gustave de Beaumont. The latter's interests leaned to the problem of racial relationships in America, while de Tocqueville was more concerned with the political theory the young Republic had evolved.

Both youths—for they were scarcely more—had an official mission to report on the American prison system, at their own expense. Both had larger objectives in mind. As a result of a visit lasting nearly ten months, during which they traveled more than 7000 miles through the length and breadth of the United States as then constituted, each wrote a book. That by de Beaumont was a now almost forgotten sociological novel entitled *Marie, ou l'esclavage aux Etats-Unis*. That by de Tocqueville, destined for innumerable editions, and translation into every important European language, was *De la Démocratie en Amérique*.

The reasons for the instantaneous and enduring success of de Tocqueville's epic work are numerous. Underlying them all was the fact that a cultured and penetrating French mind had at this early stage of independence minutely surveyed the institutions of the American people and found them of world-wide import. The thought of Montaigne, Pascal, Voltaire, Helvétius, Rousseau, and Montesquieu—especially the last—had influenced the colonial leaders, to an extent comparable with the effect of the English philosophers, excepting Locke. But prior to de Tocqueville no Frenchman, in spite of the significance of the American Revolution for that country, had seemed to realize the full meaning of the American experiment.

Moreover, Americans themselves, with the passing of the generation that had made the revolution, were becoming doubtful of the permanence of their accomplishment and were simultaneously exhibiting the inferiority complex that still remains a national characteristic. During de Tocqueville's visit South Carolina was openly threatening secession from the Union. And of Andrew Jackson's first inauguration, just three years before the young French aristocrat left Paris to inspect this wild democracy for himself, a Washington dowager had written: "The noisy and disorderly rabble . . . brought to my mind descriptions I have read of the mobs in the Tuileries and at Versailles." [8]

This disdainful lady (Mrs. Margaret Bayard Smith) would have been more at home in the Newport of the coming American plutocracy than in the unspoiled and upstanding little town of the Jacksonian era where de Tocqueville landed. In 1831 Newport was a very appropriate starting point for the tour of this student of democracy. It had been one of the four settlements in the colony of Providence Plantations actually established by a form of "social contract." Rousseau, whose writings were of course familiar to de Tocqueville, had in 1762 described the "essence" of the Social Contract as follows:

> *Chacun de nous met en commun sa personne et toute sa puissance sous la suprême direction de la volunté générale, et nous recevons en corps chaque membre comme partie indivisible du tout.*[9]

The subtlety of the phrase *en corps* makes it virtually impossible to translate this summary of the social contract theory into English, without doing some damage to the underlying thought. But the broad assertion, taking the context into consideration, is that people combine for their various undertakings under the supreme direction of a "general will," to which each individual contributes and from which he receives "conventional" as opposed to "natural" liberty. The distinction we have already drawn between "freedom" and "liberty" is in line with this thought. What Rousseau calls "la liberté conventionnelle" is really the condition of freedom, made secure by self-imposed restrictions on individual liberty, called by Rousseau "liberté naturelle." Obviously, the essential validity of Rousseau's argument does not depend upon recorded evidence that groups of naked savages covenanted with each other to define a "general will." It does require proof that men confronting primitive conditions, like the early American colonists, are individually willing to establish regulations for cooperative ends. Such proof is at hand.

[8] Quoted in Beard, *op. cit.*, Vol. I, p. 555. See also *The Life of Andrew Jackson*, by Marquis James, Ch. XXVIII.
[9] *Du Contrat Social*, Livre Premier, Ch. VI.

Rousseau's theory of social contract is much more revolutionary than Locke's guarded conclusion that Society created the State for its own advantage. And it has been bitterly denounced by many political thinkers, especially in England. Edmund Burke, for all his liberal instincts, attacked the theory as "chaff and rags and paltry blurred shreds of paper about the rights of man." Sir Frederick Pollock, writing during the present century, defines the social contract as a "plastic fiction," admitting sorrowfully that it "became one of the most successful and fatal of political impostures." [10] Even so temperate and customarily dispassionate an Englishman as George Catlin goes berserk over the social contract, repeating the charge that it is a "fiction" and saying of its author that: "The influence of this disordered, half-educated man, whose philosophy was founded upon sentimentality untrained, uncontrolled and undisciplined, is one of the major catastrophes in the history of human thought." [11]

The underlying reason for the indignant repudiation of the social contract theory by the great majority of English political writers is not far to seek. In the form expressed by Rousseau it asserts not merely that all men are equal, not merely that sovereignty rests in the people, and cannot be delegated by them even to a representative legislature, but also that no law contrary to the *"volunté générale"* can rightly be regarded as binding—*"il est contre la nature du corps politique que le souverain s'impose une loi qu'il ne puisse enfreindre."* This comes close to the doctrine of anarchy, as the French Revolution soon proceeded to demonstrate. Moreover it would knock the bottom out of the traditional English predilection for a stratified Society. What price royalty, or titles, or established Church, or primogeniture, or county family, or, most of all, "the lower classes," if actually "a man's a man for a' that"? [12]

[10] Sir Frederick Pollock, *An Introduction to the History of the Science of Politics* (1919 edition) p. 79. The quotation from Burke is given, uncited, on p. 94 of Pollock's book.

[11] George Catlin, *The Story of the Political Philosophers*, p. 444.

[12] A notable exception to the habitual antagonism of English political writers to Rousseau is Hilaire Belloc. In his study of *The French Revolution* he defines the *contrat social* as "the text" of this rising, asserting (p. 32) that "never . . .

It is no indorsement of the entire body of Rousseau's thinking to point out that those who dismiss his Social Contract as pure fiction are, on this point, themselves subject to correction. Ironically enough, it was Englishmen, on American soil, who have left us actual records of such contracts—many of them. That their existence, let alone their significance, should have been so consistently ignored by English writers is one of the most curious *lacunae* in the scholarship of that politically minded nation.

V

On this matter of social contract a Frenchman like de Tocqueville, even in his tender years, was better informed. Discussing the founding of Rhode Island, where he landed, de Tocqueville points out that the settlers "constituted themselves into a Society, and it was not till thirty or forty years afterwards, under Charles II, that their existence was legally recognized by a royal charter." And then, with one of those flashes of political insight so frequent in the pages of *Democracy in America:*

> In some countries a power exists which, though it is in a degree foreign to the social body, directs it, and forces it to pursue a certain track. In others the ruling force is divided, being partly within and partly without the ranks of the people. But nothing of the kind is to be seen in the United States; there Society governs itself for itself.[13]

In view of the frequent assertions that the social contract is a political "fiction," with no historical base, it is interesting to quote the Providence Agreement of 1636, signed by Roger Williams and his associates and coming very close to defining, for one settlement, that "*volunté générale*" for which Rousseau has been so much derided:

---

has a political theory been put forward so lucidly, so convincingly, so tersely or so accurately as in this short and wonderful book." All can agree that Rousseau has been successful in stimulating partisanship.

[13] Vol. I, p. 57 (1945 edition of Alfred A. Knopf, edited by Phillips Bradley). For a personal study of de Tocqueville and the background of his famous book, see George Wilson Pierson, *Tocqueville and Beaumont in America.*

We whose names are hereunder, desirous to inhabit in the Town of Providence, do promise to subject ourselves in active or passive obedience to all such orders or agreements as shall be made for the public good of the body, in an orderly way, by the major assent of the present inhabitants, masters of families, incorporated together into a town fellowship, and such others whom they shall admit unto them, only in civil things.[14]

The last four words are vital. For social contract in the American colonies was seldom interpreted as subordinating the individual to the general will in that spiritual field whence liberty emanates. At Newport itself, in the code of laws adopted in 1647, it was agreed that "all men may walk as their conscience persuades them." And nothing impressed de Tocqueville more, or was more continuously emphasized in his writing, than the political consequence of this essentially religious emphasis on self-government. In his words:

The partisans of centralization in Europe are wont to maintain that the government can administer the affairs of each locality better than the citizens can do it for themselves. This may be true when the central power is enlightened and the local authorities are ignorant; when it is alert and they are slow; when it is accustomed to act and they to obey. . . . But I deny that it is so when the people are as enlightened, as awake to their interests, and as accustomed to reflect on them as the Americans are. I am persuaded, on the contrary, that in this case the collective strength of the citizens will always conduce more efficaciously to the public welfare than the authority of the government.[15]

The actual vesting of sovereignty in the people, and the consequent subordination of the State to Society, was the American characteristic, in Jackson's day, that impressed de Tocqueville most and which he admired most. There were dangers, which he noted with uncanny foresight. But: "Nothing is more striking to a European traveler in the United States than the absence of what we term the government, or the administration." [16] And

[14] Quoted by Reuben J. Thwaites, *The Colonies*, p. 147.
[15] *Op. cit.*, Vol. I, p. 89.
[16] *Ibid.*, p. 70.

yet: "It was never assumed in the United States that the citizen of a free country has a right to do whatever he pleases; on the contrary, more social obligations were there imposed upon him than anywhere else." [17]

De Tocqueville, in 1831, was the first political scientist from another land, understanding the components and characteristics of political organization, to appreciate that in America the individual, retaining sovereignty, intended to fulfill his destiny through a free Society, holding the State in leash. What did it matter, then, if "clodhoppers" pushed through the wideswung doors of the White House at Jackson's inaugural? With a wealth of evidence de Tocqueville was giving Europe, in his own words, "a solemn warning that Society changes its forms, humanity its condition; and that new destinies are impending." The character of the book was such that John Stuart Mill, its first English reviewer, defined *Democracy in America* as "among the most remarkable productions of our time."

Americans of today are different from those de Tocqueville knew. One indication is in the number of contemporary college graduates who have never even turned his pages. Therefore it is not superfluous to quote the closing paragraphs of the first volume of *Democracy in America* as an illustration of the intuition that enabled this young Frenchman, well over a century ago, to foresee the ultimate challenge to the American ideal:

> There are at the present time two great nations in the world, which started from different points, but seem to tend towards the same end. I allude to the Russians and the Americans. Both of them have grown up unnoticed; and while the attention of mankind was directed elsewhere, they have suddenly placed themselves in the front rank among the nations . . .
>
> All other nations seem to have nearly reached their natural limits, and they have only to maintain their power; but these are still in the act of growth. All the others have stopped, or continue to advance with extreme difficulty; these alone are proceeding with ease and celerity along a path to which no limit can be perceived. The American struggles against the obstacles that nature opposes to him; the

[17] *Ibid.*, p. 71.

adversaries of the Russian are men. The former combats the wilderness and savage life; the latter, civilization with all its arms. The con-
quests of the American are therefore gained by the plowshare; those
of the Russian by the sword. The Anglo-American relies upon personal interest to accomplish his ends and gives free scope to the un-
guided strength and common sense of the people; the Russian centers
all the authority of society in a single arm. The principal instrument
of the former is liberty; of the latter, servitude. Their starting-point
is different and their courses are not the same; yet each of them seems
marked out by the will of Heaven to sway the destinies of half the
globe.[18]

VI

De Tocqueville's apprehensions as to the future of American
democracy were not, however, primarily based on his anticipation
of the eventual Russian challenge. With equal clarity he noted
the degenerative tendencies inherent in a democratic system, and
warned against them. The fifteenth chapter of Volume I, and the
significant closing chapters of Volume II, of this classic study,
are alike devoted to searching analysis of tendencies toward despotism in the United States.

In retrospect, the reasoning of this political philosopher is
strengthened both by the nature of the social changes that have
taken place in this country since the publication of *Democracy in
America*, and by the extent to which his predictions have already
been fulfilled. In 1835 de Tocqueville could be optimistic about
the longevity of our "democratic republic" because, for one major
reason, "America has no great capital city, whose direct or indirect
influence is felt over the whole extent of the country. . . ."[19] But
he also possessed the insight to anticipate such collectivist developments as NRA, as shown in the following thoughtful passage:

> In democratic communities nothing but the central power has any
> stability in its position or any permanence in its undertakings. All the
> citizens are in ceaseless stir and transformation. Now, it is in the nature
> of all governments to seek constantly to enlarge their sphere of action;

[18] Vol. I, p. 434. I have translated *liberté* as "liberty," not "freedom."
[19] Vol. I, pp. 289-90.

hence it is almost impossible that such a government should not ultimately succeed, because it acts with a fixed principle and a constant
will upon men whose position, ideas, and desires are constantly changing.

It frequently happens that the members of the community promote
the influence of the central power without intending to. Democratic
eras are periods of experiment, innovation, and adventure. There is
always a multitude of men engaged in difficult or novel undertakings,
which they follow by themselves without shackling themselves to their
fellows. Such persons will admit, as a general principle, that the
public authority ought not to interfere in private concerns; but, by
an exception to that rule, each of them craves its assistance in the
particular concern on which he is engaged and seeks to draw upon
the influence of the government for his own benefit, although he would
restrict it on all other occasions. If a large number of men applies this
particular exception to a great variety of different purposes, the sphere
of the central power extends itself imperceptibly in all directions, although everyone wishes it to be circumscribed.

Thus a democratic government increases its power simply by the
fact of its permanence. Time is on its side; every incident befriends it;
the passions of individuals unconsciously promote it; and it may be asserted that the older a democratic community is the more centralized
will its government become.[20]

De Tocqueville's belief that democracy is afflicted with suicidal
characteristics should, like the more doctrinaire consideration of
the same problem by Plato or Hobbes, be closely examined in the
original sources. But since the French critic's argument on this
subject is interpolated at widely separate parts of his study, an
abstract of some of his major points may helpfully be attempted
here.

A dangerous characteristic of democracy, de Tocqueville notes,
is that in giving political power to a majority it tacitly encourages
belief that there is some connection between majority opinion and
truth. This assumption is obviously fallacious. The world was
no less spherical at a time when the overwhelming majority declared it to be flat.

No political system that lends itself to fallacious direction can

[20] *Ibid.*, Vol. II, p. 294n.

be called fundamentally stable, and the instability of democracy as a political system is the more pronounced because of the constant tendency of its leaders to generalize and oversimplify in order to obtain majority support. "Complicated systems are repugnant to it [democracy], and its favorite conception is that of a great nation composed of citizens all formed upon one pattern and all governed by a single power." [21]

The majority in a democracy will always be relatively untutored and the picture of government most readily formed by it "is that of a sole, simple, providential, and creative power." [22] This illusion is fostered by those entrusted with governmental office both because it is flattering to their self-esteem and because the conception of government as creative tends to check criticism of its blunders, its wastefulness, and its suppression of individuality.

Although the democratic ideal encourages individualism, the actual operation of a democratic system produces a centralization of power hostile to self-reliance. Additionally, the vitality of local government deteriorates because: "Private life in democratic times is so busy, so excited, so full of wishes and of work, that hardly any energy or leisure remains to each individual for public life." [23] Thus there arises a class of professional but often unprincipled politicians, whose major interest in government is the prerogatives and spoils of office.

This concentration of power, in venal hands, tends to go unchecked because the majority does not like to have its electoral judgment questioned. Indeed, the principle of majority rule tends to discourage independent thinking in every field where public opinion is vocal, with results shocking to a cultured observer. De Tocqueville remarked, "I know of no country in which there is so little independence of mind and real freedom of discussion as in America. . . ." [24] The majority lives in the perpetual utterance of self-applause, and there are certain truths

[21] *Ibid.*, Vol. II, p. 289.
[22] *Ibid.*, p. 291.
[23] *Ibid.*, p. 293.
[24] *Ibid.*, Vol. I, p. 263.

which the Americans can learn only from strangers or from experience." [25]

Deterioration of the critical faculty in American political thought has kept citizens of the Republic from realizing that arbitrary power in a democracy may be just as great a menace to liberty as the outright tyranny of a dictatorship. De Tocqueville draws a nice distinction between the two: "Tyranny may be exercised by means of the law itself, and in that case it is not arbitrary; arbitrary power may be exercised for the public good, in which case it is not tyrannical." The insidious tendency in unrestricted democracy is toward both "the legal despotism of the legislature," and "the arbitrary authority" of executive officers. Thus, "habits are formed in the heart of a free country which may some day prove fatal to its liberties." [26]

"The mutability and the ignorance of democracy" in the United States contrast strangely with the intellectual "grandeur" of the men who established the Republic. Of the formative period, however, de Tocqueville observes that "public opinion then served, not to tyrannize over, but to direct the exertions of individuals." [27] Once democracy begins to operate as a political system, deference to majority control makes it almost inevitable that representative government will fall into the hands of mediocre leaders.

In short, the various reasons here summarized combine to demonstrate that the survival of the Republic is not endangered by weakness in the central government, but by popular pressure for its aggrandizement. As de Tocqueville concluded: "If ever the free institutions of America are destroyed, that event may be attributed to the omnipotence of the majority . . ." [28]

VII

While he admired the ingenuity of the checks and balances in the American system of government, de Tocqueville had little

[25] *Ibid.*, p. 265.
[26] *Ibid.*, p. 262.
[27] *Ibid.*, p. 266.
[28] *Ibid.*, p. 269.

confidence in the efficacy of constitutional restrictions on the forces
outlined above. Only the naive, he says, could "imagine that it
is possible by the aid of legal fictions to prevent men from finding
out and employing those means of gratifying their passions which
have been left open to them." [29] The likelihood that Americans
will let these passions destroy the Republic is the stronger because
of the complexity of the federal system. "In examining the Constitution of the United States, which is the most perfect federal
constitution that ever existed, one is startled at the variety of
information and the amount of discernment that it presupposes
in the people whom it is meant to govern." [30]

De Tocqueville anticipated that such intellectual discernment
would become increasingly exceptional as the nation gained in
population and material power. For the preservation of free institutions he therefore placed his faith not on the Bill of Rights
and other constitutional guarantees, but rather on continuing loyalty to that local self-government which he found so vigorous and
admirable in the United States of the early eighteen-thirties. "I
believe," he wrote, "that provincial institutions are useful to all
nations, but nowhere do they appear to me to be more necessary
than among a democratic people." And yet, with prevision of
the overshadowing nemesis that took form a century later: "I am
also convinced that democratic nations are most likely to fall beneath the yoke of a centralized administration." [31]

The distinction between centralized government and centralized administration, as made by this shrewd observer, is to be kept
in mind. Even a federal government must be centralized to the
extent that matters removed from local control, such as the direction of foreign policy, are somewhat arbitrarily decided for the
nation from its capital city. But if essentially local interests, such
as education or housing, are similarly controlled from a single
center, the result must be to add centralized administration to centralized government. "I cannot conceive," says de Tocqueville,

[29] *Ibid.*, pp. 168-9.
[30] *Ibid.*, p. 166.
[31] *Ibid.*, p. 95.

that a nation can live and prosper without a powerful centralization of government. But I am of the opinion that a centralized administration is fit only to enervate the nations in which it exists, by incessantly diminishing their local spirit. Although such an administration can bring together at a given moment, on a given point, all the disposable resources of a people, it injures the renewal of those resources. It may ensure a victory in the hour of strife, but it gradually relaxes the sinews of strength. It may help admirably the transient greatness of a man, but not the durable prosperity of a nation.[32]

Therefore, local administration, even when demonstrably backward and inefficient, is from the over-all viewpoint politically desirable. Governmental responsibility must be kept local and personal in order to foster the individual spirit of liberty. That spirit can never be externally guaranteed but must continously be internally and individually nurtured. So it followed that in the United States, as de Tocqueville knew it:

When a private individual meditates an undertaking, however directly connected it may be with the welfare of Society, he never thinks of soliciting the co-operation of the government; but he publishes his plan, offers to execute it, courts the assistance of other individuals, and struggles manfully against all obstacles. Undoubtedly he is often less successful than the State might have been in his position; but in the end the sum of these private undertakings far exceeds all that the government could have done.[33]

To read the above in the light of the political philosophy of the New Deal is to realize how fundamentally the current concept of democracy differs from that of the Jacksonian era. In 1840 the spirit of democracy was working to stimulate, rather than to repress, the activity of individual free enterprise in every kind of undertaking. By 1940 President Roosevelt could refer, with great satisfaction over the trend toward Socialism, to "the multitudinous functions that the policy-makers in modern democracy assign to administrators in modern democracy." This President rejoiced in the same centralization of administration that de Tocqueville feared. "I am convinced," Mr. Roosevelt added, "that most

[32] *Ibid.*, p. 87.
[33] *Ibid.*, p. 94.

people in the United States do have a sense . . . that we have at
least been moving forward these later years in the right direction.
. . . And one of the manifestations of that new spirit is that there
are fewer Americans who view with alarm." [34]

Thus, in the course of a single century, did the United States
come to fulfill de Tocqueville's warning "that democratic nations
are most likely to fall beneath the yoke of a centralized administration." Thus did an American President complacently attest the
validity of de Tocqueville's assertion "that a centralized administration is fit only to enervate the nations in which it exists, by
incessantly diminishing their local spirit."

It is indeed the manifestation of a new, and sadly diminished,
spirit if the dissipation of a glorious heritage is insufficient to make
the losers "view with alarm." As John Philpot Curran long since
told the Irish House of Commons:

> The condition upon which God hath given liberty to Man is eternal
> vigilance; which condition if he break, servitude is at once the con-
> sequence of his crime and the punishment of his guilt.[35]

VIII

If de Tocqueville had anticipated the decay in religious faith
that has accompanied the growth of American prosperity, he
would have been much more disposed to "view with alarm." He
raised a question that is highly pertinent today, in asking: "What
can be done with a people who are their own masters if they are
not submissive to the Deity?" And de Tocqueville did not equiv-
ocate in his answer: "Despotism may govern without faith, but
liberty cannot." [36]

The successful integration of Protestant and Catholic in the
body of American Society particularly interested this French observer. At the time of his visit he estimated that there were in
the Union "more than a million Christians professing the truths
of the Church of Rome." He was impressed by discovering that

[34] At the Jackson Day Dinner, in Washington, Jan. 8, 1940.
[35] Speech upon "The Right of Election," 1790.
[36] *Op. cit.*, Vol. I, p. 307.

in a country with a strong Puritanical background "fervent and zealous" Catholics nevertheless "constitute the most republican and the most democratic class in the United States."

A part of the explanation, de Tocqueville concluded, lies in the fact that Catholics "constitute a minority, and all rights must be respected in order to ensure to them the free exercise of their own privileges." [37] The reflection that a minority will be respected in the exact measure that it respects other minorities was intriguing to this young Frenchman and led him to the conclusion that the identification of Church and State in Europe was one of the primary causes of the decadence which he anticipated for that continent. As it seemed to him:

> In Europe, Christianity has been intimately united to the powers of the earth. Those powers are now in decay and Christianity is, as it were, buried under their ruins. The living body of religion has been bound down to the dead corpse of superannuated polity; cut but the bonds that restrain it, and it will rise once more. [38]

Religion in America, however, was viewed by de Tocqueville as a virile and vital force. He was certain that: "Unbelief is an accident and faith is the only permanent state of mankind." Religious faith, strong in the American origins, had been strengthened by the wise constitutional separation of Church and State, with the paradoxical result that "the real authority of religion was increased by a state of things which diminished its apparent force." [39]

There is good reason for Americans of this era to reconsider "the great political consequences" that de Tocqueville attributed to "the peaceful dominion of religion" in a country where no Church is privileged above another. In America he found none of those "condottieri of liberty"—a phrase reminiscent of Milton's reproach to the "banditti of liberty"—whom he had known in France. At home de Tocqueville had "almost always seen the spirit of religion and the spirit of liberty marching in opposite directions." But in this country he found them "intimately united."

[37] *Ibid.*, p. 301.
[38] *Ibid.*, p. 314.
[39] *Ibid.*, p. 309.

And so de Tocqueville, with profound admiration, reported that:

> The Americans combine the notions of Christianity and of liberty so intimately in their minds that it is impossible to make them conceive the one without the other; and with them this conviction does not spring from that barren, traditionary faith which seems to vegetate rather than to live in the soul.[40]

IX

De Tocqueville died in 1859, as clouds that he had observed during his extensive American tour were piling up to break in the catastrophe of Civil War. As we reflect upon the history of the Republic, that conflict seems to have been all but inevitable because of the almost superhuman difficulty, at that time, of resolving the underlying issue. This, of course, was formed by the antagonistic necessities of preserving the vitality of local government while strengthening the national authority for the elimination of a condition of such fundamental immorality as that of human slavery.

As to how a problem of this magnitude could be peacefully resolved without some injury to fundamental principle, de Tocqueville was himself confused. He did not offer a satisfactory solution in the neat apothegm that advised centralized government without centralized administration. So much of government *is* administration that the differentiation, while important, is tinged with unreality. If this friendly critic of American government could bring out a new edition of his classic today, however, there can be no doubt as to the major conclusion he would draw.

The pendulum has swung so far in the direction of centralization that every effort should be made to reverse its course, not only so far as the State is concerned but also in the various over-concentrated manifestations of Society.

In a general way, de Tocqueville did foresee the desirable long-range solution of the problem. Like every thoughtful man

[40] *Ibid.*, p. 306.

he recognized the systole and diastole that underlies all human activity. He saw that thesis and antithesis can be combined into a synthesis more promising than either of the opposing forces. It is this element of philosophic insight, applied to a report based upon factual and objective observation, that today makes *Democracy in America* of so much more than narrowly historical interest.

Whenever it seems necessary to strengthen the central government in a democracy, de Tocqueville pointed out, the steps taken must be directed by "discernment" of the principles upon which that democracy was established. Otherwise degeneracy into despotism, through the agency of centralized power, will be as certain as the coming of night.

In the case of our own democratic Republic, this discernment requires full appreciation of the purpose of the many impediments to pure majority rule that were intentionally made a part of the governmental system of the United States. The uncritical and unqualified adulation of "democracy," to which the American mind so readily succumbs, can only be called fantastic, in view of the scrupulous care taken to impede the realization of democracy in the operation of our government.

Fortunately, however, there does not seem to be any very determined American intention actually to practice the unqualified political democracy that officials of our government so frequently preach as a desirable system—for other people. One of the permanent "restrictions" on American democracy, which de Tocqueville of course noticed, is the Presidential veto power, "made to confer a strong and independent position upon the executive authority, within the limits that were prescribed to it." [41] If admiration of political democracy were really deep-rooted among the American people, one would be able to discern a trend, since de Tocqueville's day, toward abolishing or at least limiting this veto power. There would have been an evolution parallel to the process whereby the royal assent to legislation passed by the British Parliament has become automatic.

On the contrary, the executive veto of laws desired and duly

[41] *Op. cit.*, Vol. I, p. 155.

approved by the representatives of the people has been applied
with increasing frequency in the United States. Under President
Franklin D. Roosevelt use of the veto was actually extended to
include the cancellation of financial legislation, regarded since the
seventeenth century as the most essential prerogative of the representative assembly. The precedent set by Mr. Roosevelt was
carried even further by his successor, during the period when he
had not been elected to the office carrying the veto power.

During the first session of the eightieth congress, President
Truman successfully vetoed tax legislation not only once, but
twice, although on the second occasion more than two thirds of
the really representative House voted to override. Yet this
wholly undemocratic procedure, as it must be defined regardless
of the separate issue of whether or not the legislation in question
was desirable, was accepted as a matter of course by a people who
were simultaneously vociferously acclaiming the virtues of democracy.

The incident is no more illustrative than the continued disfranchisement of citizens who live in the District of Columbia.
But veto vitality indicates that de Tocqueville was wrong in re-
garding our constitutional limitations on democracy as of secondary importance. On the other hand, there is evidence here of
de Tocqueville's insight in his strictures on American naiveté in
the whole vital field of abstract political ideas.

Though intellectual appreciation of the limitations on democracy, in our republican system of government, is essential to the
preservation of that system, the discernment necessary for the
task is not possessed by all, and never will be. It is not a quality
packed in the baggage train of higher education, as shown by the
obviously greater success of our colleges in turning out good tech-
nicians than in making good citizens. The latter are found on
farms and in factories in just as high a proportion as under the
academic elms, which is one reason why our faith in democracy
is justified so long as it is also qualified.

Fortunately for the Republic, its permanence does not depend
wholly, or even primarily, on intellectual discernment. As de
Tocqueville clearly recognized, the American system of govern-

ment, in contrast to all the Old World forms, is founded on faith in a code of individual conduct. The moral qualities can be understood by anyone who has taken the trouble to read the New Testament, which remains the primary source book on American government, even though seldom so regarded. More fundamental than our system of checks and balances is that spiritual aspiration which justified Alexander Hamilton's assertion that: "It belongs to us to vindicate the honor of the human race."

The responsibility of every American, regardless of condition and occupation, is to play his part in making sure that the unity of the Republic does not degenerate into the uniformity of dictatorship. The overtones in this individual responsibility were fully realized by de Tocqueville. "To compel all men to follow the same course towards the same object," he wrote, "is a human conception; to introduce infinite variety of action, but so combined that all these acts lead in a thousand different ways to the accomplishment of one great design, is a divine conception." [42]

That is the conception of the Republic; that is why it may reasonably be called God's country; that is why de Tocqueville said of Americans: "Religion . . . must be regarded as the first of their political institutions." [43]

[42] *Ibid.*, Vol. II, Appendix Y, p. 367.
[43] *Ibid.*, Vol. I, p. 305.

Chapter 5

State and Society

"Man is by nature a political animal," asserts Aristotle in Book
I of *The Politics*. And, a few lines later: "A social instinct is
implanted in all men by nature." [1]

These axioms of political science are upheld by all human experience. The prolonged dependency of children, disproportion-
ately long in relation to the offspring of other species, itself
attests the validity of the two assumptions. So does the human
gift of speech, which Aristotle cites as evidence that man is more
political than the bees or other gregarious creatures. There can
be no such easy agreement, however, with his simultaneous conclusion that "the State is a creation of nature."

In the fourth century B.C., Aristotle could speak of State and
Society as though they were the same. Throughout *The Politics*
he uses the one word *polis* to represent that for which we have
the two nouns. But we must remember that Aristotle was thinking in terms of the Greek City-State, of very limited area and
population. "To the size of States," he says, "there is a limit"
and even some cities, like Babylon, are of "such vast circuit" that
they must be regarded as "a nation rather than a State" (Book
III). As to population, "a great city is not to be confounded with
a populous one." The ideal State should contain enough people

[1] Jowett translation, Oxford University Press, 1920, pp. 28-9.

to be self-sufficient, but not so many that citizens cannot personally know each other.

Moreover, by listing desirable conditions of statehood, Aristotle makes himself vulnerable to the charge that he has not discriminated between the political instinct and that which is its natural result. A natural result is not the same thing as a creation of nature. In the words of a thoughtful critic: "If the city comes of nature, it does not come of the deliberate will of citizens who get together for the purpose of achieving a certain advantage! There is an inconsistency between the principle first posited and the conclusion reached." [2]

Nevertheless, Americans should be particularly receptive to Aristotle's pioneering thought because to us, as to him, the word "State" still conveys the idea of an autochthonous political entity, with what is well described as "home rule" preserving a jealous independence or at least autonomy in the conduct of local affairs. In political science, however, this word has come to be the technical designation of the sovereign Nation-State, and in this national sense the State will be considered in this chapter.

The abiding influence of Aristotle in the field of political theory is doubtless largely responsible for the tendency to regard the State as a particular form of Society. From our differentiation between liberty and freedom, however, we have learned the importance of verbal precision in political thinking. Here again are two distinct words, representing two abstract ideas that are obviously related, but certainly not identical. In the preceding chapters State and Society have been referred to as the separate forms of human organization that they are. Now we must carefully distinguish between them, remembering Pascal's excellent advice: "I never quarrel over names, provided I am told what meanings they are given." [3]

We shall be the more on guard against confusing Society and State because American political thinking has in general drawn the clear distinction that is appropriate. The nature of that distinction conforms with the etymology of the words.

[2] Vilfredo Pareto, *The Mind and Society*, Vol. I, Sect. 272.
[3] *Lettres à une provinciale*, I, p. 6.

II

The noun "society" comes to us from the Latin *socius*, meaning a companion. And, like the related noun "association," society still carries the flavor of voluntary companionship. It would be forcing language to refer to a company of conscripts, or to the prisoners in a tier of cells, as a society. Companionship in both these cases is externally enforced (by the State, as it happens). In a society, companionship between individuals of different tastes and standards is not compulsory. On the other hand, "society . . . tends to suggest a more restricted aim, a closer union of members, and their more active participation" than does the looser term "association." [4] A common interest, a common objective, to some extent a common faith, are elements necessary to a society.

The idea of association is also involved in the noun "state," though here the association tends to be involuntary, on the basis not of free contract but of *status*, from which, of course, the word "state" derives. The place of birth determines State membership much more definitely than it does social position. In nonpolitical usage, this element of status or condition is always uppermost, as in "a state of good health" or "a state of mental depression." The same sense of subjection to circumstance applies in consideration of the political State. In Great Britain, for instance, individuals as nationals are honestly defined as "subjects," whereas the same individuals are members, not subjects, of a society like the Anglican Church.

The State, in short, subjects people; whereas Society associates them voluntarily. In a universe of rhythm and pulsation, within "the systole and diastole of Time itself," some such differentiation in human groupings is precisely what one might expect. State and Society, we shall see, are naturally and continuously in opposition. For that reason, human welfare demands the nicest balance between the appropriate functions of each.

While engaged in the important preliminary of definition, we should note that the word—and the idea—of "constitution" is

[4] Webster's *Dictionary of Synonyms*.

connected with that of "state." The "constitution" is inherent in, or literally "stands with," the physical structure. The State "stands with" its constitution and the character of that organic law, written or unwritten, determines *how* the State shall stand.

Like "state" the word "constitution" also has a physical as well as a political meaning, encouraging such picturesque expressions as "the body politic." The political constitution provides the physical linkage between the State and its subjects, with physical connection emphasized by description of a constitution as "organic" law. Indeed, every political State *must* have a constitution— though this may be as arbitrary as the personal decrees of a dictator—because the very existence of a State implies some accepted relationship, doubtless originating in custom but invariably acquiring the force of law, between government and governed. This accepted relationship, between sovereign and subject, is provided by the constitution, and a change in the constitution, by executive edict, legislative amendment, or judicial interpretation, is momentous to all because it signifies a change in that basic relationship.

As earlier noted, the great difference between the British and American systems of government is that the former has come to vest complete sovereignty in its representative Parliament, which by contraction of the power of the House of Lords has become, in effect, the House of Commons alone. In our Republic, legal sovereignty is by intent permanently divided, so that it cannot be located in any single person or organ. "The basis of law," according to Professor Vinogradoff's searching analysis, is in the United States "provided not by one-sided command, but by agreement."

Because that unique basis can so easily be undermined, every constitutional change is of greater importance in the American federal union than in less delicate governmental systems. A seemingly innocuous move to alter the method of appointment to the Supreme Court, for instance, could easily result in making the judiciary an arm of executive power. And since the judiciary has authority to check the legislature, this could in turn mean the development of executive tyranny. The vital importance of balance in the American governmental system and the ease with which it can be upset were well suggested by Justice Harlan F. Stone in his dissent in the A. A. A. case:

> While unconstitutional exercise of power by the executive and legislative branches is subject to judicial restraint, the only check on our exercise of power is our own sense of self-restraint.

Thus a great twentieth century jurist rephrased, for members of the Supreme Court, Madison's imperative reminder that we "rest all our political experiments on the capacity of mankind for self-government."

III

The State, to be a State, must have a constitution. The interlocking relationship between Society and State is indicated by the fact that practically all social organizations—religious, commercial, or merely recreational—also have constitutions. These, like a national constitution, establish disciplinary rules and regulations that may be, and often are, rigorously enforced within the particular association. The difference is that the disciplinary power of the social organization is always limited and seldom physically punitive.

A Red-Headed League, for instance, could properly exclude from membership anybody whose hirsute coloration fell short of a previously determined standard. But nothing would then prevent the deficient individual from forming an Auburn Association in the same community. Of course, the penalties inflicted by Society may be much more serious than this fanciful illustration indicates. They do not, however, effectively constrain individual liberty. Penalties by the State are designed to do just that.[5]

Society, in other words, is more fluid, more flexible, less constitutionalized, and less resolutely disciplinary than the State, which because of its supremacy possesses a power of ostracism far exceeding that of the most exclusive social organization. Between the discrimination of a governmental edict directed against Jews, and that of a social covenant with the same objective, there is a differ-

---

[5] Pareto points out that "Sunday idleness is enforced by law in the name of freedom." *Op. cit.*, Vol. III, Sect. 1554.

ence of kind rather than of degree. The inclusive discrimination of the State is tyrannical. The exclusive discrimination of a social group is merely offensive.

Nevertheless, it cannot be asserted that Society, in any of its almost numberless groupings, is particularly interested in the enlargement of freedom. Regardless of the social institution we stop to consider—whether it be the family as the oldest known co-operative unit, or an association of atomic scientists as a modern manifestation—we see similar evidences of self-imposed restraint. Husband and wife put definite limits on their individual freedom, in order to promote certain objectives, such as the rearing of children, which they have in common. And the atomic scientists in congress assembled are making comparable individual sacrifices for their particular common end. So it seems to be the nature of human association, whether voluntary or involuntary, to limit the condition of freedom for those whose association is something more than merely casual.

But when this association for a common end is voluntary, a very interesting result is wont to ensue. Although the area of individual freedom suffers undeniable contraction from association, the act of association simultaneously permits and encourages development along the lines of deepest individual interest, to an extent that would have been impossible without association. The enlargement of personality may be as inconsequential as the pleasure afforded by a foursome of golf at the country club. It may be as momentous as a general improvement of diagnostic methods resulting from a medical conference. But whatever the case in point, ridiculous or sublime, we observe that the income derived from voluntary co-operation is expected by the participants to exceed the outlay involved in such co-operation. If that were not so, we would not have voluntary co-operation, in all its myriad forms, and man would not possess the "social instinct" to the degree that makes him "a political animal."

IV

At this point we would see a distinction arising between freedom and liberty, even if it had not already been made. Voluntary association limits freedom while it enlarges liberty. That which is limited by continuous association is the indulgence of individual appetites, passions, and animal instincts—the carnal side of Man. That which is expanded by continuous association is the perfection of individual skills, ambitions, and aspirations—the spiritual side of Man. Thus continuous voluntary association may and does limit the physical condition of freedom. But it does so to enlarge the moral endowment of liberty.

During the term of earthly life, physical condition and moral endowment can never be wholly separated, for they are like body and soul. When irrevocably separated, the result is dissolution of the individual. We may suggest that this complete termination of physical freedom simultaneously brings the complete apotheosis of spiritual liberty. That would be the logical conclusion of our thought, if we were not hesitant to consider the subject of immortality in a political study already sufficiently difficult. However, we *are* concerned to point out that the quality of liberty is spiritual, and can be advanced by voluntary association, while the condition of freedom is physical, and must be limited by voluntary association. From this it follows that the individual can happily compromise with his fellows in matters of physical adjustment, but should never compromise where spiritual sacrifice is involved.

As a generality, to which many individual exceptions could be cited, Man throughout his recorded history has preferred liberty to freedom. Left to himself, his natural tendency is to limit his freedom in order to enlarge his liberty. From this tendency the observant Aristotle reasoned, more than three centuries before the birth of Christ, that: "Man is by nature a political animal."

Aristotle "first brought to bear on political phenomena the patient analysis and unbiased research which are the proper marks and virtues of scientific inquiry." [6] This early political scientist

[6] Sir Frederick Pollock, *History of the Science of Politics*, p. 2.

concentrated on the problems of a closely integrated City-State, where it was not an impossible ideal for all the citizens to know each other. Nevertheless, in Book III of *The Politics*, Aristotle was forced to the conclusion that "a State is not a mere Society," and to see further that "the good citizen need not of necessity possess the virtue which makes a good man."[7] As the State has grown in power and magnitude, to become a political aggregation that certainly would have seemed dreadful to Aristotle, the contrast between State and Society that he dimly discerned has become increasingly clear. The contrast is also increasingly important for those who assert that their national objective is to secure the blessings of liberty.

For the purpose of this study it is unnecessary to debate whether the origins of State and Society are coeval, or whether the State in primitive form was originally imposed on pre-existent social groups in order to systematize exploitation of the weak by the strong. Certain observations on the issue will be made for what they are worth. Beyond contention, however, is the obvious fact that the Nation-State has acquired characteristics that make it differ in nature as well as in degree from any voluntary social organization. The rapid extension of the authority of the State, and its increasing competence to control, discipline, and subordinate not only the individual but also all unofficial forms of social organization, was the painfully outstanding political development of the first half of the twentieth century.

V

We are now in a position to identify the components of political life as (1) the individual; (2) Society, meaning every form of voluntary association directed to the self-defined benefit of individuals; (3) the State, as the dominant organization, which has gradually acquired the power to dictate both to individuals and to social groupings under its sovereignty. From his initial entrance into family organization to his final separation from those with

[7] *Op. cit.*, pp. 106 and 119.

whom he has labored, Man has for centuries fulfilled his destiny within the framework of Society. But there are many indications that he is now exchanging membership in Society for servitude to the State.

The individual, as Aristotle pointed out, is *in* Society. Regardless of his line of endeavor or interest, he fulfills himself through various forms of social organization of which the family, giving continuity to the race, is the oldest. But a celibate brotherhood, secluded on the Tibetan side of the Himalayas, is equally a form of human Society. The occasional hermit, who seeks to withdraw from Society as well as from the world, is only the exception confirming the rule that "a social instinct is implanted in all men by nature."

Although the various forms of Society overlap and interlock, none is naturally superior to another. The local chamber of commerce and the sandlot baseball team pursue their wholly distinct activities in happy separation, with father and son leaving it to mother to bring composition into the picture at the family table. In this separation lie both the strength and the weakness of Society. The division of function makes it possible for each individual to concentrate on the activity that temporarily interests or concerns him most. But the division of function also makes it necessary to have some synthetic agency that will be less transitory than every purely social unit. To achieve permanence this artificial agency must have overriding power, either seized by it or freely entrusted to it. When that effective sovereignty has been attained, this synthetic agency is called the State.[8]

In most countries the State has evolved slowly, acquiring its power now here, now there; going through numerous structural changes before taking form as the Nation-State that came to flower in the period following the French Revolution. In the American Republic, however, the federal State was created at a given moment, by a concentrated effort of mind and will. We have already examined the procedure and we can even name the date on which

___

[8] Franz Oppenheimer, in his study of *The State*, defines six distinct stages which can usually be discerned in its evolution to the modern form.

the United States was legally established as a definite sovereign Power.[9]

Because its origin was not haphazard it was possible, in this Republic, to establish a boundary line between the powers of the new American State and those of the antecedent American Society. That boundary is drawn in the Constitution, and emphasized in the Ninth and Tenth Amendments, which may again be quoted:

> The enumeration in the Constitution of certain rights shall not be construed to deny or disparage others retained by the people.
>
> The powers not delegated to the United States by the Constitution, nor prohibited by it to the states, are reserved to the states respectively, or to the people.

Boundaries in the field of political ideas are, and must always be, elastic. Unfortunately, the elasticity that permits improvement is equally receptive to deterioration. The Constitution makes a clear distinction between the prerogative of the State and the prerogative of Society. But it also provides procedure whereby the former can be enlarged at the expense of the latter, both by open and by insidious means. In this Republic it is more difficult than in most other countries for the State to discipline and regiment Society. But one need only survey the record to realize that here, as elsewhere, the development of the State has been that of constant aggrandizement. Necessarily, that aggrandizement has been at the expense of the two other components in political life —at the expense of Society and of the individuals who create Society because it is their nature so to do. Of course, this does not mean that the State has made no contribution to social and individual welfare.

It should be noted here that in recent years there has been concerted effort to establish what at first glance seems to be a fourth component in political life—that of official international organization. But this development, of both the League of Nations and the United Nations, has so far been one of intergovernmental cooperation. There is no right of citizenship in the United Nations,

---

[9] June 21, 1788, when the ninth state (New Hampshire) gave the ratification necessary to make the Constitution effective, under the wording of Article VII.

and a national of one of its Member-States is not for that reason entitled even to cross the frontier of any other Member-State. Like its ill-fated predecessor, the United Nations does not replace the State as a political entity and does not set up a new political entity effectively depriving the State of sovereignty. Indeed, five Powers were given the right of absolute veto, precisely to prevent that development.

There was nothing accidental in the aggressive use of this veto by Soviet Russia. This Union of Soviet Socialist "Republics" does far more than the allegedly United Nations to curtail the independence of its constituent political units, and of adjacent countries within the Russian sphere of influence. And from 1945 on, the endeavor of Communist organization to break down the system of Nation-States made the U. S. S. R. a factor of transcendent political significance. To the extent that Communist organization bears directly on the individual, instead of affecting him only through the medium of his national government, the "Comintern" can properly be called a wholly new component of political life. That claim could never be made for an essentially intergovernmental organization, like the United Nations.

Whether or not Communism would triumph over Statism, in the traditional nationalistic form of the latter, had become the outstanding political question even before the close of World War II. Communism, as an antinational political party, was able, as a result of that war, to penetrate and undermine the national organization of many States to an extent which was literally "subversive." But before considering the clash between the Nation-State and the Communist International, it is necessary to give thought to the antecedent struggle between the State and Society.

The ascendancy of the Nation-State and the breakdown of Society present a pronounced coincidence. This is not fortuitous. There has been direct and causal connection between the increasing exaltation of the State and the increasing demoralization of Society. It is necessary to understand how the State has everywhere weakened Society, and how that process has in turn weakened the State, before one can intelligently consider the magnitude of the struggle between the American Republic and its Russian antagonist.

VI

It is not surprising that the State, by some writers, is still regarded as nothing more than a particular form of Society. In origin it was exactly that. Oppenheimer even asserts: "The concept of Society, as a contrast to the concept of the State, first appears in Locke," whose philosophical influence was partly due to his skill in political diagnosis.[10]

Nobody has ever been able to isolate and identify with any precision the beginnings of the State. All we know for certain is that early in the line of human evolution people began to associate for purposes that today we would call political, rather than social or biological. At some prehistoric moment the dwellers in some cave united, not to hunt animals nor to safeguard their young, but to launch an attack against the denizens of another, more desirable, location. The hairy inmates of the preferable fastness undoubtedly co-operated in resistance. Here were two rudimentary States in conflict, without names, without flags, without anything that we would today call government—nevertheless offering the prototype of all the glorious wars that fill the pages of conventional history.

But, in these uncivilized and therefore relatively harmless scuffles, primitive Society and the primitive State are all mixed up. It might be said that, at this embryonic stage, sex has not been determined. The function of Society and the function of the State is indistinguishable. "Its rudimentary forms are not so much germs from which the mature State evolves as conglomerates from which it slowly frees itself. . . . It is not surprising, therefore, that contemporary enquiries into the origin of the State bear the aspect of an uncertain and inconclusive quest." [11]

As an institution, Professor Hocking further concludes, "the State certainly did not arise in a contract," though he recognizes

[10] *Op. cit.*, Preface.
[11] William Ernest Hocking, *Man and the State*, p. 142*n*. and ff.

that the American Republic is exceptional in this respect. The State, he reasons, "can only arise as Man, looking forward, begins with conscious awareness to build for futurity not his tombs alone but his communal life also." Thus, the State "begins together with the historical sense." This thought of a prominent American philosopher is clearly derived from Hegel, as was that of Spengler when he wrote: "State is history regarded as at the halt; history the State regarded as on the move."

The theory becomes less metaphysical, and therefore more convincing to the unphilosophic mind, if we reduce it to particulars. At some unascertainable period the individual presumably began to reflect on what would happen, after his death, to the group with which he was associated. We may reasonably conclude that this thought was early prominent in the minds of those who in some way had acquired positions of leadership, and with that eminence the sense of responsibility that leadership tends to foster. Evidently this dawning individual awareness of a group future must have followed some definition of the group as such—in other words, Society does antedate the State. We may guess that it was the corpse of a mate that first aroused in the mind of primitive man the fearsome thought of what would happen to the helpless offspring if the survivor also were slain by a saber-toothed tiger or falling rock.

It is important to realize that this particular form of anxiety about the future was neither narrowly selfish nor superstitious. It was, on the contrary, social and mundane. Accepting his own physical extinction as an eventual certainty, Man sought some procedure whereby after his death his accomplished work could still contribute to the welfare of his group. Here was the first problem in statecraft, and its solution involved creation of the State. Moreover, the gregarious instinct that underlies Society led naturally to the formation of the State.

Because of its voluntary nature, Society is fluid. And because of its fluidity, Society could not create the desired element of permanence. The head of a primitive group, whether patriarch or matriarch, whether warrior or magician, could do something to provide shelter, weapons, bodily covering, and even fuel and food that would be available after the individual leader's death.[12] But a nomadic organization of hunters, fishermen or even predatory herdsmen did not have the continuity necessary for significant accumulation. Like the neighborhood "gang" of modern boyhood, the primitive group was always subject to the disintegrating processes clearly characteristic of voluntary organizations, wherever or whenever found. The condition of freedom was present, but not that sense of responsibility for the future that is a concomitant of liberty. It was not until men ceased to be wholly nomadic, and began to settle down as cultivators, that the means of introducing permanence into social organization became available.

The most intractable enemy of Man is man himself. The seed of the modern State can be detected in the groupings of primitive man for offense or defense against his fellows. The seed could flower only for a season, however, prior to the agricultural stage of social development. Husbandry provided the condition of continuity that gives the State, as offspring, characteristics that Society, as parent, does not possess. And with the rise of the State, as a permanent institution, the arts of peace and those of war alike begin that tremendous development traced by recorded history. "The roots of modern civilization are planted deeply in the highly elaborate life of those nations which rose into power over six thousand years ago, in the basin of the Eastern Mediterranean, and the adjacent regions on the east of it." [13]

VII

So the State, as a human institution, has a definite and rational objective: to offset mortality by means of an agency that can be expected to go on functioning without reference to the individual

[12] Because irrelevant to present consideration, we intentionally evade argument as to the location of directive power in primitive Society. For a scholarly and searching review of the whole subject, the reader is referred to Bertrand de Jouvenel's *Du Pouvoir*, an important study of the evolution and growth of political power. Sir James G. Frazer's *The Golden Bough* remains fundamental.

[13] James Henry Breasted, *History of Egypt*, p. 3. See also, Oppenheimer, *op. cit.*, Ch. II.

life span. This objective was always distinct from the will to personal aggrandizement, for at least a part of the underlying purpose was to make available to survivors those fruits of labor that men cannot take with them when they leave this world. But there were implications to this creation of the State that, as we look backward, are horrifying.

To achieve the objective of permanence it was essential, in the first place, to endow the State with a collective power far beyond that which any individual, or any ephemeral social group, could hope to exercise. As Dr. Breasted says, civilization took root as the first States of which we have definite knowledge "rose into power." But evils, as well as blessings heretofore unknown to Man, also rooted as this concentration of power took place. It is suggestive that the long history of political thought is more concerned with the restraint, than with the exercise, of power entrusted to the State.

The State, in origin, was a projection of power in the field of time. Because time and space are related, the time-projection involved a projection of power in the field of space.[14] Since such spatial projections were certain to intersect, on this small planet, it was foreordained that the State system would be a war system, and that the more highly developed this system, the greater the probability of friction between its units. The fact that the State system is a war system in turn made it certain that each developing State would do everything possible constantly to enlarge its power "in self-defense." As the human source of this power was the individual, State aggrandizement necessarily pointed toward human enslavement. As Man enslaved the power of the beast, so the State proceeded to enslave the power of Man. But some beasts cannot be enslaved, and neither can some men.

Aside from its tendency to monopolize power, and its tendency to wage war with other States, the nature of the State harbors a third inherent danger to the happiness, and even the existence, of Man. This third danger arises from the bestowal of artificial im-

---

[14] Political science, with its tendency toward ontological method, has given inadequate consideration to the implications of the Time-Space Continuum. Cf. John Dewey, *Logic: The Theory of Inquiry*, pp. 482-6.

mortality on a human institution. Because of its permanence the State has gradually established for itself a dubious moral authority. This spurious authority, which will be closely examined in the following chapter, is based on the State's assumption of the divine attribute of immortality. But while Man derives from his Creator a moral sense, the State, which is the creation of Man, has none. Power it has, and force, and techniques to make its commands effective. Through the agency of the State, also, the moral as well as the bestial side of Man can be encouraged. But with morals *as such*, as distinct from the imposed prohibitions of man-made law, the State is not, has never been, and never will be concerned. The State is a physical and not a moral instrument. It is therefore antipodean and always latently hostile to the instrument of human conscience, which is moral and not physical.

It is, of course, true that as an instrument the State may be utilized to forward morality and to oppose immorality. It is true that administrators with the highest personal ideals may, like Marcus Aurelius, temporarily go far to meet Plato's requirement of a philosopher-king. But since the State has no conscience, and is primarily a continuing mechanism of material power, the human welfare side of State activity should blind no thoughtful person to its underlying menace. And the potential of the State for "The Abolition of Man"—to use the telling phrase employed by C. S. Lewis—is the greater because Man himself has created and directs this juggernaut that rolls over him.

Idolatry is always blind, and never more so than when it seeks to cloak a human creation with mystical significance. It was the tragedy of the German genius to carry worship of the State to the stage where Hegel could reason that: "The State is the Divine Idea as its exists on Earth." [15] If literally interpreted this thought could lead logically to the assertion of Nazi Minister Robert Ley: "Truth is whatever benefits the State; error is whatever does not benefit the State."

The monstrous perversion in this axiom was not due so much to any particular national aberration as to a general tendency to

[15] Introduction to Lectures on *The Philosophy of History*.

exaggerate the potential of the State for good, and to underestimate its capacity for evil. Goethe's countrymen, of all people, should have realized that it is the bargain of Faust to sell one's soul, which is one's self, for an enlargement of temporal power. Even a bargain with Mephistopheles is less surely a losing proposition than one in which the individual surrenders his soul to the State. For Satan has forbidden fruit of his own to distribute, while the State, in the last analysis, has absolutely nothing to offer that it has not already expropriated from its subjects. So, in worship of the State, men sacrifice their souls to a false god that can give them in return only what has already been placed by the worshippers themselves on this sacrilegious altar.

If this indictment seems strong, it is primarily because Americans have so largely ceased to reflect upon the implications of the unconditional surrender of power to political government. We have seen that such surrender is wholly contrary to the principles of the Republic. But even without that patriotic justification there would be good reason for men to rise in opposition to State aggrandizement. It is a case of selling the human birthright for a mess of pottage.

For the instrumentality of the State is only relatively immortal. And there is reason to believe that not only are particular States on the road to dissolution, but also the Nation-State as an institution. The State is afflicted with a disease that can be called hypertrophy of function. And the germ of this disease of overgrowth appears to be inherent in its nature.

VIII

The outstanding characteristic of the State, regardless of its place in time, its location in space, its form of government, is monopolization of physical power. To endure as a political entity the State must be in a position to enforce its laws, however adopted or decreed, on all persons and private organizations resident or operating within its boundaries or, as we say, "under its flag." While retaining social value as a symbol of fidelity and loyalty, the flag has also become increasingly emblematic of national sovereignty—of the State's possession of power and its corporate will to make that power effective.

War, in which the flag is an important emotional asset, is the classic device by which the State most rapidly augments its power. There is an exhilarating gamble in the process, because war is simultaneously a device whereby a State may be utterly destroyed. Through war, again, new States have not infrequently achieved independence, our own being an example. But not every attempt to establish a new State by force of arms has succeeded, as is also illustrated in American history by the failure of the Southern Confederacy. The importance of war in the creation and development of States has been sadly neglected by many who have labored devotedly to secure stabilized peace within the State system. As already suggested, it is doubtful whether that system was ever really compatible with international peace.

We must also realize that the strength gained by a victorious State through war is in large part taken not from the enemy but from its own people. All of the private elements in Society—the family, the church, the press, the school, the corporation, the union, and other co-operatives—are subject to special discipline by the State in wartime. The pressure of this discipline depends on the urgency of the wartime emergency, which the State itself defines. The phrase "total war" accurately expresses the evolution to its logical conclusion of a State-building activity obviously antisocial to the extent that State and Society have opposing interests and objectives. Total war, arriving in our lifetime, is the perfected means for building the totalitarian State. And it is scarcely necessary to emphasize that once an emergency control has been established by the State, all sorts of arguments for making it permanent are forthcoming.

That the State moves consistently to augment its power is indicated not only by the entire course of history, but also in everyday parlance. We speak of "Great Powers" and "Small Powers," using the noun "Power" synonymously with "State," and evaluating the quality of the State by that single material attribute. Regardless of how the State originated, it has evidently developed into a final repository of power, with the exercise of this over-riding power its fundamental and characteristic function. Only that conclusion can explain the pronounced unwillingness of States to yield sovereignty, even when it is of clear social advantage that some aspect of sovereignty, such as preventive measures against epidemics, should be administered by a nonpolitical international body.

Moreover, insistence on national sovereignty grows stronger as the power of the State augments. The strong, not the weak, nations were the ones that insisted on maintaining a governmental veto in the work of the United Nations.

IX

The word "power," however, implies much more than physical supremacy. There is also moral power and intellectual power. Some individuals are also granted a magnetic power of personality that may have moral, intellectual, or physical basis, yet is never-theless seemingly independent of all these attributes. But every form of human power, however exercised, involves some influ-ence over others, whether that influence is positive or negative, for good or for evil, as defined by the standards of the period.

Intellectual power is obviously a higher form than the merely physical. It had been frequently harnessed to the service of the State long before Machiavelli advised Lorenzo the Magnificent that: "Whoever becomes the ruler of a free city and does not destroy it, can expect to be destroyed by it, for it can always find a motive for rebellion in the name of liberty . . ." [16]

The adjective derived from Machiavelli's name reminds us that the State develops its physical supremacy with utter disregard for morality. A Machiavellian policy is simply one in which in-tellectual ability is wholly divorced from moral considerations. And there is no doubt that, as the State has gained in power, the inclination to follow the teaching of Machiavelli has increased. "We live today in the shadow of a Florentine, the man who above

[16] *The Prince*, Ch. V.

all others taught the world to think in terms of cold political power." [17]

Quite naturally, the tendency of the State to exploit intelligence for its own uses has given rise to increasing official suspicion of unregimented thinking. Instances of this are seen in the effort to suppress "dangerous thoughts" in prewar Japan, and in the disciplinary action taken in postwar Russia against writers, artists, and composers accused of "poisoning the consciousness of our people with a world outlook that is hostile to Soviet Society." [18] Incidentally, this accusation identifies Society with State, intimating that in Russia the State has definitely engulfed Society.

It is noteworthy that conscientious objection to State supremacy is still treated somewhat more tolerantly than other forms of hostility. Undoubtedly this is because conscientious objection is negative, and impartial as between rival States, while objection based on material considerations may lead to active support of another government against one's own, which in war is defined as treason.

In her case study of *The Meaning of Treason,* Rebecca West asserts that: "All men should have a drop or two of treason in their veins, if the nations are not to go soft like so many sleepy pears." But this defense of the individual against the State clearly bothers Miss West, for she adds immediately: "Yet to be a traitor is to be most miserable." This generality is absurd, for there is ample evidence to show that neither George Washington nor Robert E. Lee were ever made miserable by their treason, successful in the one case and unsuccessful in the other.

Miss West's rather muddled argument is nevertheless significant, because of the illuminating overtones in the conclusions to which she is driven. The summation of this English writer is that the unsavory traitors whom she analyzes deserved a certain sympathy because they "needed a nation which was also a hearth." In other words, their treason was excusable to the extent that they had not been comforted and consoled by a welfare State of their

[17] Max Lerner, Introduction to *The Prince* and *The Discourses;* Modern Library Edition.
[18] Quoted by Brooks Atkinson, *New York Times,* October 6, 1946.

own. The suggestion is that the more maturely reasoned and self-sacrificial an act of treason, the less pardonable it becomes. We are not concerned with debating this belief pro or con, but merely with pointing out that it reflects the general European assumption that the higher the intelligence, the more imperative is its subordination to the service of a particular State.[19]

X

We owe some further consideration to the element of moral power, meaning the force that impels the individual to observe certain idealistic standards of conduct regardless of their conflict with his physical or intellectual desires. Like intellectual power, that of morality has been increasingly pre-empted by the State for political purposes. Thus we have reached the stage where an ill-assorted group of victorious governments can assert a moral basis for the indictment, trial, and execution of the leaders of a defeated nation who were responsible for "crimes against humanity." But the same governments placidly ignore the presumably equally criminal character of comparable actions by their own States against other human beings, or even reward such actions with decorations, when carried out under the direction of their own leadership.

In the Christian religion, as contrasted with the political life of nominally Christian countries, morality is regarded as an even-handed force of universal applicability; one which cannot properly be nationalized or made subservient to either physical or intellectual power. Indeed the social contribution of Christ may be summed up by saying that in the hierarchy of values he places Love first, denying merit to all forms of power centering on that hatred of other peoples which governments so often seek to stimulate.

In this Christian doctrine, of course, are found both the origin and the justification—perhaps the only valid justification—of democratic theory, dismissed by many philosophers, ancient and

[19] *Op. cit., passim,* especially pp. 306-7.

modern, as politically impractical. The logic of Christianity has never attempted to deny that men are unequal in their physical and mental endowments. It has emphasized that such differences do not prevent them from associating in full comradeship in many social undertakings where the solidarity of the human species is more important than its differentiations. "The Idea of a Christian Society," in the words of a great poet who has thought deeply on the subject, "is one which we can accept or reject; but if we are to accept it, we must treat Christianity with a great deal more *intellectual* respect than is our wont; we must treat it as being for the individual a matter primarily of thought and not of feeling." [20]

We have had occasion to note the profound, though declining, influence of Christianity on American political thought. Yet even in the various activities of private Society the exercise of ruthless power has been none too successfully restrained by the moral suasion of Christianity. This inclines one to reflect on the use that would be made of the almost unbelievable physical power of the United States, if its control were concentrated without restriction in a strongly centralized government. Power in the hands of the State is less inhibited morally and more destructive physically than in Society. The State, not Society, is responsible for the design, development, and utilization of the atomic bomb.

State power, no matter how well disguised by seductive words, is in the last analysis always coercive physical power. And since the Industrial Revolution this form of power, unlike that of mind or morals, has grown with increased physical wealth. The greater the material resources over which it can exercise absolute control, the greater the potential power of the State. From this arises the tendency to develop and pyramid governmental controls in order to augment power. As we come to recognize that the State is the repository of coercive power, and by its nature works ceaselessly to enlarge that power, much that seems shameful and senseless in the world today becomes intelligible, though not for that reason cheerful.

[20] T. S. Eliot, *The Idea of a Christian Society*, pp. 4-5.

XI

Let us now briefly consider World War II as a strictly political phenomenon, isolated from its heavily encrusted emotional overtones. The hostilities were launched in the historically familiar pattern of a struggle for national power among contending States. But the duration, intensity, and bitterness of the war completed that disintegration of European Society which the war of 1914-18 previously had done much to advance. With this social collapse the entire State system of Europe was undermined. Unfortunately, American political thinking was slow to adjust itself to the fact, and still slower to realize the implications, of this unprecedented situation.

Sociologically, the essential difference between World War I and World War II was that the latter far more extensively drained the reservoirs on which the State depends both for its strength and sustenance. This drainage was only in part due to physical destruction on the "home front," a phrase itself tellingly descriptive of the modern State's wartime impingement on social institutions. Society everywhere was also weakened by National Socialist controls, which were applied universally, though not always upheld as shockingly as in the country that first made State Socialism a religion. Nevertheless, in every belligerent nation, and necessarily also among those preserving an uneasy neutrality, social welfare and governmental policy were arbitrarily assumed to be identical. Bureaucratic thinking everywhere paid the Nazis the flattery of imitation, in spite of the more guarded phraseology used by the officials of countries with a more virile heritage of individualism.

Responsibility for making the drainage of European social strength complete, however, must be said to rest on those who enunciated and enforced the doctrine of unconditional surrender, never before applied in modern warfare between sovereign States. This doctrine said, in effect, that the German people would not be allowed to admit military defeat until their government had been utterly destroyed. In practice, this meant the destruction of the society over which the enemy government had secured totalitarian control. Had there been any Anglo-American plan for reconstituting the social institutions of the German people, or if they had been allowed to do this for themselves, a moderate degree of European recovery could have been achieved fairly soon. As shown by the event, there was no such plan, though fortunately for ourselves the policy of social pulverization was not carried to the same extreme in the case of the other major enemies —Italy and Japan.[21]

The tragic significance of this coercive dissipation of social strength lies in the fact that Society, in all of its activities except State building, is naturally international or, to be strictly accurate, supranational. To see American and Japanese babies playing together, or French and German mathematicians discussing their professional problems, is to realize that their common social interests do not naturally divide along national lines except to the extent that the easily surmountable barrier of language may prove an obstacle. It follows that the destruction of a toy factory or a scientific library, whether located in France, Germany, or Tasmania, is in the last analysis a deprivation for children or for mathematicians as such, even though State-controlled "Ministries of Enlightenment" may insist that the loss to one "enemy national" is somehow a gain to his opposite number across a frontier. Undoubtedly this fiction can be impressed on gullible human beings, but no individual, and no society, is the healthier for being deceived as to the nature of the disease that is draining strength away.

The drainage of social strength in the course of World War II resulted, throughout nearly all of Europe, in an unprecedented national disintegration. Its effects were almost as pronounced in the victorious as in the vanquished countries. Nor was the stark and elemental picture of social degeneracy long concealed by the frantic efforts of bankrupt governments to re-establish some orderly basis for the lives of their demoralized peoples. Additional governmental controls merely added further handicaps to an economic recovery that would have been difficult at best. Along

[21] The farrago of unworkable penalties set down by Mr. Henry Morgenthau, Jr., in *Germany Is Our Problem*, cannot be dignified as a plan.

with the structure of European Society, its State system had been so weakened that reconstitution, in anything like the nineteenth century form, was never to be expected. And restoration of this decadent system was always the less probable because of the abundant evidence that Soviet Russia did not intend to permit recovery in the old, outworn pattern.

In 1939, as in 1914, Western Europe was the seat of four "Great Powers"—Great Britain, France, Germany, and Italy. In spite of the changes brought by World War I the decisions of each of these four governments continued to count, in the conduct of international relations, on the same plane as the decisions of Japan, Russia, or the United States.

Of these seven erstwhile "Great Powers" three—Germany, Italy, and Japan—have been reduced to negligible status from the viewpoint of that material strength which is the essence of statehood. The position of France is not very much better and the preposterous effort to cast China in a Great Power role could never be taken seriously. Great Britain retains the shell of its former physical vitality but actually, and even more relatively, has sunk in the scale by comparison with either Russia or the United States. These last two nations alone possessed the resources to survive the wastage of two World Wars as wholly independent sovereignties. All the remaining States have emerged as what in the last analysis must be called the willing or unwilling satellites of one or the other of the two political constellations that dominate the postwar darkness.

The wheel comes full cycle. Like Frankenstein's monster, the hydra-headed Nation-State has brought a dreadful retribution on the European Society that created it.

Chapter 6

The Issue of Authority

This study is necessarily concerned with the careful use of words employed to convey political ideas. For if the currency of our language is debased, our thinking will be corrupted with it. In a representative republic, corruption of political thought must necessarily lead to corruption of government, and thereby endanger continuation of a political system dependent upon popular understanding of the ideas on which it is based.

So we have been at pains to distinguish between *liberty* as an individual aspiration and *freedom* as a general condition. We have made the necessary distinction between *Society* and *State* as different genera of co-operative organization. Now it is in line with the development of our subject to give close consideration to the nature of what we call *Authority*. The reason why this is politically important will soon become clear.

The root of the noun "authority" is the Latin *auctor*, from which we also derive the word "author." A completely acceptable definition of the latter offers no difficulties. Every English-speaking person would agree that an author is one who originates or creates. While the word is most frequently applied to a literary composer, its applicability of course goes far beyond this secondary category. A deeper meaning of the word is well brought out by the familiar lines in the hymn "America":

> Our fathers' God, to Thee,
> Author of Liberty, to Thee we sing.

By virtue of his creation an author becomes an authority. The significance of the authority is reflected in the nature of the creation. A chef who concocts a new recipe for a soup is certainly a creator and by his accomplishment becomes an authority in culinary matters. With a difference of degree, rather than of kind, Euclid made himself a mathematical authority, recognized as such after twenty-two centuries by the enduring character of what is still called Euclidian geometry.

Because it is influential, in the literal sense of something which "flows in" upon us, Authority is therefore a form of power. But it is clearly a special sort of power: one which does not need to employ physical coercion and is on the whole willingly rather than unwillingly recognized. There is thus a clear and vital distinction between Authority and Force. As well expressed by Joseph Michael Lalley: "We obey authority, in the sense that we listen to it and respond with the will; we *submit* to force and are, as it were, sent under." [1]

This means that the less force involved in Authority, the more truly authoritative it is. And the more that physical force is necessary to sustain Authority, the less authoritative it really is. Hence it follows that if the virtue of Authority can be successfully challenged it ceases to be Authority, even though it may still retain the means of physical coercion. True Authority must have a general acceptance, which of course may be passive rather than active.

The validity of this distinction between acceptable and unacceptable Authority has long been recognized by the common law. For instance, most civilizations have made it customary that parents should have authority over their minor children. Because they are the authors of their children, parents are regarded as having a natural authority over them. But it is also customarily held that this authority involves and is dependent upon a lively sense of responsibility. Modern Society agrees that an insane, inebriate, or otherwise irresponsible person may properly be deprived of parental authority. If injuriously exercised that authority becomes reasonably questionable. Certainly it would be

[1] *Faith and Force*, THE HUMAN EVENTS PAMPHLETS, No. 4, p. 5.

difficult to argue that authority over children is justified merely by the exercise of a physical force sufficient to intimidate and coerce. In this case, and many others could be cited, the common law is directed in accordance with instincts that of themselves indicate the presence of an Authority higher than the individual, the Society, or the State.

Of course Authority is never completely unquestionable. The most important characteristic of the human mind—that which is responsible for all the progress of the race—is its almost irrepressible tendency to question. Acceptable Authority is a power that cannot be *intelligently* or *reasonably* questioned, and the emphasis is on the adverbs. The most conscientious parent knows that his or her authority over children can and will be questioned, by obvious resentment and resistance even before there is aptitude to form an issue in words. Nor is it always easy for a parent to draw the line of demarcation between the unreasonable and reasonable questions. "Why can't I play with matches?"—is clearly an example of the former. "Why can't I finish this chapter before I go to bed?"—is a more debatable case.

It is precisely because all authority is questionable that the distinction between what should be accepted and what should be repudiated becomes of such tremendous political importance. Discrimination in this field is made easier by starting from the relatively easy distinction between Authority and Dictation. Authority allows itself to be questioned, but withstands the test. Dictation does not allow questions primarily because it cannot withstand them.

No authority is less questionable by man than that ultimate power that rules the lives of all of us. No authority is more questionable than the absolute power that is the objective of the authoritarian State. In the first case we have a true authority against which our questions will always break in vain. In the second case, we have a false authority, which discourages questions because they would lead to its undoing.

Thus we are led to consider whether cumulative encroachments of false upon true authority provide the underlying cause of the breakdown in our era.

II

If Man were a more ideal creature, and if the conditions of his social life were less exacting, he could be governed, with relatively little political complication, by the authority of God alone. But the Ten Commandments, even if scrupulously obeyed, together with all the detailed ordinances that follow in the Book of Exodus, would of themselves be inadequate for the government of a modern community. Because of human shortcomings this ideal authority was not even effective as civil government for the primitive nomadic groups that proudly called themselves the Chosen People. The theocracy developed by the Israelites after Moses was, indeed, conspicuously unsuccessful in preserving either the moral law or—what in the long run is the same thing— the conditions necessary to secure the blessings of liberty.

But the Hebrew nation, like our own a federation founded on a voluntary covenant, introduced into political thinking one concept of profound and far-reaching influence. This, in Lord Acton's words, was "the principle that all political authorities must be tested and reformed according to a code which was not made by Man." [2] Since the time of the Hebrew prophets, political authority has never been safely absolutist. Regardless of the sanctity attributed to the State, brave men have for centuries reserved to themselves the right to take an appeal from its government to the higher authority of conscience. When the occasion has seemed to warrant, they have not hesitated to say: "If this be treason, make the most of it."

The belief that governmental absolutism is tolerable only if governmental performance is honorable is nevertheless becoming retrogressively and deplorably feeble. The whole theory of the authoritarian State is that the individual is subject in every respect and has no recourse, political or spiritual, from the edicts of his rulers. To achieve this end the Communist hierarchy, immediately after gaining control in Russia, began its crusade against religion as "the opiate of the people." Though the reasoning is

[2] Essay on "The History of Freedom in Antiquity."

almost unbelievably arrogant, yet it is also undeniably logical. God, the Communists argued, is an idea that has attained reality in the mind of Man. Conscience is that which he "knows with" God. So if the idea of God can be obliterated, conscience will also be undermined and it will be far more difficult for men to find any basis for an appeal against tyranny on the part of Caesar.

Fortunately for the survival of liberty, however, the early Jewish insistence on the right of appeal to God is not the only inherited support of liberalism. Mankind has thought out and established other, though allied, political principles as a part of the defense against false authority. When the iron curtain of Asiatic despotism closed over Jerusalem, and the Jews were carried into captivity, the City-State of Athens came to the fore as the center of humanitarian thinking. While the poor, as well as the slaves, were there excluded from office, Solon [640-558 B.C.] nevertheless gave all citizens a voice in the election of their magistrates, and the right of criticizing the performance of these rulers. "This concession, apparently so slender, was the beginning of a mighty change." [3] Theretofore the only effective obstacle to arbitrary government had been religious. Now the idea that the citizen is in that capacity the guardian of his own interest was established as a further check to political absolutism.

With the advent of Christianity there comes another, and mightier, forward stride. It is of transcendent political importance for two reasons. In the first place Christ, speaking as the son of God, gave to mankind an assurance more inspiring than that brought by any other religious leader. He preached, in very simple language, that if men will learn to govern themselves it is possible—though never easy—to conduct mundane activities on the divine pattern. God the Creator, the final Authority, is not to be slavishly feared nor blindly worshipped. His will, rather, is to be understood and advanced in the field of human relations, to the end of social as well as individual regeneration. "For God sent not his Son into the world to condemn the world; but that the world through him might be saved." [4]

[3] Acton, *ibid.*
[4] John 3:17.

In the second place, the case for resistance to temporal force, wherever the latter can be shown to conflict with the Law of God, was enormously strengthened by acceptance of the divinity of Christ. If Jesus were merely an unusually moral human being, his exhortations could be observed or disregarded in conformity with the judgment of the individual intelligence. But once the divinity of Christ was accepted—and until relatively modern times it was never questioned by Christians—a moral authority superior to every earthly political rule was established for all who regard Christ as Master. Conscience was confirmed as the guide of conduct. And human allegiance was thus divided between the sovereignty of God and that of Caesar.

III

For nearly twenty centuries, the effort of political philosophy in the Christian world has been to reconcile the dilemma posed by the latent antagonism between Divine Authority and mundane authorities.

Some individuals, whom we may class as mystics, have always so far as possible ignored the governmental regulation of daily activity, concentrating their whole attention on the development of an inner life. Other individuals, whom we may call the agnostics, endeavor to be indifferent to the existence of Divine Authority, though willing to admit that all humanity is subject to certain obviously inescapable controls, such as the force of gravity. In consequence, the agnostic, though not necessarily law-abiding, tends to obey without spiritual protest whatever the local political force commands. A third type, still numerous among Americans, accepts the challenge of Christianity with greater or less enthusiasm and energy. People in this category really endeavor to reconcile the mandates of divine and human law. The quality of their striving determines first the practice and eventually the form of representative government.

The Marxist effort to undermine, and if possible destroy, the idea of God is certainly doomed to failure. One comes to this conclusion because distinction between Divine Law, capitalized, and man-made laws, in lower case, is so deeply ingrained in human understanding.

Indeed, the anthropologists tell us that the distinction is universal for human beings, in space as well as time. Greek philosophy was deeply concerned with the nature of the ultimate Authority that directs men's actions. The quest for justice, as the touchstone of moral law, is the theme of Plato's *Republic*, with its concluding admonition to "hold fast ever to the heavenly way." Blackstone, at the outset of his famous *Commentaries on the Laws of England*, asserts flatly that the "law of nature being co-eval with mankind, and dictated by God himself, is of course superior in obligation to any other." The law of nature, as a set of uncodified commands implicitly accepted by the mind and conscience of every reasonable person, is merely the concept of Divine Law under another name. Time and again the law of nature has been dismissed as mere fantasy. But time and again it has operated to overthrow entire systems of positive law.

> Thus the contents of the law of nature vary with the ages, but their aim is constant, it is justice; and though this species of law operates not in positive enactments, but in the minds of men, it is needless to urge that he who obtains command over minds will in the end master their institutions.[5]

We may therefore conclude that Authority will always have its final *locus* beyond the reach of the sheriff and the tax collector. Up to a point men will obey the regulations imposed upon them by the State and undoubtedly the field of their submission can be greatly extended by terrorization. There comes a time, however, when civil regulations become so numerous or so absurd that they conflict too sharply both with the moral and the intellectual sense. It may be a law that prohibits men from taking advantage of the natural process of fermentation. It may be a law demanding that on his eighteenth birthday a boy shall be conscripted for military service. It may be a law that fixes an arbitrary price for a pound of butter. The occasion is less important than the result, which is at first individual, and finally collective, rebellion.

[5] Sir Paul Vinogradoff, *Common-Sense in Law*, Home University Library, p. 245.

From the viewpoint of political science, the point at which such rebellion may be expected is as important as is the tensile strength of metals to the engineer. No earthly government can be so authoritarian and no people can be so regimented as to eliminate the tendency to rebel against what their inmost instincts deem to be injustice. This tendency, define it as we will, is at bottom the personal recognition of an Authority higher than that of mortal kings and commissars. And since we cannot dispense with political regulations, the art of government is seen to be that of keeping these regulations in general conformity with Divine Law.

But the law of nature is dynamic as well as eternal. Therefore the problems of political government will never be finally solved; will be in process of solution so long as Man continues to exist as "a political animal."

IV

The aspiration of bringing earthly government into conformity with Divine Law has always been particularly pronounced among the American people. It could scarcely have been otherwise, considering the important part which the passion for religious freedom played in the settlement of the colonies.

Nathaniel Morton, contemporary historian of the first years of the Plymouth settlement, has left us the wording [in New England's Memorial] of the social contract by which the Pilgrims established the first political community of white men in New England. Its stated purposes were, in descending order, "for the glory of God, and advancement of the Christian faith, and the honour of our King and country." When, "in the course of human events," it became necessary to dissolve the political bonds connecting America and Britain, the task was easier because the primary American political allegiance had from the outset been given to Divine Authority. Loyalty to the British sovereign had always been secondary in the minds of most colonial Americans.

The importance of the role played by the clergy during the period immediately preceding the Revolution is more than interesting. It is also convincing evidence that our government during its formative period was being directed toward the fulfillment of Divine Law, so far as this can be understood by earnest Christians. In his book entitled *They Preached Liberty* the Reverend Franklin P. Cole has collected an anthology of quotations from the sermons of New England Ministers during the middle decades of the eighteenth century. These divines sought diligently to confirm a connection between Christian doctrine and political arrangement.

A favorite text, Mr. Cole observes, was: "Where the spirit of the Lord is, there is liberty." It was utilized, in particular, by Jonathan Mayhew. On January 30, 1750—the anniversary of the execution of King Charles I—Mayhew preached a remarkable sermon, in the West Church of Boston, afterward widely circulated under the title of: "A Discourse Concerning Unlimited Submission." It asserted that:

> Those in authority may abuse their trust and power to such a degree that neither the law of reason nor of religion requires that any obedience or submission be paid to them; but on the contrary that they should be totally discarded, and the authority which they were before vested with transferred to others, who may exercise more to those good purposes for which it is given.

The belief that civil power is only provisional, and should at all times be subordinate to intangible Authority, of course led to, and will always lead to, many difficult political problems. Civil law can be codified and given a relatively uniform judicial interpretation much more easily than is possible with Divine Law. The only practical way to make the latter effective as a form of jurisprudence is either to give political allegiance to a universal church, with a governing head more powerful than any national potentate, or else to create a theocracy in which a qualified priesthood exercises political command. Mankind has tried both of these methods, but not in this country. From the beginning, sectarian separation was of the essence in American Protestant thinking, as the New England Puritans found when they tried to impress on others the same sort of doctrinal unity that they had themselves so deeply resented in the Mother Country. And the strength of sectarianism in turn made separation of Church and

State inevitable, regardless of the deep respect accorded the ministerial profession as such.

In practice, it was impossible to elevate a single sacerdotal class empowered to interpret and apply Divine Law for all Americans. But it was equally impossible for the colonial mind to accept a civil authority empowered to disregard and override Divine Law as interpreted by the various religious bodies. Therefore, with the genius for practical solutions characteristic of a frontier people, a part of the problem was eliminated by severely limiting the powers of civil authority. We have already emphasized that the limitation of official power is a central characteristic in the American way of life. But we have not heretofore considered the extent to which religious thought is responsible for that limitation.

The evidence in this matter is abundant. A few instances may be taken from the rich storehouse of Mr. Cole's anthology.[6]

In 1765, the Reverend Edward Dorr asserted from his Hartford pulpit the "melancholy truth" that "the rulers of this world have generally set themselves in opposition to the interest of true religion and the cause of Christ." In 1771, the Reverend John Tucker, of Newbury, Massachusetts, told his parishioners in an election sermon that: "Unlimited submission . . . is not due to government in a free state. There are certain boundaries beyond which submission cannot be justly required, nor is therefore due." In 1773, the Reverend Charles Turner said in Duxbury that: "Unlimited power has generally been destructive of human happiness. The people are not under such temptations to thwart their own interests, as absolute government is under to abuse the people." And in 1777, in a sermon as cogent today as when it was delivered, the Reverend Samuel Webster warned in Salisbury, Massachusetts, that:

> . . . encroachments on the people's liberties are not generally made all at once, but so gradually as hardly to be perceived by the less watchful; and all plaistered over, it may be, with such plausible pretenses, that before they are aware of the snare, they are taken and cannot disentangle themselves.

[6] *Op. cit.*, pp. 70, 81, 83, 84-85.

Mr. Cole has done a great service in assembling material that shows how sharply the clergy of the Revolutionary period denounced exaltation of the civil power. Their attitude was of course instrumental in curbing the wishes of those centralizers who, like Alexander Hamilton a few years later, sought to establish a strong national government. But it must not be thought that this faith in home rule developed only when the breach between America and Great Britain made it popular to attack the government in London. The distinctively American political philosophy was apparent long before there was any idea of political independence.

In his preliminary sketch for the government of West New Jersey, which foreshadowed the later government of Pennsylvania, William Penn wrote, in 1676, that: ". . . we lay a foundation for after ages to understand their liberty as men and Christians, that they may not be brought into bondage but by their own consent; for we put the power in the people . . ."

Six years later, in the first "Frame of Government" for Pennsylvania, Penn developed even further the idea of civil government as a social contract between men subject primarily to God. One provision was too liberal for many of his own Quakers to approve:

> That all persons living in this province, who confess and acknowledge the one Almighty and Eternal God to be the Creator, Upholder and Ruler of the world, and that hold themselves obliged, in conscience, to live peaceably and justly in civil society, shall, in no way, be molested, or prejudiced, for their religious persuasion, or practice, in matters of faith and worship; nor shall they be compelled, at any time, to frequent, or maintain, any religious worship, place or ministry whatever.[7]

No people can be entrusted with power unless their minds have dwelt deeply and reverently on its inner nature. So it is important to remember that generations of political thought and experimentation had made their mark upon the American character

[7] The political documentation on Penn is conveniently collected in Chapter IV of *Remember William Penn*, published in 1944 by the official William Penn Tercentenary Committee of Pennsylvania.

before Benjamin Franklin summed up the dominant conclusion in an apothegm that stands the test of time: "Man will ultimately be governed by God or by tyrants."

V

To "put the power in the people," with any degree of permanence, it was necessary for the colonists: (1) to establish a system of government in which the individual would not be subjected by the State; (2) to develop a form of Society in which the individual would be inclined to restrain himself through recognition of an alternative and higher authority. The first of these connected tasks, being essentially negative in nature, could be achieved at a stroke, when the separation from Great Britain had been accomplished. But the positive duty of developing self-government, in the literal sense of the phrase, remains as a continuing obligation for citizens of the Republic. Nevertheless, it was believed with good reason, at the close of the eighteenth century, that Americans on the whole had learned how to govern themselves according to the moral law, and would retain and improve their capacity for self-government in a condition of political independence.

Enough has been said about the specific measures taken to insure that political government, while powerful enough to maintain a stable republic, should be neither strongly centralized nor in any way omnipotent in the United States. It is at least equally important to understand the motives that molded the Constitution as devised and accepted. These motives were to a very considerable extent spiritual, and therefore as valid today as in 1787. They were inspired by, and were in turn integrated with, the Christian doctrine that every man has in himself not only a copious measure of original sin, but also at least a trace of the divine. The problem of the Republic was, and is, how best to cope with the former while nurturing the latter. The first and fundamental decision was that this problem can never be solved by governmental agencies alone.

The heavy responsibility thereby placed upon the individual is the foundation of the liberal position, using the word in its true, historical sense. A person who maintains that the State should solve, by necessarily coercive methods, any problem that individuals are capable of solving voluntarily, is, of course, the very opposite of a liberal. The esssence of tyranny is reliance on external, as opposed to internal, compulsion.

Liberalism as a political creed is simply an application of the Christian doctrine that Man has within himself the seed of his own salvation. The liberal obeys Paul's admonition to: "Stand fast therefore in the liberty wherewith Christ hath made us free." To be liberal is to have faith in human decency, without qualification of creed or color or circumstance. It is to possess a sense of justice that applies as well to an enemy as to a friend, and an intellectual discrimination that can admit and admire excellence wherever found. Liberalism is of course an aristocratic attitude which does not suffer fools gladly. In paying tribute to wisdom, however, the liberal demands that it be combined with integrity. His concept of aristocracy is one that includes not only wisdom but also character and conduct. The liberal repudiates class distinction based upon financial status, along with the fantastic assumption that superiority of any kind can be devised from father to son.

The smugness and complacent self-righteousness of the Pharisees could easily taint the surface virtues if there were no element of self-restraint in the composition of the liberal. What distinguishes him most clearly, however, is abiding faith in that self-imposed discipline which, explicitly or implicitly, he regards as a test of loyalty to Authority superior to any on this earth. The liberal knows that self-discipline is necessary, not merely to perfect his own capacities but also to enable him to live co-operatively with other men. Indeed, the exercise of self-discipline is the very center and well-spring of the liberal creed. It develops a sincerity that may not be strong enough to prevent sin, but does guarantee dissatisfaction with perfunctory outward observance of any code, whether civil or religious. The liberal cannot believe that the end justifies the means and must at all times maintain a critical attitude, toward his own philosophy in the first instance but also toward that of other men.

It follows, from these characteristics, that in any place, at any time, the liberal is likely to be a member of the minority. Liberalism is an intellectual philosophy as well as a religious faith. Relatively few people are likely to possess the tenacity, the wisdom, or even the capacity for reflection essential to combine these attributes. Moreover it takes moral courage to give primary allegiance to an Authority that is unseen. Inevitably this elusive loyalty makes the liberal a thorn in the flesh of those who exercise temporal power. Between the man who makes political office his highest aim and the man who tends, no matter how delicately, to deride political office, there will always be an underlying antagonism. So the State machinery operates to discourage liberalism, and liberals become a shining target of State coercion as this instrumentality seeks to enlarge its scope and power over individuals.

Liberalism is neither a proletarian, a bourgeois, an agrarian, nor even necessarily a clerical characteristic, and from its individualistic nature the philosophy cannot survive identification with the spurious aristocracy that demands class loyalty. For that reason England, in spite of the magnificent contribution of many Englishmen to the development of liberal philosophy, has not maintained itself as a stronghold of liberalism. Class government, whether Tory or Labour, is fatal to a doctrine that repudiates the theory of social classes and, consequently, that of class war. There is nothing accidental in the way the Liberal Party in Great Britain has been pulverized between the millstones of Conservatism on the one hand and Socialism on the other.

VI

Our system of government was consciously designed to protect and encourage the liberal attitude as outlined above. This purpose is apparent in the elaborate dispersion of political power both between the federal government and that of the states, and among the executive, legislative, and judicial functions in all of them. There is far more to the picture, however, than is found in the constitutional setup. Even more significant, because more illustrative of unrestricted popular will, has been the character of party organization in the United States.

As noted in Chapter 2, political parties in our country have from the beginning divided along lines of philosophic principle rather than of class interest. This is not to say that our politicians have been philosophers, any more than were the Honorable Samuel Slumkey and Horatio Fizkin, Esq., of whose "spirited contest" for the honor of representing the borough of Eatanswill the Pickwick Papers have left us a no less spirited account. And to say that political parties in the United States have philosophic significance is not to assert that they are devoid of class attachment. The self-interest of slaveowners certainly played a part in the early days of the Democratic Party; the charge that Big Business has dominated the Republican Party contains enough truth to give that indictment ample sting.

Nevertheless, it remains true that no major American political party has ever attempted to identify itself with the welfare of a single element of the body politic: as in England the Tories associated themselves with the landowners; the Whigs with the mercantile and manufacturing interests; the Labour Party with the wage earners. American politics, by contrast with those of Europe, have not been a class struggle as to who should control the machinery of the State but much more a continuing conflict as to how extensive the authority of the national government should be. Though often only half-realized, and always obscured by local or temporary considerations, the real division in American parties has been between those who regard liberty as more important than security, and those who maintain that without security there is no meaning to liberty. To put it sardonically: The Republican Party has not been primarily interested in extending democracy, nor the Democratic Party in preserving the Republic. Yet the interplay of these forces has so far served both to extend democracy and to preserve the Republic.

We are now in a position to realize the fundamental nature of our two-party system of government. The cleavage is really over the issue of Authority and it may divide even families [8] ac-

---

[8] Cf. Matthew 10:35; Luke 12:53.

cording to whether the individual believes that Man should work out his destiny in accordance with the laws of God, or whether he believes that Man's primary allegiance is to a political artifact. There is no danger to the country in this division. On the contrary, balance is preserved by a clear-cut opposition of political forces. The danger would arise if there should ever cease to be a major party resolutely opposed to centralization of government. For instance, when Democrats abandon states' rights, and if Republicans do not move in to support home rule, then the anomalous and disturbing result is a federal republic in which neither major party upholds the basic principle of federalism.

Liberals, who could not be so defined if they lacked the aspiration of liberty, know perfectly well that their primary allegiance is to political principle and not to any particular political party. If the party of their allegiance deserts the principles of liberalism, then they will leave that party for one that conforms more closely to the liberal tradition. If for a time there is no such party, then one will probably be constructed, as the States' Rights Party was, after the Democratic National Convention of 1948.

If the people as a whole finally abandons the liberal tradition the problem will become more difficult, for one cannot move to another country as one can to another party. But there were many loyal Germans who fought National Socialism to the death in Germany. There are many patriotic Russians and others who are willing to do the same wherever the Communist tyranny controls. In the United States, where political authority has always been suspect, the proportion of honorable rebels would probably be even higher if the necessity should arise. There will be no such necessity if a resolute minority of Americans rally to save their system of government before it is too late.

VII

There are many liberals who are not Americans and there are many Americans who are not liberals. But the American system of government is particularly favorable to the development of liberal thought. To say that the system encourages liberalism, however, is not to assert that all the results of the system operate to that end.

In this seeming paradox, indeed, is found the very heart of our present discontent. By limiting political authority the American system has released tremendous energies, which have made our country, from every material viewpoint, the envy of the world. Yet this concentration on material improvement has itself lessened American allegiance to the ultimate Authority in behalf of which the power of political government was circumscribed. The natural result of concentration on the production of material wealth, and of the unequal distribution of the product, has been increasing popular demand for some sort of "New Deal."

In practice, as we have bitter reason to realize, the phrase is likely to mean only a return to the oldest and most impoverishing of tyrannies—the elevation of political at the expense of spiritual authority.[9] It is, nevertheless, idle to expect the masses to learn anything from the lessons of history if they are not applied and made clear by those who have had opportunity to reflect upon them.

The blessings of liberty turn quickly into dust and ashes unless they are disseminated among the people, to whom the power of government has been distributed. So there is need for something deeper and more spiritual than socialistic rationing of wealth or capitalistic profit-sharing devices. Without production, there will be nothing to distribute, either in the field of morals or in the field of economics. Therefore it is an individual responsibility to be a producer of moral as well as of material wealth. Perhaps there is room for argument as to whether private enterprise can produce material goods as efficiently as the State. But it is certain that, in the production of moral wealth, private enterprise is far more productive than the State can ever be.

The reason for this is rooted in the nature of Authority. The character of the State, as noted in the preceding chapter, is essentially amoral. Certainly its machinery outlaws and punishes

[9] The shopworn principles of arbitrary government employed by F. D. Roosevelt's Administration are critically and refreshingly examined by Henry J. Haskell in his study entitled *The New Deal in Old Rome*.

what is considered to be evil conduct. But the State accepts no responsibility for the active promotion of good conduct. The Authority of Christ, on the other hand, is wholly devoted to the improvement of individual behavior. Here is a moral code repressive of that which is degrading; productive of that which is uplifting. So the emphasis of true Authority is on increased individual production of the nonmaterial wealth without which the condition of freedom is meaningless and the aspiration of liberty stultified. The emphasis of forceful government, on the other hand, is increasingly on material production, in order to meet the rising cost of government, even though governmental procedures actually serve to restrict rather than to encourage output.

One may read every line of *The Great Stalin Five-Year Plan* for the Soviet Union without finding any advocacy of the production of spiritual wealth. This plan provides, among countless details, that: "The capacity of the cotton textile mills in Stalinabad shall be expanded by 18,500 spindles." [10] But there is not a word about expanding the capacity of the people of Stalinabad for self-government. That is because authoritarian government cannot afford to recognize Authority external to itself.

VIII

It is important to realize that the aggrandizement of the State has to a large extent resulted from what we vaguely call democracy. And this is bitterly ironical, for the State as such is inherently hostile to democracy and, once it has achieved sufficient power, will destroy democracy, in fact if not in name.

As a result of our failure to differentiate between Society and State, the word "democracy" itself has come to have two distinct meanings, dependent upon whether our usage of the term is primarily social or primarily political. In the social sense, democracy signifies a daily application of the doctrine of human equality —that *égalitarianisme* for which the English language, perhaps because it was developed by a class-conscious people, has no sim-

[10] *The Great Stalin Five-Year Plan*, published by the Washington Embassy of the Union of Soviet Socialist Republics (June, 1946), p. 28.

ple equivalent. That which is "undemocratic," socially speaking, is any practice tending to deny the assumption that one man is "as good" as another. Vernacular expression is often beautifully exact, and certainly is so in this instance. For to say that one man is "as good" as another does not mean that his intelligence is as quick, or that his bank account is as substantial. It merely means that in the sight of God, as the source of good, the differences between the pauper and the millionaire, the black and the white, the Russian and the American, are negligible. All are subjects of the same "natural laws." All are brothers under the Fatherhood of God.

Social democracy is thus at bottom a religious conception, enormously strengthened by the precepts of Christianity; therefore indigenous for the American people and also strengthened by conditions of life in this country during the formative period of American institutions. No dogmatic assertion has been received more favorably by American ears than the one in the Declaration of Independence that states as a "self-evident truth" that "all men are created equal." And this has been not only an article of faith, but also a rule of social practice on the part of most Americans who take their ideals seriously. For a long time "equalitarianism," except for slaves, was to a notable extent achieved as well as acclaimed. "During my stay in the United States," de Tocqueville wrote in his introduction to *Democracy in America*, "nothing struck me more forcibly than the general equality of conditions among the people."

But, "democracy" has a political, as well as a social, meaning. Politically speaking, the word can only mean a system of government under which the laws are made and administered in accordance with the will of the majority, so far as this is mechanically ascertainable. So democracy as a political system may be defined as truly representative government with unrestricted majority rule. For propaganda purposes, and to promote the semasiological confusion that has been so helpful to their cause, the Communists maintain that the dictatorship of a small minority is actually democratic. To accomplish this *tour de force*, however, they must reason that there is no opinion where no expression of it is allowed.

If all opposition to a decree of the Politburo is outlawed it can
indeed be asserted that the official viewpoint accords not only with
that of the majority but even with the *volunté générale* so far
as it is expressed. However, common sense, as well as common
usage, rebels against the attempt to call this political democracy.

Common sense, however, should also rebel against the attempt
to call our system of government democratic. For to deserve that
term several conditions, lacking in the United States, must be
present.

Obviously a system of government cannot properly be called
democratic unless the law-making power is wholly under the control of a majority of freely and periodically elected representatives. The number of these representatives, in a democracy, should
be in proportion to the number of citizens and the franchise should
not be denied by any arbitrary or discriminatory regulation. And
since democracy means rule *of* the people—not rule *for* the people
—the democratic principle would seem further to require a continuously compliant attitude on the part of elected representatives,
in contradistinction to Edmund Burke's famous argument that
"Your representative owes you, not his industry only, but his
judgment." [11]

In this country the members of the more representative House,
whether in the state or national legislatures, can be said to show
habitual compliance with the majority will, or at least with that
of the local party organization. But few of the other essential
characteristics of democratic government are fulfilled. Until
1913, the election of members of the federal Senate was indirect.
And the Seventeenth Amendment of course did nothing to rectify
the highly undemocratic arrangement whereby a Senator from
Nevada, with fewer than 125,000 inhabitants, can cancel out the
vote of a Senator from New York, representing (in 1940) 112
times as many people. In the matter of overriding a Presidential
veto—itself a serious dereliction of the democratic principle—it
actually takes the vote of both Senators from New York to match
that of one from Nevada. The Greek name for a political order
of this character was polity, not democracy.

[11] Speech to the Electors of Bristol, November 3, 1774.

The sharp restriction of democratic processes in the American system of government was both intentional and well reasoned. We have already quoted Edmund Randolph's observation that "a good Senate seemed most likely" to check "the turbulence and follies of democracy . . ." Argument in behalf of an undemocratic Senate is less provocatively set forth in Numbers 62 and 63 of *The Federalist.* According to the latter, "history informs us of no long-lived republic which had not a senate" and gives "very instructive proofs of the necessity of some institution that will blend stability with liberty." The conclusion is "that liberty may be endangered by the abuses of liberty as well as by the abuses of power."

The Senate, moreover, is by no means the only one of our governmental institutions designed to prevent "a mutable policy," which "poisons the blessing of liberty itself." [12] Even less democratic than the Senate, designed to represent states rather than citizens, is the institution of the Supreme Court. This permits nine appointed judges, or rather a bare majority thereof, effectively to nullify any legislation that may be deemed contrary to our written Constitution. Finally, and most important, the theory of democracy is directly flouted in numerous clauses of the Constitution, especially in the first ten amendments (the Bill of Rights). These flatly deny to the representatives of the people any power to curtail freedom of speech, right of assembly, and other individual privileges, no matter how unwelcome to the majority these may be.

During the life of the Republic there has been some tendency to democratize its institutions. But changes like the direct election of Senators, or the extension of suffrage to women, have been offset by such undemocratic procedures as the disfranchisement of the District of Columbia and the increasing use of the presidential veto. On balance, it is impossible to assert that the American people show any strong desire to see their system of government made more democratic. When President Franklin D. Roosevelt sought to push through the notorious Judiciary Bill of 1937 he was justified in saying demagogically that: "If we would keep faith with

[12] *The Federalist*, No. 62.

those who had faith in us, if we would make democracy succeed, I say we must act—Now!" [13] But Mr. Roosevelt apparently failed to realize that Americans did not want the sort of democracy that would have made the judiciary subject to the executive by having the Supreme Court "packed" with servile nominees. And this devious legislation—a good example of a tyrannical measure depicted in seductive terms—was defeated.

There is, of course, an underlying reason for the seemingly illogical American habit of continuously exalting "democracy" while carefully modifying its practice as a political system. The egalitarian flavor of the word supports the stimulating belief that each and every one of us, regardless of handicaps or limitations, may by honorable effort progress toward whatever goal we set for ourselves. Since such progress is always primarily dependent upon individual endeavor, it is wholly in accordance with liberal philosophy to praise "democracy" in this discriminating sense. But it is equally important to remember that true liberalism insists on protecting the individual from tyranny of every variety, and that tyrannies are almost always imposed on minorities with the acquiescence of majorities—in other words, by democratic means.

IX

Democracy and liberalism have much in common; but they are not the same thing, regardless of whether we are considering Man as a member of Society or as a subject of the State. The distinction between the democratic and the liberal attitudes is very important, and again it hinges on understanding the nature of Authority.

Both democracy and liberalism are opposed to privilege, but the opposition springs from different motives. The hostility of democracy is directed against the supremacy of an estate—whether it is legally recognized, as a hereditary nobility or an "established" Church, or whether it is something vague and indeterminate like "Wall Street" or the "leisure class." But while the instinct and desire of democracy are to destroy the vested interest, it generally has no formula of replacement. Demos is apt in

[13] Democratic Victory Dinner, March 4, 1937.

destruction but unskilled in reformation. Its emphasis is always on distribution rather than production; on rights as contrasted with responsibilities. "To the victor belong the spoils."

It is a fundamental characteristic of democracy to believe that there is some virtue in a majority as such. Psychologists tell us that this behavior pattern results from the herd instinct. If animals of any kind group together, whether to build an anthill, to construct a hive, or to establish a colony, the action of the individual must be disciplined to the purpose of the group. So the case for democracy is not undermined by suggesting that as often as not the majority opinion, at any given moment and on any given issue, is demonstrably false. To avoid complete frustration the group, as a group, must frequently take decisive action. If one believes that the individuals forming the group are fundamentally of equal worth, then the majority opinion is for that reason alone worthy of respect.

But "the cardinal quality of the herd is homogeneity." [14] So it follows that once a direction has been chosen, pressure is brought to bring all opinion into conformity with the choice. Critics and skeptics must be silenced; the more resolutely if their questions are effective. This effort to enforce uniformity is too universal to be casually condemned. It has been as pronounced in the conduct of the Society of Friends, where a member formerly could be expelled for joining the Army even in time of war, as in the Army itself, where the same individual could be shot for showing the same independence of mind at the expense of similar group welfare.

This natural desire of the group for uniformity provides the opportunity of the demagogue, who is both the product and the menace of democracy. For it is the ambition of the demagogue to exploit the natural regimentation of a democracy in behalf of his personal leadership, utilizing and developing the disciplinary machinery of the State to that end. As State controls become more plausible, more far-reaching and more effective, the tendency of democracy to succumb to the demagogue becomes ever more pronounced. This degenerative tendency has been present from the

[14] W. Trotter, *Instincts of the Herd in Peace and War*, p. 29.

beginning of political organization. Indeed no modern writer could analyze it more clearly than did Plato, in the Eighth Book of *The Republic:*

> The people have always some champion whom they set over them and nurse into greatness . . . This and no other is the root from which a tyrant springs; when he first appears above ground he is a protector. . . . At first, in the early days of his power, he is full of smiles and he salutes everyone whom he meets;—he to be called a tyrant, who is making promises in public and also in private! Liberating debtors, and distributing land to the people and his followers, and wanting to be so kind and good to everyone! . . . then he is always stirring up some war or other, in order that the people may require a leader. . . . Has he not also another object, which is that they may be impoverished by payment of taxes, and thus compelled to devote themselves to their daily wants and therefore less likely to conspire against him? . . . And the more detestable his actions are to the citizens, the more satellites and the greater devotion in them will he require? . . . Thus liberty, getting out of all order and reason, passes into the harshest and bitterest form of slavery.[15]

As one reflects upon this discerning passage, written more than 2300 years ago, it is difficult to avoid identification of Plato's hypothetical tyrant, "wanting to be so kind and good," with outstanding politicians of our own day.

X

It is on this question of majority rights, and the leveling process that they imply, that the liberal separates from the democrat, even to the extent of opposing enlargement of political democracy. So long as the struggle is against conservatism as such; so long as the desired reform is directed toward the elimination of arbitrary privilege, or monopolistic practice, the liberal and the democrat are allied. They part company as democracy slides into socialism, which it must do to the extent that the democrat trusts and employs the State as an agency for the rectification of social abuses.

Liberalism believes in equality of opportunity, but does not

[15] *The Dialogues of Plato;* Jowett's translation. Vol. III, pp. 274-9 *passim.*

assume that equality at birth means automatic equality throughout life. There is stimulus in the assumption that "all men are born equal." There is repression in the illogical corollary which asserts that men *remain* equal, regardless of their individual effort for self-improvement and self-government. This secondary assumption is denied by something more than all the evidence of biology, which even questions the literal accuracy of the basic premise. A belief in automatic and continuous equality is also wholly at variance with Christian doctrine, which emphasizes throughout that intense and persistent personal struggle is necessary for salvation. "He that shall endure unto the end, the same shall be saved." [16]

As Croce points out, liberalism has gained in strength, as has democracy, with the decline of privilege as a class prerogative. But liberalism is far more careful than democracy to avoid the substitution of a new form of privilege for that which is eliminated. The liberal, as a case in point, fought side by side with the democrat to establish the right of collective bargaining. The liberal was as staunch in advocacy of the principle of free association as the conservative was stubborn in his opposition. But liberals maintained their principles when State intervention was called in to make trade unionism compulsory. Croce has defined the line of demarcation: "Liberalism is in contrast to democracy in so far as democracy, by idolizing equality conceived in an extrinsic and mechanical way, tends, whether it wishes to or not, toward authoritarianism. . . ." [17]

It is the idolization of equality that has produced what Ortega y Gasset has called "hyperdemocracy," developing that mass mind which contributes little or nothing, but nevertheless vociferously demands "security" as a right. This is the meat on which our Caesar feeds. And the mass man is, by definition, always a member of the majority whereas the liberal is, as we have seen, habitually a member of the minority. The democrat, whose emotional urge is always stronger than his critical faculty, is more in danger

[16] Matthew 24:13.
[17] Benedetto Croce, *Politics and Morals*; essay on "Liberalism as a Concept of Life."

of being pulled over into "hyperdemocracy." And because of this pull he is often "unaware that the select man is not the petulant person who thinks himself superior to the rest, but the man who demands more of himself than the rest, even though he may not fulfill in his person those higher exigencies." [18]

Liberalism, in short, is a reasoned philosophy, bolstered by faith in the essential goodness—or God-ness—of Man, whereas democracy is tinged with a passionate quality to the extent that resentment and jealousy can easily overwhelm the necessarily dispassionate sense of justice. Consequently, the aspirations of democracy can never be satisfied unless and until mankind is reduced to a single plane, of which the level would at best be that of mediocrity. And since the instinct of liberty rebels against the dull oppression of the mass, there will always be a latent conflict between democracy and liberalism. In this conflict, moreover, the thorough democrat will often be more hostile to the liberal than to the selfish conservative. The self-interest of the latter can be intelligently exposed and advantageously denounced. But the position of the ideal liberal is both morally and logically unassailable. So liberal opposition to the aspirations of democracy can only be countered by contemptible denunciations of motive and character—in a word, by "smearing."

Thus there is something tragic in the thoughtless acclaim given to democracy as a political movement. As soon as it overthrows one impediment to egalitarianism, another arises. When a hereditary nobility is destroyed, "economic royalists" are seen to usurp the stage. As these are struck down, an elite of Nazis or Commissars moves in. Abolishing privilege by purely political means, by either legal or illegal force, is like killing the hydra. Even if two evils do not arise for one eliminated, at best the original oppression continues in another form. Its name is changed, but not its essential character. Thus many well-intentioned democrats are pitifully confused when the Communists say, with some reason, that they have achieved democracy, wherever their writ runs. It takes a discerning mind to realize that the Soviet system *is* political democracy, brought past the transition into tyranny.

[18] José Ortega y Gasset, *The Revolt of the Masses*, p. 15.

A few years after the establishment of our Republic the people of France rose in a spontaneous upheaval, of which the record has been carefully compiled; from which important lessons are still to be learned. Spurred by American accomplishment, goaded by almost incredible injustice, the French revolutionaries moved to destroy the *Ancien Régime*. On their banners and on their lips was a ringing phrase, as eloquent of democratic aspirations as it was destined to be fatal to human welfare. *"Liberté; Égalité; Fraternité,"* the people chanted. But very soon equality strangled liberty; and fraternity passed swiftly into atrocity. The Reign of Terror indicated the absence of some essential ingredient, necessary to transmute democratic yearning into liberal accomplishment.

Americans had carried that missing ingredient with them, to the New World. It was not, is not, a national monopoly, for Frenchmen, too, were Christians. But around the Court of Louis XVI it was not Christianity, it was merely the Church that counted. So there was excuse for the forlorn decree transforming Notre Dame into a "Temple of Reason" and it was understandable when, on the 17th Brumaire, Year II, the President of the Assembly declared that, "The worship of Reason should in future be the national religion." [19]

The sequel showed that nothing is more unreasonable than Reason, when it forgets the nature of Authority.

[19] Louis Madelin, *The French Revolution*, p. 388.

Chapter 7

The Meaning of Self-Government

Sweeping assumptions were made by the men who founded the American Republic. They held some "truths to be self-evident," also asserting in the Declaration of Independence "that all men are created equal, that they are endowed by their Creator with certain unalienable Rights, that among these are Life, Liberty and the pursuit of Happiness."

As the era of Science has succeeded that of Faith, these "self-evident truths" have been increasingly questioned. Many have demonstrated, in action if not in words, that they do not regard all men as having a fundamental claim to equality. And while there has been increasing lip service to the doctrine of Natural Rights, we demonstrate in many ways that such rights are not regarded as "unalienable." Indeed it is argued with increasing vigor that the individual has *no* rights that cannot properly be alienated by the State.

Of course the founders of the Republic were not all as idealistic and personally disinterested as is often suggested. The Declaration of Independence, in particular, was as much a propagandist as a philosophical document. Its signers subordinated complete sincerity to their primary purpose of justifying a particular course of action. Among those who sponsored the assertion that "all men are created equal" were some who indorsed the practice of human slavery. It suited their convenience to define liberty as an "unalienable Right," even though they were personally opposed to dissemination of its blessings among many of their fellow creatures.

But such individual hypocrisy did not minimize the value of the Declaration as an assertion of principle. Its essential value was not as a statement of the way things were, but rather as a proclamation of the way things should be. The actual, as opposed to the ideal, is full of inconsistencies. The importance of the Puritan attitude, so deeply rooted in the fiber of American life, lies in its assumption that it *is* practical "to grasp this sorry Scheme of Things entire." The skepticism and defeatism of the Orient, so alluringly portrayed in Edward Fitzgerald's translation of the Rubaiyat, is wholly alien to the main stream of American thought. The costs of revolution, of civil war, of world-wide combat against alien tyrannies, have never disheartened Americans. So far as our people give any consideration to the "scheme of things" they still on the whole believe that it is possible to "re-mould it nearer to the Heart's Desire." It can't be done—but here it is!

This national characteristic, so stimulating to idealists, so exasperating to skeptics, is of course essentially an expression of faith. And very noteworthy is the fact that this underlying faith has not yet, in the United States, really been undermined by the advance of science. On the contrary, the endeavor has been to harness science to the service of faith. Obviously that faith is frequently crude in its conception and materialistic in its application. But it is still faith—still an essentially religious conviction that Man, for all his inner failings and in spite of all the outer handicaps, remains the master of his destiny.

Blunders and myopia and consequent disillusionment spot almost every page of American history since July 4, 1776. But now, as then, the average American continues to respond to the belief that there really are natural rights and: "That to secure these rights, Governments are instituted among Men, deriving their just powers from the consent of the governed."

II

Without equivocation, the Declaration of Independence maintains that the purpose of government, as an institution, is "to secure" certain "unalienable Rights." Some of the less restrained advocates of "free enterprise"—in the narrow commercial sense of the term—would do well to remember that fact. The "American way"—if that means policy sanctioned by tradition and justified by solemn pronouncement of the Founding Fathers—does not preclude governmental intervention in private affairs. On the contrary, it justifies such intervention, since the basic purpose of government is said to be "to secure these rights."

But Thomas Jefferson, as the chief author of the Declaration, was well aware of the tendency of government to destroy natural rights under the pretext, or with the honest intention, of securing them. Even without this perception it would have been logically impossible for the signers of the Declaration to deify the State as such, in a document primarily designed to justify American rebellion against the British State. So contemporary political necessity combined nicely with permanent political philosophy in the passage of the Declaration that immediately follows the statement on the purpose of government. This passage asserts, as another "self-evident truth":

> That whenever any Form of Government becomes destructive of these ends, it is the Right of the People to alter or to abolish it, and to institute new Government, laying its foundation on such principles and organizing its powers in such form, as to them shall seem most likely to effect their Safety and Happiness.

The supreme value of that assertion lies in its classification of government as a controlled institution, entitled to continue in a particular form only so long as that form is satisfactory to those who are governed. The principle laid down makes it improper to regard any political administration with reverence. This principle makes it an actual civic duty—not just a mischievous pleasure—for the citizen to assume a critical attitude toward his government;

local, state or national. The American political tradition holds that not merely a particular administration, but also the whole political system—the "Form of Government"—is there on sufference. "It is the Right of the People to alter or to abolish it"; preferably to alter by orderly election, but if necessary to abolish by violent revolution. The power in the people is only provisionally delegated to officers of State.

Such a philosophy could easily produce intolerable political instability. And it is significant that the American Communist Party has seized on this endorsement of revolution as a justification for its "Americanism." As Earl Browder observed when national chairman of the Party (with that lack of subtlety which had so much to do with his fall from grace) "American Communists have long been ... reviving the study of American history in the light of today's problems." But Mr. Browder's underlying purpose was a little too obvious in his suggestion that Thomas Jefferson was a Communist; that "the Communist Party has its place in the great American tradition" and that Americans should be eternally grateful for "this revival of the American tradition by the Communists." [1]

The American tradition is of course completely opposed to authoritarian government, whether sponsored from the Left or from the Right. The theory of an elite governing class has had profoundly different superficial characteristics in Great Britain on the one hand and in Russia on the other. The Victorian belief in government by a titled aristocracy is seemingly far removed from the Communist principle that a handful of tyrants are entitled to dictate in the name of the proletariat. But from the American viewpoint both are based on the same underlying fallacy. Both assume that political office is something sacrosanct and that those who wield the power of government are for that reason alone worthy of respect. The American conviction is that the "Safety and Happiness" of the governed takes precedence over every governmental prerogative and that deference is not necessarily owing to those temporarily in a position of political command.

[1] Earl Browder, *Victory—and After*, pp. 94, 95, 101.

In Jefferson's words: "When a man assumes a public trust, he should consider himself as public property." [2]

III

Between the principles enunciated in the Declaration of Independence, and the practices established by the formulation of the Constitution, there was a space of time and a development of political thinking.

The doctrine that men are important in themselves, and that government is subject to overthrow if it controverts their happiness, was in accord with revolutionary conviction. But after twelve difficult years, of war and virtual anarchy, most Americans became convinced that a national government was both necessary and desirable. Even so, in the establishment of that government the greatest care was taken to insure both the individual citizen and the "sovereign states" against complete subordination to central political authority.

As every student of the Constitutional Convention knows, it was a painfully difficult task to bridge the gap between the popular insistence on responsive local government and the simultaneous necessity for a stable general government. On this issue the convention more than once came near to breaking up. Indeed it is doubtful whether it could have held together without the patient and luminous guidance continually exerted by James Madison. The issue was clarified for all the delegates when Madison said, during the critical discussion on July 17, 1787:

> The necessity of a General Government proceeds from the propensity of the States to pursue their particular interests, in opposition to the general interest. This propensity will continue to disturb the system unless effectually controlled. Nothing short of a negative on their laws will control it.

But no constitutional device could alone have reconciled the particular and the general interest. The achievement of this synthesis was really more a matter of national character than of

[2] Quoted in Rayner, *Life of Jefferson*, p. 356.

governmental design. It was possible only for a people who had been trained, and who had trained themselves, in the virtue of self-government. Without that training it would have been impossible to harmonize the philosophic assumptions of the Declaration of Independence with the practical controls of the federal Constitution.

It has been emphasized that the American Revolution was the third of its kind to be attempted by liberty-loving Englishmen over a period of a century and a half. The English Civil War established the desirability of representative government, as opposed to that of "divine right" monarchy, even though the Puritans were too politically inexperienced, too divided by faction, and often too intolerant to consolidate the gains they had won. The bloodless revolution of 1689 again uprooted the growth of royal dictatorship and confirmed Parliamentary supremacy. By developing the mechanism of party it also made representative government workable in a manner impossible until men had learned to associate their individual political convictions with a continuing organization. The third of this sequence of revolutions was fought out on American soil. Again it was necessary to extirpate—this time completely—the pretensions of the Crown. Again it was necessary to fight for the principle of representative government. But at the third attempt an enduring triumph for the principle of self-government could be narrowly achieved—because in the New World men had learned how to govern themselves.

This was not because Americans were, or are, a superior breed of men. From the beginning the people of this country have, as a generality, lacked the polish, the flavor, the intellectual subtlety —what may broadly be called the culture—characteristic of a minority in older nations. But in compensation Americans as a whole have possessed, more strongly than any people stratified by class or caste, a historically unusual ability to govern themselves. The outward conditions of American life certainly helped to develop this ability. But it has also been greatly strengthened by the doctrine of the Holy Spirit, which rooted firmly in the American colonies during their formative years.

IV

The doctrine of the Holy Spirit was accurately, if contemptuously, described by Thomas Hobbes when this seventeenth century advocate of political absolutism said of the early Quakers, that "every boy or wench thought he spoke with God Almighty."

It is precisely this sense of continuing communion with God that has given the Society of Friends a spiritual strength wholly out of proportion to its numerically trivial membership.[3] With absolute conviction George Fox maintained that the Spirit of God —the Holy Spirit—is permeative. "Now the Lord God opened to me by his invisible power that every man was enlightened by the divine light of Christ; and I saw it shine through all."[4]

The central core of the Quaker faith lies in the belief that this revelation is immanent; that it can come to the individual independent of priest or Scripture; that its coming is an inward experience that cannot fail to have profound effect on personal conduct. As Fox goes on to say in his *Journal:* "These things I did not see by the help of man, nor by the letter, though they are written in the letter, but I saw them in the light of the Lord Jesus Christ, and by his immediate Spirit and power, as did the holy men of God, by whom the Holy Scriptures were written." These things are, indeed, "written in the letter," never more beautifully than in the passage that says: "Behold, I stand at the door and knock: if any man hear my voice and open the door, I will come in to him, and will sup with him, and he with me."[5]

But the issue that above all others split the Puritan movement of the seventeenth century was whether the Spirit and the Word can properly be separated. Can the believer be directly inspired by God, as the Quakers and other Separatists maintained, or is revelation possible only through the scriptural word of the Apostles, as the main body of Puritanism asserted?

Today this issue may seem somewhat rarified, partaking of the

[3] About 110,000 in the United States; 40,000 in the British Isles; under 200,000 throughout the world.

[4] *Journal* (1901 edition), Vol. I, p. 34.

[5] Revelation 3:20.

cloister rather than the forum, lacking in applicability to the problems of a world jeopardized by the atomic bomb. Reserving judgment on that viewpoint, it must nevertheless be emphasized that the Puritan Revolution in England failed because those who made it split over theological differences. Three centuries ago theology was politics and politics was theology. That fact is worthy of our closest attention, because of the many indications that the troubles of our own time are rooted in a moral decay that cannot be countered either by mechanistic devices or by surrender to irreligious absolutism.

If one says, with more conviction than a parrot, "I believe in the Holy Ghost," what does this mean? Trinitarian doctrine explains that it is necessary to believe in God the Father as the creative power; in God the Son as the redemptive power, and in God the Holy Ghost, or Spirit, as the sanctifying power. Many deeply religious thinkers have concluded that the really distinguishing feature of Christianity is the conception of God as Spirit.[6] Certainly this conception is ingrained in American political thinking.

The signers of the Declaration of Independence proclaimed their "firm reliance on the protection of Divine Providence." The continuity of faith is shown in the not wholly perfunctory practice of opening every meeting of both Houses of the federal legislature with a prayer. It is still true, as noted by de Tocqueville, that: "Religion in America . . . must be regarded as the first of their political institutions."

These institutions properly leave it to Society to thrash out such dogmatic differences as those that separate the trinitarian and the unitarian. But in this country care has been taken to insure that he who believes in the Holy Spirit shall not be regarded as a nonconformist. For those receptive to this belief, the turn from darkness to light becomes very largely a matter of personal choice; a matter of self-government. Because self-government can bring a spiritual, as well as a political, rebirth it seems probable that, with increasing national complexities, increasing numbers of

[6] Cf. Josiah Royce, *The Problem of Christianity*.

Americans will seek to make this turn. It is at hand for every man, at any time.

Science has certainly weakened the anthropomorphic conception of God. Science has probed the mysteries of matter and energy so deeply as to make it seem that the nature of the Creator can best be defined as coldly abstract thought, most readily comprehended by a mathematical mind.[7]

Belief in the authority of Jesus, as the son of God, has also been weakened, not so much by scientific as by political development. However much we may dislike, or hesitate, to admit the deification of the Nation-State, acknowledgment of the growth of this idolatry is ineluctable for the courageous mind. The power of the State could not have been so tragically exalted if so many men, following the example of Peter, had not first denied Christ, saying in effect: "I know him not."

But belief in the Holy Spirit has not and cannot be lessened, unless Man is willing to reduce himself to the level of the brute. For the Holy Spirit is only a somewhat exalted synonym for the moral sense, in which even the atheist takes pride as he paradoxically denies the Authority from which it comes. While Right and Wrong may be variable in Space and Time, they are always antipodal at any given place and moment. That much we know, even without benefit of clergy. We know it, and knowing are able to live on a more inspired level than that of the wild animals— because of the Holy Spirit and for no other reason.

God may be denied, and Christ may be denied, but to deny the Spirit is to dissolve Society and to re-establish a system of thinly disguised slavery in its place. No human authority could prevent this outcome, for the more absolute the political dictatorship attempted, the less the field of sovereignty reserved for moral law. And when that law is completely repealed all voluntary co-operation, and therefore all human accomplishment beyond the scope of slavery, becomes impossible.

It follows that repudiation of God the Father, and God the Son, can only serve to emphasize the importance of God the Spirit.

[7] Cf. Sir James Jeans, *The Mysterious Universe*, Ch. V.

We can sidestep creation and we can refuse redemption. But sanctification we cannot deny, for to do so is suicide of the soul.

V

The divergencies in Puritanism must not deceive us as to the unity of its central core. Puritanism was "a determined and varied effort to erect the holy community and to meet, with different degrees of compromise and adjustment, the problem of its conflict with the world."[8]

This effort failed in England, where external opposition to the entire movement was strong and where internal unity was destroyed in the day of victory by dogmatic differences. But in America the Puritan revolution succeeded, partly because the movement was stronger and favored by isolation from European traditions; partly because American political leadership was wise enough to keep any single sectarian viewpoint from gaining the upper hand. There is nothing haphazard in the wording of the First Amendment to the Constitution: "Congress shall make no law respecting an establishment of religion, or prohibiting the free exercise thereof."

This provision was not inserted because the framers of the Constitution regarded the practice of religion as superfluous, but because they knew it to be essential. George Washington was merely stating the general conviction of his fellow-citizens when in his Farewell Address to them he said:

> Of all the dispositions and habits which lead to political prosperity, Religion and morality are indispensable supports. . . . And let us with caution indulge the supposition that morality can be maintained without religion. . . . reason and experience both forbid us to expect that national morality can prevail in exclusion of religious principle.

Church and State were separated in this country not to diminish but to augment the power of religious practice. Here was a tremendous power that the American State was *not* allowed to arrogate to itself. On the contrary, it was believed that sectarian

[8] A. S. P. Woodhouse (Ed.), *Puritanism and Liberty*, Introduction, p. 37.

competition would continue to develop moral self-reliance, and with it that capacity for self-government on which, as Madison said, we "rest all our political experiments."

The essence of spiritual power is found in personal conviction and conviction is strengthened by freedom of choice. The men who fashioned the Republic regarded monopoly of every kind as evil. They therefore sought to avert this evil in every field of social action—political, economic, educational, and religious. They realized, furthermore, that an evil is most dangerous when it can plausibly be portrayed as good. The monopoly of an established church encroaches most insidiously on freedom of choice because the trespass seems to have sanctification. For that reason disestablishment, though implicit in the Constitution as adopted in 1787, was also specified in the clearest possible language in the first article of the Bill of Rights.

Disestablishment was thus a vital part of the procedure insuring that the American Revolution would be successful where its predecessors in England had failed. In his later years this was constantly emphasized by Thomas Jefferson, whose fight against privilege for any particular church lies at the bottom of the foolish charge that he was irreligious. "While the English people had to accept some of the inheritance of the past," wrote Jefferson, "our Revolution commenced on more favorable ground. It presented us an album on which we were free to write what we pleased." [9] Jefferson's insistence on disestablishment was unquestionably influenced by Locke's doctrine of civil rights, but he concluded that Locke did not go far enough. The deeper reliance placed by Jefferson on natural rights is blazoned in the very text of the "Act for Establishing Religious Freedom," adopted by the Virginia Assembly under his guidance in 1786. This declares "that the rights hereby asserted are of the natural rights of mankind; and that if any act shall be hereafter passed to repeal the present, or to narrow its operation, such act will be an infringement of natural right."

[9] Letter to Major Cartwright. Quoted by Gilbert Chinard in *The Commonplace Book of Thomas Jefferson*, Introduction, p. 61. See also Dumas Malone, *Jefferson the Virginian*, Ch. XX.

Separation of Church and State solved the problem that had proved fatal to the Puritan Revolution in England. Americans could adhere to a trinitarian or a unitarian creed, according to their own individual conviction. They could maintain with the Presbyterians that the Holy Spirit operates through Scripture, or they could follow the Quaker belief that the Spirit of God is implanted in every man, including heathen and sinners. Such differences of opinion, if held sincerely and with mutual respect, were deemed to be helpful rather than harmful to religious faith.

There was, however, a chink in the armor of this doctrine of tolerance. The tendency of man to place small value on the things for which he does not have to struggle has been the Achilles' heel. There is much basis for the contention that freedom of religion is a natural right. There is also basis for the contention that a natural right, like one prescribed by civil law, evaporates if it is never asserted. But who can maintain a natural right, and how?

VI

A natural right can be asserted but cannot be maintained by act of government. It is within the province of arbitrary government to deny that there are *any* natural rights, or to destroy those—such as the right to life—that seem most undeniable. It is not within the power of the State either to create or to enforce a single right that seems to come to us from nature. Those rights are the work of God, however we may define Him. Their assertion is the work of something within the soul, or self, of the individual possessor. That something is the spirit of liberty.

The assertion of one's own right, however, is always likely to involve encroachment upon the right of another. The lives of men are inextricably intermingled, and further complicated by problems of sex relationships. Even the anchorite cannot liberate himself from the world without affecting the hopes and happiness and health of others, as Charles Reade pointed out so poignantly in his great story of *The Cloister and the Hearth*. So there must be some balance wheel, which the State cannot provide, to see that liberty is secured, not only for oneself but for one's neighbor.

The State alone can never provide this balance, no matter how much it emphasizes the general welfare as the objective of its government. For the State, though more powerful than the most ruthless individual or corporation, can protect the rights of some only by infringing upon the rights of others. Since all the power of the State is derived from Society, it follows that the more one group is privileged, the more the rest are penalized. No matter how evenly the balance is held, in the ceaseless quest for justice, a governmental service to one group in the community is sure to be discriminatory. When the State restricts imports in behalf of domestic manufacturers, the agricultural element pays higher prices for its tools of production. When the farmers in turn obtain a subsidy from the State, the wage earner finds that his food costs more as a result. When the State moves to protect wage earners, through various forms of what is dubiously called "insurance," the manufacturers find that the costs are largely imposed on them.

These are simple economic illustrations of the fact that in helping one interest in a complex Society the State necessarily tends to injure other interests. But the vicious circle is so pervasive that it actually represents a law. The State cannot possibly grant privilege to some without at least tacitly depriving others. Even if titles of nobility are awarded only for truly distinguished service, nevertheless there is discrimination against those whose faithful labor does not attract the royal attention. Even if a Church is given pre-eminence for the loftiest reasons, yet those who conscientiously dissent from its particular ritual are placed in an invidious position as "nonconformist." Even when justice is dispensed with the most scrupulous care, the exaction of due punishment will work a form of injustice on those near and dear to a criminal whose personal guilt is undeniable.

There is that within Man which is forever aspiring to a better way of life. And it is apparent, though perhaps insufficiently remarked, that this ambition for improvement is social as well as individual. Many who are really not interested in personal gain are nevertheless sincerely anxious to see the condition of others advanced. It is not at all unusual for people to spend more truly sacrificial effort on a general cause than they would think of devoting to their own purification. This social aspiration, which cannot be suppressed and should be guided rather than discouraged, is behind the pathetic belief that civil government, if sufficiently strengthened and enlarged, can somehow vastly improve the lot of mankind.

The tragic fallacy in this illusion is clear. Encroachment on the rights of others is not prevented by withdrawing the power to encroach from individual hands and vesting it in government bureaus. What happens, under the fancied panacea of socialism, is merely that the exercise of power becomes more impersonal, more arbitrary, more inhuman and therefore inevitably more ruthless. This soon becomes apparent, but from the original false diagnosis it is then reasoned that the trouble lies in failure to grant *sufficient* power to the State. So the tendency, especially where democratic processes are wholly unchecked, is to move down the blind alley with increasing speed. When the completely authoritative State is achieved there comes realization that totalitarian government and human liberty are incompatible. But it is then too late.

Clearly the remedy lies in better appreciation of the simple fact that no individual right can be justified without acceptance of an equal and balancing individual responsibility. Most people realize this instinctively, but equally instinctive is the unwillingness to draw appropriate conclusions. The exercise of a right is always more pleasurable than the acceptance of a responsibility. And thus arises the truly fatal tendency to claim the right as an individual while passing the inseparable responsibility over to officialdom.

The men who framed the American republic saw this dilemma with remarkable clarity. They did not foresee that their posterity would be less perceptive. They did not realize that the very perfection of their work for self-government would lessen appreciation of the importance of self-government. They did not anticipate decay of the spiritual element which alone gives full understanding of the beautiful political mechanism that they built. No mechanism can be expected to operate successfully for very long, unless the operators understand its nature.

VII

So reason alone compels us to conclude that religious observance is not just a perfunctory matter for Americans. It is not a superfluous organ, a sort of vermiform appendix in the body politic, which can be removed without affecting the remaining parts.

But religious observance will be largely the passive action of an observer, lacking in the rich contribution of a participant, unless something more than the routine of a formal ritual is involved. Merely to sit through a church service means little. It may be called the spiritual counterpart of casting a ballot on election day. Neither action fulfills its true importance in the field of government if it is performed as a mere convention. There must be active political interest to make the ballot significant in the field of representative government. There must be vital religious interest to make church attendance significant in the field of self-government.

Every executive is painfully familiar with the type of employee who is reasonably regular in punching a time clock, who observes the requisite working hours, who goes through the motions of participating in an enterprise, but who is nevertheless wholly uninterested in his or her work. People of that sort load the payroll of every commercial undertaking and if their pay is negligible their value to the operation is even more so. Such time-servers are inert themselves and only the greater inertia of the organization, or arbitrary regulations forced on its management, secures their employment.

The larger the enterprise, and the more complicated its character, the higher the proportion of its employees who are likely to be mere "job-holders." Size adds an additional stultification by making it difficult for the individual to sense the significance, if any, of what he is doing. This frustrating tendency comes to a climax in what is grandiloquently called "government service." It provides little or no competition to disturb natural inertia and in government there is also a definite short-range political advantage to the establishment of superfluous, duplicating, and sometimes positively harmful jobs.

A somewhat similar frustration is apparent when we turn to a consideration of the duties of citizenship. Here there are many who do not even take the trouble to make conventional observance, for it is much easier to drift along without voting than it is to survive without working. The perfunctory attitude, however, is pronounced even among those who go through the motions at the polls. It is explained that the candidates are machine-picked and that a choice between them is largely meaningless. But when this charge is justified it really means that the electorate has become too indifferent to interest itself in, and to improve, the procedures by which opposing candidates were selected.

With the decline of spiritual vitality, a great deal of religious observance has also sunk to this same level of purely mechanical performance. In many cases there is not much conviction behind either the selection of a church, or attendance after the choice is made. And, increasingly, many Americans do not bother to join or participate in the work of *any* church. Often these absentees are the same people who do not bother to vote. They would not bother to work if "the government" could be prevailed upon to keep them provided with ham and eggs, a heated apartment, comic strips, and a plug-in radio—television preferred.

This sort of person—negative in his religion, his citizenship, his work, and even in his taste for entertainment—is the mass man who swarms in the great cities that characterize the machine age. By the sheer weight of indifference the mass mind must, in time, drag down and destroy any system of government that depends on the sense of individual responsibility for its successful operation. The mass mind is allergic to responsibility, but is insistent on rights that have no reality when they are divorced from responsibility. Always there have been men whose dominant aim has been to get more from the common pot than they contribute to it. But this failure of self-government has become more dangerous socially with the triumph of representative government. For this system tends to vest authority in those who will conform automatically to the level of the mass.

The trouble is far too deep-rooted to yield to any panacea, or to permit an indictment leveled at one particular point in its development. If the mass mind is a concomitant of the assembly line, then those who devised the assembly line certainly have some responsibility for its shortcomings. It is not how the mass mind was produced, however, but how it is to be enlightened, that is the present problem. Certainly there is no hope in a political doctrine suggesting that because many have failed to meet personal responsibility, all should be made personally irresponsible. Yet this is precisely what has come to be widely advocated for the Republic.

Americans should feel indebted to the Communists, the Fascists, and the Nazis for having so clearly shown, by parallel demonstrations, just where the various avenues of socialism eventually lead. In each case, with only minor variations, it is assumed that the individual is incapable of self-government, with consequent measures designed to keep him so. Since the mass man fears personal responsibility, his irresponsibility is encouraged. Then all individuals who dare to carry social responsibility are sweepingly denounced in such opprobrious generalities as "economic royalists" or "capitalistic exploiters." In this manner the groundwork is laid for governmental dictatorship to take over.

The reasoning is based on good psychology and it is noteworthy that Communists and National Socialists have often used parallel phraseology to express their parallel thought. Thus the Theses of the Communist International, as adopted in Moscow during the summer of 1920, proclaimed that:

> The preparation of the dictatorship of the proletariat demands . . . the replacing of the old leaders by Communists in all kinds of proletarian organizations, not only political, but economic, co-operative, educational, etc., . . . In every organization . . . groups or nuclei of Communists . . . must systematically train themselves, the party, the class and the masses by such multiform work.[10]

Whether or not Hitler had read this, when four years later he wrote *Mein Kampf,* he certainly had the same idea of exploiting the mass mind in behalf of the *Fuehrer Prinzip.* "One thing we must get through our heads," Hitler told his fellow Nazis:

[10] *Blueprint for World Conquest,* p. 49-52.

If a certain total of a peoples' energy and vigor seems to be concentrated on one goal, and thus is definitely removed from the inertia of the broad masses, these few per cent rise to be overlords of all. World history is made by minorities, if this numerical minority embodies a majority of will and determination.[11]

VIII

American political theory also asserts that progress in every line of endeavor comes from the effort of that small minority of men who are alert, intelligent, determined, and self-sacrificial in their desire to raise mankind in the scale of animal life. The value of minority opinion is recognized in the provisions of the Constitution designed to protect minorities—of every kind. But there is an antipodean difference in the American and the totalitarian attitude toward minorities. The American theory is that every man has within him the potential to make a significant contribution of some kind to human welfare. Therefore every minority, which is usually a grouping of individuals connected by some common belief, must be protected against the ever possible tyranny of mass opinion. The minority is not given this protection because it *is* making a significant contribution, but because it is always possible that it may do so. Thus the promise of tomorrow in every line of endeavor is kept bright in America.

Totalitarianism, whether Communist, Fascist, or Nazi, has no faith in the virtues of minorities as such. The characteristic of this system is that it exalts one single minority, and seeks to subjugate all others to the will of that unified group. This group may claim to speak for national welfare, like the Italian Fascists; for racial welfare, like the German Nazis; for proletarian welfare, like the Russian Communists. But these apparent differences are only variations on a single theme. In each case a minority that regards itself as elite seeks not merely to dominate other minorities, but also to bind the entire population to its will. This minority sincerely believes that it has found the formula of salvation. All that is necessary is to subject everybody to that formula. The

[11] *Mein Kampf* (Stackpole Edition), p. 387.

fundamental questions have all been answered—by Mussolini, Hitler, Karl Marx, or somebody—and henceforth mankind need only follow the leader. Disagreement with the party line is heresy. Thus the maximum promise of tomorrow in a totalitarian State is some material improvement.

Stated this way, the philosophical basis of totalitarian doctrine is seen to be puerile. But the doctrine has made, and continues to make, such headway that one must analyze the reasons for its success. They are not far to seek.

In the first place we can readily see that the malaise is universal. America, for all its relative political health, has plenty of native Nazis who firmly believe in the superiority of their particular racial group. We have our native Fascists, who blandly identify the national interest with their personal advantage. We have our native Communists, easier to identify because they more openly proclaim their disloyalty to American institutions. In using these labels it is, of course, important to concentrate on their essential meanings, and not to be confused by emotional overtones. Thus a Zionist minority can be fundamentally racial in its thinking, even as it denounces the Nazi form of racism. Similarly, a business group, seeking to establish a monopoly, may condemn Italian Fascism even though its techniques are identical with those that Mussolini advocated.

We have native Fascists, Nazis, and Communists primarily because it has now become customary for people to place their whole faith in material well-being. That is the low common denominator making surface differences within the totalitarian species a relatively secondary matter. And insistence upon material well-being, divorced from any sense of personal responsibility, has become a dominant American characteristic. If materialism continues to be increasingly emphasized, we may and should expect our native totalitarians to increase in number. There is justification in the Communist claim that free enterprise must, in the long run, be suicidal. If free enterprise has only a materialistic meaning, then it is doomed.

For the murder of free enterprise, however, two antecedent preparations are necessary. The State must be exalted at the expense of the individual and there must be an increase in religious indifference. The procedure in exalting the State is steadily to augment its physical power at the expense of Society. The more that power can be concentrated, the more perfect the State becomes as an instrumentality of suppression in the hands of those who believe in suppression. Here is the point at which the real liberal and the amiable Socialist divide. The analytical liberal realizes that the Welfare State is the agency through which totalitarianism takes over. The kind-hearted Socialist sees only the humanitarian possibilities of State control—until the thoroughgoing Marxist tells him where to get off.

But more than possession of the machinery of physical power is necessary for a totalitarian triumph. It is not enough to exalt the State. It is also essential to debase the individual. To accomplish this his religious instincts must be weakened, for it is these instincts that alone give substance to the spirit of liberty. Politicians in whom the religious element is lacking are frequently glib in demanding that liberty be provided by government. Liberty, however, cannot be manufactured, packaged, and distributed —not even by nationalized industries. Liberty is not a commodity, but a quality. Only one form of government can nurture liberty, and that is personal self-government.

Here is the explanation of the political importance of Christianity. That religion demands consistent subordination of self to the welfare of others. In so doing it emphasizes the superiority of Divine Authority to "the insolence of office"; the importance of self-government as opposed to external regimentation. Admittedly the standards of Christianity are painfully exacting for human nature. The fact that they are so exacting is itself part of the evidence of the divinity of Christ, for no mortal can be expected never to transgress his teachings. Allowance for this is made by the incorporation of mercy, forgiveness, and redemption in the Christian system.

Precisely because Christianity emphasizes self-government, every advocate of totalitarianism is either openly or tacitly anti-Christian. But a frontal attack on religious observance is not necessary from the totalitarian viewpoint. The growing emphasis on materialism itself weakens Christianity. Man cannot serve both God and Mammon, and when service to the former is made subordinate, the road of the dictator is made smooth for him in advance. Therefore it is more subtle for the Marxist to emphasize materialism, where he can exploit the sense of justice to strengthen his case, than it is to attack the churches as such.

Both exaltation of the State and destruction of religious faith are necessary to undermine the American system of government, as a preliminary to the coming of dictatorship. But of the two procedures, exaltation of the State is the more emphasized, because it is reasoned from the evidence available that Americans can be expected to abandon their religious faith without much prompting; and of their own free will.

IX

A few months before his death, which took place on August 13, 1946, a very influential English author published a truly tragic confession. The writer was Herbert George Wells and his final essay was entitled *Mind at the End of Its Tether*.

The far-ranging thought of H. G. Wells made a deep impression during the half-century that preceded achievement of the atomic bomb. Both his scientific fantasies and his sociological novels were of more than transient influence. No other scientist could so clearly portray to the average mind the weird developments to be expected from concentrated laboratory research. No other Socialist could describe more winningly the Utopian emancipation anticipated from the breaking down of personal self-restraint, and the substitution of always pleasantly vague governmental controls.

At the close of his remarkable *Outline of History*, written with the hope of bringing some helpful moral out of the catastrophe of World War I, Wells became characteristically lyrical about the future:

> History is and must always be no more than an account of beginnings. . . . Life begins perpetually. Gathered together at last under

the leadership of man, the student-teacher of the universe, unified, disciplined, armed with the secret powers of the atom and with knowledge as yet beyond dreaming, Life, for ever dying to be born afresh, for ever young and eager, will presently stand upon this earth as upon a footstool, and stretch out its realm amidst the stars.

Wells will long continue to be an interesting figure, for reasons that have nothing to do with the quality of his imagination and his literary skill. What makes this prolific and stimulating thinker of unusual importance is something that he perhaps never realized. Wells was the great popularizer of positivist philosophy. His apostasy, in this final essay, is therefore indirect affirmation of the vital importance of those difficult abstractions on which the American system of government depends.

The parents who named him Herbert George were a small shopkeeper and a domestic servant, occupations that placed the boy at the very bottom of the curious social pyramid that was Victorian England. Yet Wells' brilliant creative mind brought him, by middle life, world acclaim as well as plenty of honor in his own country. He symbolized a significant change in social outlook. The barriers of class and caste, always resented in America, were also breaking down in England. Here, in the person of H. G. Wells was the triumph of the democratic over the aristocratic principle. But here also in the same person is a solemn warning to those who rest their faith on the assumption that the removal of external barriers to individual advancement is of itself enough.

This popular writer was very definitely lacking in spiritual qualities. Perhaps this attrition was partly due to the effort Wells had to make to raise himself from ignoble obscurity. Certainly his reverence for the progress of science magnified the deficiency. Whatever the reason, the deficiency was there. It is apparent in much that Wells wrote, but nowhere more nakedly than when, in the *Outline of History*, he turned to discuss the rise of Christianity. Here he says: "About Jesus we have to write not theology but history, and our concern is not with the spiritual and theological significance of his life, but with its effects upon the political and everyday life of men."

Wells' pathetic attempt to separate the inseparable—to departmentalize "positive" and "negative" knowledge as in the barren system conceived by Auguste Comte—is characteristic of the fatal fragmentation of our times. In the case of Wells the moral is made plain for all to see because, like Comte, the democratic English author had a well-developed ethical instinct. Often his writing protests injustice. Yet, paradoxically, he never seeks the source of the concept of Justice. "After all," he writes in *Mind at the End of Its Tether*, "the present writer has no compelling argument to convince the reader that he should not be cruel or mean or cowardly."

Thus, for lack of a developed sense of spiritual values, Wells at the close of his life was forced by his fine intellect to assert morosely that: "the human story has already come to an end . . . Homo sapiens, as he has been pleased to call himself, is in his present form played out." Previously he had "liked to think that Man could pull out of his entanglements and start a new creative phase of human living." But as the shadows closed in on this mind of undoubted genius it could see only "a jaded world devoid of recuperative power." And most of what he had written to the contrary, Wells bitterly concluded, "may now go down the laboratory sink."

X

For its deep sincerity, as well as for the underlying moral that it unconsciously points, *Mind at the End of Its Tether* may be expected to survive the oblivion to which H. G. Wells consigns "the greater bulk" of his writing "upon the fundamental nature of life and time." But our concern is with the vicious circle in which this brilliant mind was caught and to which, at the end, it so tragically succumbed.

That fate, we are now in a position to assert, is the inevitable and foreordained result of trying to separate spiritual significance from "the political and everyday life of men," as Wells himself tells us he sought to do. Although the tragedy is commonplace it is particularly stark in this case. The legend of Prometheus reminds us that punishment is nicely calculated to the degree of

the offense against the moral law. The ordinary recusant does
not suffer as did Wells when his courageous mind reached the
end of a tether a little longer than that vouchsafed the average
man.

But, in greater or less degree, the same cause produces the
same consequence. Therefore self-government can never properly or safely rely on the direction of intelligence alone. And
the need for external support becomes the greater when mankind
has struggled up to the stage where intelligence is respected for
itself. The emancipation brought by democracy, in other words,
immediately emphasizes the need for submission to an Authority
higher than that which has been displaced.

So we reach the conclusion that self-government is something
even more than the only method by which the enjoyment of what
we call natural rights can be assured. It is also a continuous, not
occasional, act of individual sublimation. Christ explained the
formula simply enough to the woman of Samaria, as they talked
beside Jacob's well:

> God is a Spirit: and they that worship him must worship him in
> spirit and in truth.[12]

Without this spiritual content the greatest intelligence is hopelessly inadequate. With it, even the most humdrum mind will
experience satisfactions beyond the purchase of any bank account.
And the moral here is a matter of practical precinct politics. Self-
government must be spiritually directed in order to be effective.
Without effective self-government no political system, no matter
how ingeniously designed, can hope to secure life, liberty, or the
pursuit of happiness, in the deeper sense of those rich words. So
the spiritual quality, demanded by the American political system,
must be brought back into active production, even though no
federal bureau is able to measure the individual output. If, as a
people, we have lost the sense of spiritual values, then the very
basis of our material values is also gone. When it becomes a matter of consolidating strength to meet a challenge, the foundation
of our civic strength must first be re-examined and repaired.

[12] John 4:24.

The abandonment of faith in behalf of undirected reason leads swiftly to a second, and final, apostasy. The mind does come to the end of its limited tether, and then there is nothing but black despair beyond. Then it happens that men forget the meaning of self-government and surrender themselves—willingly or despairingly, according to temperament—to be absorbed into and directed by the totalitarian State.

Against such an outcome, the American Republic stands as mankind's last substantial defense.

Chapter 8

Free Enterprise

Writing at the end of the colonial period, Adam Smith remarked: "It has been the principal cause of the rapid progress of our American colonies towards wealth and greatness, that almost their whole capitals have hitherto been employed in agriculture."[1]

From this observation the Scottish professor of moral philosophy moved logically into his famous consideration (Book III) "Of the Different Progress of Opulence in Different Nations." The following passage contains more than a suggestion of the causes destined to bring the American people to a position of world leadership:

> According to the natural course of things . . . the greater part of the capital of every growing Society is, first, directed to agriculture, afterwards to manufactures, and last of all to foreign commerce. . . . But though this natural order of things must have taken place in some degree in every . . . Society, it has, in all the modern States of Europe, been, in many respects, entirely inverted . . . and manufactures and foreign commerce together, have given birth to the principal improvements of agriculture. The manners and customs which the nature of their original government introduced, and which remained after that government was greatly altered, necessarily forced them into this unnatural and retrograde order.[2]

[1] *The Wealth of Nations*, Modern Library Edition, p. 347.
[2] *Ibid.*, p. 360.

Adam Smith goes on to explain that this inversion of "the natural course of things," in Western Europe as distinct from its offshoot in North America, was a direct consequence of the catastrophic fall of the Roman Empire. The disruption that then ensued destroyed the entire social fabric of Western Europe. When a system of social order was restored, it was along lines, and according to principles of government, from which American thinking later broke away.

In our own era, in which human blunders have again produced a disaster comparable to that of the fall of Rome, there is a natural temptation to re-examine what Gibbon called the "most awful scene in the history of mankind." There is certainly a warning for contemporary Americans in the degeneration that this great historian attributes to "the artful policy of the Caesars, who long maintained the name and image of a free republic." And the responsibilities forced upon the United States, in the era following World War II, also make apposite Gibbon's picturesque description of Rome as the sixth century of the Christian era drew to its dismal close: "The lofty tree, under whose shade the nations of the earth had reposed, was deprived of its leaves and branches, and the sapless trunk was left to wither on the ground." [3]

It is not forcing a historical parallel to uncover background that explains the deeper nature of contemporary problems. The fall of Rome is important to us primarily because the resulting chaos set Western Europe on a course of development from which the American Republic eventually departed. The significance of that departure cannot be realized without some survey of what was left behind. And even an outline brings out the profound difference between the basis of the European and the North American civilizations.

[3] *The Decline and Fall of the Roman Empire*, Ch. XLV. The reference to the Caesars is at the conclusion of Ch. LXXI.

II

The dissolution of the Roman Empire was followed, for a protracted period, by conditions so terrible that even the records are, almost happily, fragmentary. Flourishing cities fell into ruins and, over large areas of Western Europe, country once cultivated reverted to wilderness. Here and there throughout the Dark Ages organized Christianity was able to maintain some degree of social order. But the general picture, not for a few years but for five centuries, is one of continuous violence and insecurity; of utter poverty, ignorance, depravity, and barbarism. It is relieved only by the heroic, though futile, effort of Charlemagne to found an Empire of the West—the first of the many post-Roman failures to give Western Europe political unity.

After the death of Charlemagne, in 814, there was a complete dissolution of civil law. But out of this chaos, as a result of the banding together of men in self-protection, slowly emerged the system that we know today as feudalism.[4]

By contrast with the preceding anarchy, feudalism in time brought a very real advance, placing a premium upon good faith and encouraging co-operation through the mutual obligations gradually developed in the reciprocal services of lord and vassal. Nevertheless, two other characteristics of the feudal system gave rise to handicaps for Western Europe from which it has never become fully emancipated. One of these stultifying characteristics was the concept of status. Allied with this was the denial of free enterprise. It is not surprising that the order which succeeded the Dark Ages should have had those characteristics. Acceptance of status seemed a small price to pay for some security in life, and free enterprise had been for centuries primarily a matter of theft and murder.

Under the feudal system a measure of order returned to the European countryside. But it was an order of stagnation, not far

---

[4] Perhaps the best general study of the feudal system, and that most relied upon in this summary, is still to be found in the first volume of Henry Hallam's *View of the State of Europe during the Middle Ages.* F. W. Maitland: *The Constitutional History of England,* has also been useful.

removed from slavery even for many who were nominally free-
men. In return for service, military and otherwise, the lord
promised, and to the best of his ability provided, protection for
the villein. Thus the degree of local security improved, to the
extent that the land, and with it the dispensation of justice
through private courts, came under the unchallenged control of
the feudal proprietor. There was, however, a constant tendency
for these proprietors to become more powerful, and fewer in
number, as—in the absence of any effective central authority—
one lord conquered his neighbor and took over the retainers together with the estates.

Both the theory and practice of feudalism required monopolization of the land, ideally in the hands of the king from whom
the barons nominally held their fiefs, actually by these "over-
mighty subjects" who so frequently repudiated any exercise of the
royal authority in their own domains. Therefore, to perpetuate
land monopoly, the devices of primogeniture and entail, unknown
to the Romans, were developed: the first preventing an estate
from being divided at the death of the lord; the second blocking
alienation during his lifetime.

These stereotyping devices helped to insure that the interest
of the feudal proprietors, monastic foundations excepted, should
not be that of production. In the eyes of the feudal nobility,
agricultural labor was at best a debased occupation and the class
distinction, between those who labored and those who led, became
ever more pronounced as the meticulous code of chivalry came
to place exclusive emphasis on the knightly virtues. Increasingly,
the effects of primogeniture and entail were to emphasize the
proletarian and enslaved condition of those who actually tilled
the soil. Feudalism, for all its virtues, produced an inert social
order. The only feasible way to change this order, in Western
Europe, was by the development of centralized governments
sufficiently powerful to subordinate the Lords Temporal and Spiritual to the Crown.

Under feudalism the monarch was nominally the supreme lord.
In reality the king was merely first, and not always that, among
equals. Hallam lists five prerogatives of the French baronage

that "during the prevalence of feudal principles" were exercised wholly independent of the Crown. These were (1) the right of coining money; (2) the right of waging private war; (3) the exemption from all taxation except feudal aids; (4) the freedom from legislative control; (5) the exclusive right of original judicial procedure. "Privileges so enormous and so contrary to all principles of sovereignty might lead us," in the conclusion of this historian, "to account [medieval] France rather a collection of states, partially allied to each other, than a single monarchy." [5]

As actually happened in Germany and Italy, all of Western Europe might easily have developed into a patchwork of petty principalities, because of the divisive characteristics of feudalism. And it is well to realize that this is no mere academic consideration, without practical bearing on the lives and fortunes of present-day Americans. When national governments were eventually formed, in Italy and Germany, they were the more strongly absolutist because of the background of fragmentation tracing to feudal times. Behind movements like Fascism and Nazism there is a long line of predisposing causes, and American boys died in Italy and Germany in part because of the feudal heritage in those countries.

As the solutions of today determine the problems of tomorrow, so the problems of today are the result of conditions created in the past. Free enterprise, specifically, is not likely to be preserved in the American Republic unless we realize why it took root so much more readily here than in Western Europe.

III

It was the revival of urban life that eventually shattered the feudal system in Western Europe.

Even during the Dark Ages a measure of trade and simple manufacture continued in the stricken towns. Then, gradually, fortifications, raised by community effort, turned back all but the strongest of marauding bands. There had been a large degree of municipal autonomy under the Roman Empire and the spirit of

[5] *Op. cit.*, (fifth edition) Vol. I, p. 227.

independence was fostered by the anarchy that seethed throughout the countryside. Slowly, the corporate structure was strengthened by the necessities of the medieval monarchs. To gain
support against the great feudal lords the Crown devised the
plan of granting charters, with broad immunities and powers, to
the towns. These municipal charters, granted by the monarch,
may be called a precedent for those which later established some
of the American colonies. But it is obvious that the feudal charters are in sharpest political contrast with the social contracts
whereby these colonists actually founded settlements in the wilderness.

With the royal charters the medieval burghers became the
legal as well as the natural allies of the king, bound by a common interest in resisting the pretensions of the territorial nobility.[6] And to gain further strength the municipal governments of
medieval Europe actively encouraged the villeins, though bound
to the soil by feudal law, to escape to the walled cities. In Hallam's words: "One of the most remarkable privileges of chartered
towns was that of conferring freedom on runaway serfs, if they
were not reclaimed by their masters within a certain time."[7] Oppenheimer summarizes the whole process: "The city as an economic, political body undermines the feudal system with political
and economic arms. With the first the city *forces*, with the second
it *lures*, power away from the feudal master class."[8]

So it was from the towns, with the active support of the Crown,
that a measure of commerce and general prosperity penetrated
into and over the baronial countryside. The beginnings of national government spread out along the "King's Highway,"
linking the seat of the throne with the self-governing towns.
And in reviewing this development, Adam Smith concluded: "It
is thus that through the greater part of Europe the commerce
and manufacture of cities, instead of being the effect, have been

[6] Sir Walter Scott's novel *Quentin Durward* centers on the alliance between
the town of Liège and Louis XI of France, in opposition to the Duke of Bur-
gundy. The same important reign is the theme of Victor Hugo's *Notre Dame
de Paris.*

[7] Hallam, *op. cit.,* Vol. I, p. 306n.

[8] Franz Oppenheimer, *The State* (Vanguard Edition) p. 238.

the cause and occasion of the improvement and cultivation of the country." [9]

IV

In the economic growth of the United States, on the other hand, agricultural development came first. The way, as well as the will, to create a new form of Society was open in the New World. Certainly it was not easy to clear and cultivate the land around the early settlements. Nature was none too gracious and occasionally there was bitter resistance from the aborigines. But the intractability of these obstacles itself served to elicit unusual individual effort. And the reward of this effort was not expropriated, to anything like the degree that ruled in Western Europe, by overlord or tax collector. Except for slaves and temporarily indentured servants, the fruits of American labor actually accrued to those who labored. Thus free enterprise became a characteristic that permeated American life as thoroughly as status had permeated feudal Europe.

The progress of European civilization had been from town to country; here the movement was from country to town. Generations of American tourists, charmed by the antiquity of the walled cities of Western Europe, have been prone to ignore what those fortifications so strongly suggest. Here there was no hostility, and therefore no need for physical barriers, between urban and rural leadership. It has been of the utmost significance to humanity that Americans were never forced to immure free enterprise.

On the continent of Europe, and to a somewhat lesser extent in England, where feudalism did not entrench itself so strongly except in respect to land tenure, that system caused men to place security ahead of liberty. Exactly the opposite was happily true in the United States, where the early colonists sought liberty first. From that profound difference of emphasis emerged the very different attitude toward centralization of power, and other political contrasts not less pronounced because Americans continued to speak a European language. The difference was well expressed

[9] *Op. cit.*, p. 392.

by Henry Hallam when, as far back as 1818, he summed it up—
from the European viewpoint—as follows:

> From these feelings engendered by the feudal relation has sprung up
> the peculiar sentiment of personal reverence and attachment towards a
> sovereign, which we denominate loyalty; alike distinguishable from
> the stupid devotion of eastern slaves, and from the abstract respect
> with which free citizens regard their chief magistrate. Men who had
> been used to swear fealty, to profess subjection, to follow, at home and
> in the field, a feudal superior and his family, easily transferred the same
> allegiance to the monarch. It was a very powerful feeling, which could
> make the bravest man put up with slights and ill treatment at the
> hands of their [sic] sovereign; or call forth all the energies of dis-
> interested exertion for one whom they never saw, and in whose char-
> acter there was nothing to esteem. In ages when the rights of the
> community were unfelt, this sentiment was one great preservative of
> Society; and, though collateral or even subservient to more enlarged
> principles, it is still indispensable to the tranquillity and permanence
> of every monarchy.[10]

It does not minimize the value of the loyalty that Hallam emphasizes to point out, as he does, that this loyalty differs fundamentally "from the abstract respect with which free citizens
regard their chief magistrate." The primary American loyalty
was always directed much more to God than to the monarch.
This pregnant fact cannot be fully understood without realization
of the strength of the feudal heritage in Europe, abandoned by
the judicious choice of the American colonists.

Therefore the American Revolution was a much more significant upheaval than any of the mutually suicidal wars of European nations which followed the firm establishment of statehood
on the Continent. In the long perspective these will be seen as
quasi-feudal struggles, in which centralized governments sought
to impose their punitive will upon each other much as the rival
baronies had sought to do a few centuries earlier. The change in
European warfare, from feudal to modern times, was much more
in the method than in the meaning of conflict. But the American
Revolution, for all that the actual fighting was only a series of

10 *Op. cit.*, p. 323.

skirmishes, arose from the impossibility of reconciling two entirely different sets of loyalties. The profound difference between the two is not lessened by the fact that a large number of individual Englishmen preferred the American way, and vice versa. We have already seen that the American Revolution, which succeeded, was at bottom a continuation and completion of the two previous revolutions in England, neither of which achieved the republican ideal.

The different set of loyalties that came to dominate in the United States was greatly strengthened by the individual enterprise fostered in a civilization with a basis of free agriculture. All the economic historians of Europe, even those as far apart in their conclusions as Adam Smith and Karl Marx, are in agreement on one indisputable point. The urbanization of Europe was greatly stimulated by the stereotyping of agriculture under feudalism. Marx, being bitterly opposed to the whole concept of free enterprise, makes a defense of feudalism. He must do so, in order to argue that "wage slavery" is worse than "the guarantee of existence afforded by the feudal arrangements." But Marx agrees with Adam Smith that the stagnation of feudalism operated to concentrate energetic producers in the "sovereign towns," which the philosopher of socialism calls "the highest development of the Middle Ages." [11]

What appealed to Marx in urbanization, however, was its encouragement to centralized power, furthering security at the expense of freedom. While the villein had no freedom, security of a sort he did possess under the protection of his lord, and therefore Marx saw good in feudalism. Better security was provided for the burghers by the walls behind which they sheltered, and by the restrictive mercantile guilds, which so strongly favored the privileged membership at the expense of general progress. Still more security, on a broader basis, was promised by the gradual centralization of all political authority under the national king. All that seemed necessary to Marx, to complete what looked like natural evolution, was to proceed from the royal and local to the proletarian and universal dictatorship. It is the role

[11] *Capital*, Ch. XXVI.

of private capital, according to Marx, to make that further step toward social security inevitable.

> One capitalist always kills many. Hand in hand with this centraliza-
> tion, or this expropriation of many capitalists by few, develops, on an
> ever extending scale . . . the entanglement of all peoples in the net of
> the world-market, and with this, the international character of the
> capitalistic regime. Along with the constantly diminishing number of
> the magnates of capital . . . grows the mass of misery, oppression,
> slavery, degradation, exploitation; but with this too grows the revolt
> of the working-class, a class always increasing in numbers, and disci-
> plined, united, organized by the very mechanism of the process of
> capitalist production itself.[12]

To the American contemporaries of Marx, and indeed to most Americans until recent times, this type of reasoning simply made no sense. In a civilization which was building its cities on an agricultural base, it was absurd to argue that "one capitalist kills many." On the contrary, every capitalist was helping to create others, and this with a restless energy and rapidity that amazed European observers. "What most astonishes me in the United States," de Tocqueville wrote, "is not so much the marvelous grandeur of some undertakings as the innumerable multitudes of small ones. Almost all the farmers of the United States combine some trade with agriculture; most of them make agriculture itself a trade." [13]

De Tocqueville, however, was keenly aware of the long-range social and economic implications of the democratic urge. He clearly foresaw that American insistence on equality would mean a general demand for manufactured articles, and that they must be manufactured cheaply in order to facilitate a general distribu-tion. Therefore America was from the outset destined to become a center of mass production, involving both the development of crowded cities and the replacement of individual craftsmanship by a minute division of labor. In the famous passage that opens *The Wealth of Nations*, Adam Smith had dilated upon the ad-

---

[12] *Op. cit.*, Ch. XXXII.
[13] *Democracy in America*, Vol. II, p. 157.

vantages of having "eighteen distinct operations" in the manufacture of a pin. De Tocqueville asked caustically: "What can be expected of a man who has spent twenty years of his life in making heads for pins?" And then, replying to his own question: "In proportion as the principle of the division of labor is more extensively applied, the workman becomes more weak, more narrowminded and more dependent. The art advances, the artisan recedes." [14]

V

It was not long before the art of American manufacture advanced, and the individuality of American artisans receded, to an extent that seemed to make the observations of Karl Marx more reasonable to Americans, as well as to Europeans. Certainly the basis of American civilization remained different, but an enormous industrial superstructure was rapidly developed on the agricultural base.

By the dawn of the twentieth century, as we can see in retrospect, the still unsolved dilemma of the Republic was already foreshadowed. On the one hand the blessings of liberty had been secured, for at least a large proportion of the population, by a carefully-balanced governmental system that placed a minimum of restrictions on individual enterprise. On the other hand Americans, thus liberated, had almost unconsciously developed an industrialism which by its very power was likely to lead to centralized governmental restraints. Meantime, as the Republic grew ever richer in material wealth, its thinking, political and otherwise, became less discriminating and more standardized. Here was a portent that, in the name of liberty, liberty would be circumscribed.

This sardonic result was made the more likely by the democratic character of American society. Happily for progress, its members do not regard themselves as born to any "station" in life. Great waves of immigrants poured in from Europe essentially for the same reason that had moved their ancestors from

[14] *Ibid.*, p. 159.

feudal serfdom to the relative freedom of the chartered medieval cities. They came not to exchange one status for another but in the belief that as Americans, by the application of energy and shrewdness, they could exploit their individual talents to the full. As the pages of *Who's Who in America* attest, many have done precisely that.[15] But, as is true also of native talent, the very rapidity of success has often meant a subordination of qualities that are as important to the Republic as is mere acumen.

Titles of nobility were prohibited by the Constitution. That prohibition did not make it desirable to forget that the device of nobility had overtones, of which our general use of the word gives evidence. The phrase *noblesse oblige* possessed substantial meaning. Too many successful Americans have failed to realize that in eliminating prerogative there was risk of eliminating also all sense of obligation to those less favored in character or circumstance.

For those who think only of climbing, it has never been difficult to reach a certain eminence in American life. And by admiring one's own skill as a climber, by forgetting that the ascent involves the co-operative assistance of other human beings, it became easy to regard material success itself as a virtuous accomplishment. It was particularly easy to make this moral error in a society that for good reasons gave free play to the acquisitive instinct. The fundamental components of Society—the Home, the Church, the School—could have emphasized the ethical counterpart more strongly. Indeed, they sought to do so. But parental standards were themselves too often uninspired. The churches were frequently more jealous of each other than of the spiritual welfare of their parishioners. The schools and colleges, with honorable exceptions, worked into the rut of vocationalism. And so the man of "business"—of busyness with purely material production—rode merrily on toward fortune and the fall that was his in 1929.

The subsequent tragic turn toward reliance on governmental planning was also inherent in the nature of democracy, viewed as a matter of some established "right" to equality. To many

[15] The 1930-31 edition shows that 9.02 per cent of those listed were foreign-born. This percentage has tended to remain remarkably constant.

people such a right is meaningless, unless it becomes operative in terms of material possessions. For some reason, deep-rooted in the nature of Man, there is little incentive to memorize the Twenty-third Psalm just because one's neighbor knows it by heart. But it appears highly desirable to have an electric washing machine or a hydroidiotic car, if others on the same street are thus equipped. It is the material and not the nonmaterial possession that inspires envy. People are not made unhappy by an unequal distribution of talents. Often there is no apparent desire to make the individual effort required to emulate superior intelligence, or superior morality. An unequal division of material possessions, however, appears to many as a personal deprivation and therefore "undemocratic." Neither ability, nor assiduity in its application, is envied in a democracy. Covetousness is reserved for the fruits of applied knowledge.

We are concerned with understanding, rather than with appraising, the seeming miracle of American economic development. Here was a society, wholly agricultural in origin, all members of which had to produce in order to live. Its first indigenous holy day was Thanksgiving, set aside in appreciation of conditions facilitating material production. Among such a people the virtue of producing was always the more likely to lead by imperceptible gradation into the vice of acquisition without ulterior purpose. It is equally understandable that, since their society was democratic, these people should the more strongly resent the inequalities of distribution, justifiable or unjustifiable, which are inevitable under any economic system. And, finally, there is no mystery about the very dubious resort to governmental controls, eventually chosen to bring about a more even distribution of material wealth.

The widespread desire for more material possessions can be met only by the large-scale development of industry. For such a development American conditions were particularly appropriate. There was the mechanical genius of a people who had to be skilled in contrivance in order to meet the rigorous demands of frontier life. There was the general spate of invention that brought what we call the Industrial Revolution coincident with the achievement of complete political independence. There was the tremendous encouragement to individual enterprise that resulted from eliminating the restraints of the British mercantile system. There was the impetus given by the establishment of a federal republic, strong enough to maintain order, but carefully designed to minimize its coercive or directive power over the individual. By placing the power in the people, individual energies were released for productive enterprise, of every kind, in a manner for which history shows no parallel.

All this pointed to and explains the development of mass production. The extent to which that mass production has been developed, and the speed with which it came, undoubtedly constitute one of the most remarkable phenomena the world has ever witnessed. Americans themselves, unaccustomed to philosophizing about their activities, have given little thought to the magnitude of their accomplishment, for good and evil. Peoples of other countries had even less realization of the gigantic strength that America was building up. Until it was actually demonstrated, during World War II and its aftermath, there had been nowhere any adequate appreciation of the fact that 6 per cent of the world's population, in the United States, could outproduce the other 94 per cent; could not merely provide fabulous conveniences and luxuries for their own people, but could also simultaneously fight a global war and afterward supply the necessities of life to millions in destitution on other continents.

Not much that can be called consideration was given to the almost incredible nature of this accomplishment as it was being developed. And wonder, rather than understanding of the portent, was the general reaction when the physical strength of the United States was finally made unmistakably apparent to friend and foe alike. Americans themselves have scarcely begun to reflect upon the deeper meaning of the enormous power that they control—the meaning both for their own Republic and for the world at large.

VI

The mass production of the United States has provided extraordinary material well-being for the American people as a whole. But it has also brought a truly disturbing industrial concentration. Although the basis of our civilization remains agricultural, and although our political institutions still conform to that basis, the industrial superstructure is now so great as to jeopardize the foundations on which we have built. Here is the explanation for many of the social problems, and much of the justified uneasiness, of our times.

At the risk of repetition, let it be emphasized that there has been nothing unnatural in the capitalistic concentration that has taken place in American life. Popular demand, native ability, and continental setting combined to develop both the billion dollar corporation and the million population city. Both of these have contributed to the comfort and amenity of American living. But both the big corporation and the big city have brought grievous problems in their train. To say this is not to idealize a past that was in many ways crude, raw, and far more inimical than modern life to cultural and spiritual values. Nor is it to deny the tremendous advantages and merits of a material prosperity that has percolated through the entire body politic to a degree that has no precedent. Here we merely observe that our national development has tended to concentrate power; and concentration of power, whether clerical, political, economic, financial, or social, is at variance with both the purpose and the nature of the Republic.

The cult of bigness, though wholly natural in a big country, has done great damage to American civilization in two directions. In the first place, it has given mere numbers, whether of dollars in a bank account or of wage earners crowded into city slums, a wholly fictitious and false importance. In the second place, it has led to a quantitative competition in which the value of the individual effort as such is consistently minimized. Big Business, for instance, has logically evoked Big Unionism. And to a "Public Be Damned" attitude on the part of both must be attributed at least some responsibility for the original acceptance of Big Government as a remedial device. Long before the "New Deal" it was pointed out that industrial feudalism would inevitably lead to the subordination of this neo-baronial class by the State.

The distinguishing characteristic of American civilization is the subordination of centralized power in behalf of individual liberty. But the blessings of liberty cannot be firmly secured unless there is limitation of social and economic, as well as of political, power. The Constitution seeks to restrain the latter and combines with the native intelligence of the American people to make pretensions of social pre-eminence meaningless. For the restraint of economic power, however, whether acquired by determined individuals or groups, there is no effective mechanism. The spirit of the Constitution is as hostile to economic monopoly as to that of any other kind. But within the letter of the law, as we know from many somber pages of our national history, its spirit can be easily and successfully flouted. The history of the Sherman and Clayton Acts, admirable as was their intent, is clear indication that legislative defense against monopoly is not enough.

All Americans to whom the definition of liberal can properly be applied have realized that freedom is indivisible. Therefore, freedom cannot be preserved in the political and social spheres, if it is lost in that of economics. The American mind and the American morality alike respond to the assertion of Justice Brandeis: "Our business is not to make goods but to make men." [16] President Hoover rose above the political arena when he said that: "Liberalism is a force truly of the spirit proceeding from the deep realization that economic freedom cannot be sacrificed if political freedom is to be preserved." [17] Professor Hocking reduced the whole issue to a thoughtful aphorism when he wrote:

> . . . human beings, while they can endure sometimes to reduce others to items in their own calculations, cannot endure to be so reduced by them. . . . Hence the general habit of considering the other man so far as he is useful to me and no further is a trait which, given sole

[16] Statement before Commission on Industrial Relations, 1914, Sen. Doc., Vol. XIX, p. 1003.
[17] Speech at Madison Square Garden, October 31, 1932.

sway in any community, would reduce it in time to its elemental dust. Economy alone could destroy, it could not create the nation.[18]

These parallel assertions, by a jurist, a statesman, and a philosopher, indicate that every line of careful thinking leads to an identical conclusion on the subject of economic freedom. Industrial and commercial conditions must not be allowed to frustrate the individual spirit of liberty. Otherwise it is worse than deceit to define these conditions as "freedom." It is worse than deceit because, as the Communists have helpfully taught us, trickery with words designed to convey thought is the perfect way to turn Society into that chaos from which dictatorship must emerge.

VII

Freedom is not an abstraction, like liberty, but an underlying condition of life that cannot be fragmentized into four or any other arbitrary number of parts. Lincoln realized this when he told the American people, quite simply, that this nation could not continue "half slave, half free."

But while freedom is indivisible it may at any given time be present or absent in various spheres of human activity, such as the political, the religious, or the economic. It is doubtful, however, that freedom can be broken up within any particular field so as to justify the Marxist assertion that capitalists can be free while wage earners are enslaved. Again Lincoln went to the heart of the matter in saying that the chain which fetters the slave is also fastened to the master.

Certainly it is false to say that economic freedom has two sides, corresponding to two aspects of the economic process, commonly described as production and consumption. Actually these functions are inextricably interwoven and people in their economic activities cannot properly be divided into textbook illustrations of producers and consumers.

The device that establishes the underlying unity of man as producer and consumer is the market, which is as old as Society itself.

[18] William Ernest Hocking, *Man and the State*, p. 293.

To be free, either as producer or consumer, the individual must have open access to a market in which he can exchange what he has to offer for what he wants to obtain. The offerings and the wants are alike expressions of the spirit of liberty and when they complement each other satisfactorily the condition of freedom is established. So the market, though only an economic instrument, is actually a device essential for securing the blessings of liberty, which in the aggregate constitute the condition of human freedom.

The offerings and wants exchanged in the market assume innumerable forms, because of the infinite variety of the power in the people, both as creators of and as consumers of wealth. But whatever the product the market will tend to embrace it and facilitate its exchange for other products. It is the market that permits men to produce without reference to their animal needs. It is the market that permits men to satisfy esthetic yearnings as consumers.

But the market is only a trading place. Impersonally it receives whatever goods and services are offered. Impersonally it utilizes a mechanism whereby things in demand can be conveniently exchanged. That mechanism is the price mechanism. This may be as primitive as barter, or as refined as the various forms of credit. Similarly the market itself may be as variegated as an eastern bazaar, or as specialized as a commodity exchange. The tendency, in every advancing civilization, is for the market and its price mechanism to move from a rudimentary to a perfected stage, in the sense that the exchange of goods and services is facilitated.

It follows that in an advancing civilization the objective with regard to the market will always be the removal of restrictions to trade. In other words, competition will be encouraged. When sellers compete with one another, and only then, is the buyer truly sovereign, as he should be under a political system in which no organ is allowed to usurp sovereignty. This economic sovereignty can be exercised only in a free market, responsive to the constant extension of competition.

Unrestricted competition is essential to economic freedom. Indeed, it can be said that competition *is* freedom, as distinct from the personal attribute of liberty.

It is impossible to refute the legal apothegm, older than our

Republic, which declares that "necessitous men are not free men." [19] But the thought behind those words can be more generally phrased by saying that those who are unable to compete successfully inevitably lose a measure of their freedom. Competition is always and necessarily ruthless, for all men. It is inhuman, in the sense that it pays no attention whatsoever to human weakness or human failings. But competition could not perform its essential service for Society as a whole if it were not "cut-throat" for individuals.

The unrestrained ability to compete is freedom, in every human undertaking, from the planting of potatoes to the painting of portraits. And when we speak of free enterprise what we mean is enterprise unfettered by restrictions, conventional or legal, directed to the limitation of either production or exchange. At one time the operation of a free market, through the price mechanism, will favor the individual as producer; that is the case when demand in any line is strong, and prices rise because of scarcity. At another time unrestricted competition will favor the individual as consumer; that is the case when demand is met from relative abundance and prices consequently fall.

Indisputably these fluctuations work tragic individual hardship. Undoubtedly they favor those who are unscrupulous as well as those who are farsighted. The very responsiveness of the market to human wants must tend to penalize those who are uninformed as well as those who are incompetent. And it is precisely because of this impersonal operation of the market that Christianity becomes a factor of economic as well as of political importance.

Christ laid particular emphasis on the responsibility of the fortunate in respect to those who are unable to compete in the market, or whose offerings the market rejects. If that sense of social responsibility is absent, or inadequate to the spiritual need, the inhumanity of the coldly mechanical operation of the market becomes obvious. It is a perfect mechanism. Left to itself the market will accurately evaluate the services of every individual and impersonally fix the price of every commodity that is offered

[19] Opinion of the Lord Chancellor in Vernon *v.* Bethell (1762). Quoted by Edward S. Corwin, *Liberty Against Government*, p. 5.

for sale. But the mechanism can do this only according to the standards that Society sets. And the free market will set values on only those things that can be bought and sold.

There is much in life that cannot be defined as merchandise. So the incompetence of the free market in pricing nonmaterial values is one factor that makes men turn to the State to control or even destroy the market operation. The fallacy in that recourse is clear. The market does not become more humane under the direction of the amoral institution that we have seen the State to be. Only as humanitarian considerations are brought to the market by those who trade there is its mechanical perfection really adapted to human needs. State intervention destroys the freedom of the market. But the mere absence of State intervention does not mean that the free market will be preserved. Those who cannot compete are also men. And to the extent that Society disclaims responsibility for them, the State, always impinging on the market, will enlarge its paternalistic role.

Thus it becomes axiomatic that the less significant the spiritual element in business, the greater will be political intervention in the economic sphere.

VIII

If we look for a common factor in all the developments that have tended to impinge on freedom in the United States, we shall find it in concentration of power.

In a predominantly agricultural society, such as in this country when its form of government was established, there can be no significant concentration of economic, as contrasted with political and social, power. That is why those who wrote the Constitution gave only inferential consideration to the problem of economic concentration, leaving this problem to posterity to confront in accordance with the general objective of securing the blessings of liberty for all Americans.

Under no system of government has it ever been possible to concentrate and maintain significant economic power on a purely agricultural base. But concentration of power is to a considerable extent imperative, as well as easily accomplished, in the operations of modern industry. And the larger those operations become, the more formidable is the potential threat to freedom. It is not eliminated by the breakup of combinations in restraint of trade, for organized labor has shown itself as apt in dictation as management ever was. Nor is the problem of concentrated power solved by distributing legal ownership among many shareholders, as in a big corporation, and still less so by spreading ownership among the entire body of taxpayers, as in a nationalized industry. With such absentee ownership, industry is actually operated by a small managerial group, the more likely to be arbitrary because it is deprived of the discretion of personal ownership. When industry is nationalized, management becomes still more arbitrary, because all power of effectively resisting or opposing the managerial group must then be denied to the rank and file of employees.

So concentration of economic power has become an issue of the first magnitude for the Republic. Historically, this happened as the center of political gravity moved from the agricultural base to the towering industrial structure imposed upon it. Concentration of power was the motive force behind the nineteenth century trust. It was the motive force behind the rise of industry-wide unionism, which has certainly done as much to fix prices arbitrarily as was ever accomplished by any trust or cartel. Finally we must realize, if we are interested in preserving free enterprise as a vital expression of liberty, that concentration of power in the State was the uniform motive force behind every aspect of the so-called "New Deal."

Early in his first administration Mr. Roosevelt tacitly disclosed his intention of destroying economic freedom in the United States, charging in the manner of Karl Marx, though more obliquely, that this condition has in it more of evil than of good. In the foreword to his book entitled *On Our Way*, describing the first year of the New Deal for popular consideration, this President said:

> In spite of the necessary complexity of the group of organizations whose abbreviated titles have caused some amusement, and through what has seemed to some a mere reaching out for centralized power by

the Federal Government, there has run a very definite, deep and permanent objective.[20]

Further on, in this revealing memoir, the chief architect of the New Deal explained the nature of its "definite, deep and permanent objective." The "emergency" of 1933, wrote Mr. Roosevelt:

> . . . went to the roots of our agriculture, our commerce and our industry; it was an emergency that had existed for a whole generation in its underlying causes. . . . It could be cured only by a complete reorganization and a measured control of the economic structure. . . . It called for a long series of new laws, new administrative agencies . . . all of them component parts of a fairly definite broad plan. . . . We could never go back to the old order.[21]

For freedom immediately, for liberty eventually, the New Deal cure was far more dangerous than the disease it sought to eradicate. The ailment was concentration of power. Stripped of disarming phraseology, the remedy found by the Roosevelt administrations was simply to increase the concentration of power, to a degree for which there was no parallel in American history, and even less warrant in American political philosophy.

The steps that have been taken to concentrate economic power in the federal administration, and their cumulative effect in the undermining of free enterprise, are matters of recent history. The documentation is exhaustive and the material easily available. It is not our purpose to examine these measures in detail, but merely to fit the historic significance of Mr. Roosevelt's "broad plan" into the long perspective of this study. How did it harmonize, for instance, with James Madison's conclusion that "we rest all our political experiments on mankind's capacity for self-government"?

For succinct answer to this question it would be difficult to improve on the brilliant summarization made, as early as 1944, by Garet Garrett, in his pamphlet entitled: *The Revolution Was.*[22] Here it is pointed out that the Roosevelt "Revolution"—it was a

---

[20] *Op. cit;* Foreword, p. xii.
[21] *Op. cit.,* pp. 35-36.
[22] Obtainable from the Caxton Printers, Ltd., Caldwell, Idaho.

counter-revolution—"took off from nothing that was implicit in the American scheme. . . . The design was European. . . . The end held constantly in view was power."

Mr. Garrett then sets forth nine separate "problems" that had to be solved by the New Deal before the United States could be converted into a unitary socialistic State, exercising what Mr. Roosevelt had euphemistically called "a measured control of the economic structure." In order to gloss the projected regimentation of the market, each of these problems was publicly represented as one of economic recovery. But each problem also represented some phase of the seizure of power from the people; of the liquidation of local government; and of the consequent concentration of the captured power in the hands of a strongly centralized, unrepresentative, and irresponsible "elite." The nine "problems," recasting Mr. Garrett's wording somewhat in the light of subsequent official disclosures, were as follows:

First, peacefully to capture the center of governmental power and then rapidly to enlarge its functions with the consent of a malleable Congress.

Second, to seize the major controls of economic power by instituting a "managed currency," involving progressive governmental usurpation of private banking functions; and devaluation.

Third, to organize and promote, through governmental agencies, vilification of all who asked that these problems should be intelligently and dispassionately examined, in the traditional American and liberal manner.

Fourth, to undermine the independence of the American farmer by lavish subsidies and controls, simultaneously making labor organization compulsory and provisionally giving to union leadership powers more autocratic than business management had ever possessed in its most concentrated form.

Fifth, simultaneously to shackle business, taking every advantage of its vulnerability to criticism in order to center more and more of the power of private enterprise in the State.

Sixth, to destroy the American tradition of individualism by making every citizen dependent on State benefits and by creating conditions under which nobody, irrespective of ability, could hope to achieve that degree of personal security which encourages men to speak their minds, without fear or favor.

Seventh, to weaken the federal system by systematically reducing the area of state sovereignty and the powers of all governmental agencies except those of the centralized administration, concentrating all these usurped powers in the White House.

Eighth, to promote inflation by continuous deficit financing, with the well-reasoned conviction that rapidly rising prices would popularize the argument for government controls and thus further strangle free enterprise.

Ninth, to debilitate capitalism by confiscatory taxation deliberately calculated to make capital formation increasingly difficult, thus facilitating the steady development of State enterprise as free enterprise became increasingly anemic.

In these, and other ways that the reader will recall for himself, the very bone and marrow of American civilization were corrupted from within. Even so, except for the windfall of World War II, it is doubtful whether the New Deal could have broken down the strong fiber of Americanism to the extent that it did. But it is important to realize that the disintegration had been carried far, before Mr. Roosevelt broke the precedent against a Third Term. In his Second Inaugural Address, on January 20, 1937, he felt able to say publicly:

> Nearly all of us recognize that as intricacies of human relationships increase, so power to govern them must also increase. . . . In fact, in these last four years, we have made the exercise of all power more democratic; for we have begun to bring private autocratic powers into their proper subordination to the public's government. The legend that they were invincible—above and beyond the processes of a democracy—has been shattered. They have been challenged and beaten. . . . In taking again the oath of office as President of the United States, I assume the solemn obligation of leading the American people forward along the road over which they have chosen to advance.

But, in spite of the lures so successfully held out to the electorate, it cannot be called certain that the American people have so definitely "chosen to advance" along this well-worn road to serfdom.

IX

Those who would build up the State to break up private concentrations of economic power are making essentially the same mistake that Europe made when it developed absolute monarchy in place of feudalism. The remedy does not lie along that road. It will not come from without, but from within. If Americans would save the Republic, they must realize that: "We rest all our political experiments on mankind's capacity for self-government."

To transfer power to the State may temporarily seem to break its concentration. Actually the process serves only to monopolize power in wholly irresponsible hands. When the State achieves mastery it is no longer possible even to identify those in the maze of bureaucracy who actually wield the power of government. If the exercise of power seems less flagrant than in the hands of industrial autocrats, that is only because the processes are more surreptitious and because the cost of inefficiency and corruption is concealed; to be made up later under the whip of the tax collector. To expect the dictatorial State to break a monopoly, and to restore the benefits of competition, is almost the height of human folly. The State from its very nature is, and must be, monopolistic.

So the tendency of the American people to turn to political authority for the solution of their economic problems was tragic. It was tragic, in the first place, because there is no solution, nor even any reasonable hope of solution, in this fancied remedy. The disease from which our Society suffers is overconcentration of economic and financial power. The remedy is to break up concentration, not to magnify it in political hands.

Acceptance of State Socialism as a remedy was the more tragic because once a people are lost in the recesses of this blind alley, they will learn that it is almost impossible to find a way out. The big fortune, the big corporation, the big union, all carry in themselves the seeds of their own liquidation. Certainly, devices can be established to keep them intact, as in the case of primogeniture with landed property. So it is a proper function for the State to remove all arbitrary interferences with natural distributive tendencies.[23] But even without noncontroversial measures for making perpetuation of private power more difficult, there is a natural process of disintegration that tends to liquidate it. A trust fund may guard the income of a prodigal son, but cannot keep him from wasting inherited substance in a manner injurious primarily to himself. And one of the most able and inveterate foes of corporate bigness has pointed out that:

> When . . . you increase your business to a very great extent, and the multitude of problems increases with its growth, you will find, in the first place, that the man at the head has a diminishing knowledge of the facts and, in the second place, a diminishing opportunity of exercising a careful judgment upon them. Furthermore . . . there develops a centrifugal force greater than the centripetal force. Demoralization sets in; a condition of lessened efficiency presents itself. . . . These are disadvantages that attend bigness.[24]

In this passage Justice Brandeis suggests the essential difference between private and State enterprise. In the former, at one point or another, decentralizing forces outweigh those of centralization. The point at which concentration is dispersed comes later in finance and industry than in agriculture, but if competition is preserved concentration eventually breaks down of its own weight. As the most superficial study of American business will show, the change in its pattern is continuous. Under State controls, however, exactly the opposite is true. The very nature of the State demands an ever-increasing centralization. The State monopoly outlaws competition. The centrifugal tendency is crushed. And every aspect of life becomes centripetal. Indeed, this is apparent even before the stage of State monopoly is reached. For governmental regulation always tends to weigh more heavily on small than on big business, and in consequence actually forces business mergers and consolidations.[25]

[23] An interesting development of this point is worked out by Fred I. Raymond, in *The Limitist*.

[24] Quoted by Alpheus T. Mason, *Brandeis and the Modern State*, p. 58.

[25] *Cf.* Federal Trade Commission, "A Summary Report" on *The Merger Movement*, 1948.

Enlargement of the area of State authority therefore does not enlarge, but definitely contracts, the condition of economic freedom. Since freedom is indivisible, this contraction of a part also contracts the whole. Since the spiritual urge of liberty demands the physical condition of freedom in order to be effective, contraction of freedom is at best debilitating—and will eventually prove fatal—to liberty itself. The loss of liberty is the more probable because, once the State has assumed a function, the deprivation suffered by Society is likely to be permanent. A relative immortality has been bestowed upon the State. So the advantage of this false god over every form of social organism is enormous and devastating.

The situation is evil in itself. It is obviously evil in Russia, where the cult of Bigness, through State domination, has achieved complete mastery. It is evil in those other countries where the liberal tradition still struggles feebly against Socialist encroachment. But in America the evil of centralization under governmental control is actually greater than anywhere else. For here more is at stake. Here this malignant growth has jeopardized the only political experiment that was ever consciously directed to the end of securing the blessings of liberty for the people as a whole.

X

We are now ready to look more closely at that beautiful but much-abused phrase "free enterprise"; to consider what it means —and what it implies.

As shown by the etymology of the word, an enterprise is not so much an *under* taking as a *between* taking, for the noun is compounded of *entre* and *prendre*. It comes to us from medieval France and something of the original flavor of chivalry still lingers. An enterprise is less humdrum than an undertaking and less exciting than an adventure. The word implies something arduous, requiring initiative, resource, and energy to carry it through. In an adventure these characteristics are suddenly demanded by some external circumstance. In an enterprise they are more sustained; exerted not to meet an objective emergency but to achieve a subjective purpose. Beyond tenacity, moreover, there is a spiritual quality to enterprise, which explains its close association with liberty. Enterprise is needed to give substance to liberty. Liberty is needed to animate enterprise.

It is natural that enterprise has come to have a particularly commercial connotation. The entrepreneur, whether miller, shoemaker, or smith, was the man who in some capacity bridged the gap *between* producer and consumer. The prevalence of family names like those just cited is suggestive. They point up the relatively primitive nature of early enterprise. In the telephone directory one does not find the names "Accountant," "Controller," or "Basingpointer." But the Bakers, Carpenters, Stablers, and so on by their very names are reminders that the development of the free market is the reason why most of us are alive today. Even if the evidence on the connection between free enterprise and population growth were not abundant it could be surmised from the number of occupation names, in every European language.

Moreover, the spirit of enterprise, as distinct from that of adventure, could not take hold until the Industrial Revolution had made an intricate division of labor possible. And to make headway even then it was necessary to have a political system in which the enterpriser would not be held back by the superior authority of vested interests or estates. The circumstances have been well summarized by John A. Hobson:

> The warrior-noble, the sportsman, the churchman, the landed-gentleman, who gave example and direction to the feelings, thoughts, and activities of our ancestors in the Middle Ages, had no feeling for "profit", and gave no regular accumulative impulse to the production of wealth. The mental and moral equipment of the *entrepreneur*, required for the conduct of modern capitalist industry, demands a special valuation and outlook upon life, possible to very few even in the more developed industrial cities of the Fourteenth and Fifteenth Centuries. Not until the Eighteenth Century was his character sufficiently evolved to enable him to take full advantage of the new industrial conditions.[26]

In America, both the timing and the circumstances were right for the entrepreneur. Nowhere else has it ever been so easy "to

[26] *The Evolution of Modern Capitalism*, p. 23.

take full advantage" of conditions that were naturally favorable and made more so by the character of our federal government. But in exploiting their advantages Americans have tended to forget that gain in one direction is loss in another. Energy spent in material progress is energy taken from other forms of advancement—unless the increased leisure that accompanies material progress is used to good advantage.

And good advantage, it may be emphasized, means literally God's advantage. Americans are entitled to boast of their inventive and organizing skills. In conjunction with the democratic character of our Society and the restraints placed upon our State, these skills are responsible for the prodigality of American material production. But this form of wealth is offset by an intellectual and spiritual poverty that causes the more anxiety because it reflects retrogression from earlier standards. There is a paucity in the American contribution, outside the field of commodities. Over a century ago de Tocqueville was disturbed to find that "hardly anyone in the United States devotes himself to the essentially theoretical and abstract portion of human knowledge." [27] Relative to the enormous increase in material wealth, this national deficiency is even more pronounced today.

We must assume that the Creator is pleased by creativity. The Universe, so far as we can understand it, is replete with dead matter and empty space. But this tiny fragment of Earth that Man inhabits in filled with extraordinary subtleties of movement and color, rhythm and pulsation, change and stability, growth and decay. Since Man, alone of all the animals, is interested in all those subtleties it must be concluded that the Creator wishes him to explore them. The exploration of earth's resources is not the same thing as their exploitation.

For spiritual exploration, as well as for material exploitation, free enterprise is essential. It must be so, for while political government can easily repress all kinds of creative thought, no official has ever been able to decree its accomplishment. At the same time, free enterprise must really be enterprise. That is, it must be

[27] *Op. cit.*, Vol. II, p. 42.

co-operatively exerted—*between* people—to the end that there is
a general understanding of its purpose as well as a general sharing
of its fruits.

Over a space of years, or even decades, free enterprise can be
constrained to the base of material advancement. Indeed for a
time it must concentrate on such limited objectives as the housing,
feeding, and clothing of men, for without such elementary facili-
ties there can be no advance in more significant matters. But disaster looms when a people who are permitted free enterprise see
in it—as seems to have happened in ancient Rome—only an efficient device for the development of personal adornment, luxury,
and display. Enterprise is a function of liberty and liberty was
not given to Man merely for the enlargement of his ego. If free
enterprise is directed only to physical satisfactions, discounting the
service that the created owes to his Creator, then doom is certain.
"Economy alone could destroy, it could not create a nation."

XI

Here is the weakness in the case for free enterprise as commonly presented. It is of course true that the absence of governmental restraints encourages productivity. The theoretical case
for the free market, and for competitive price fixing through the
relationship of supply and demand, is indisputable. One should
not require personal experience with ration cards and queues
and bureaucratic bungling to appreciate the practical superiority
of the free enterprise system over any form of State-directed economic planning. The defenders of free enterprise, however, have
made a dual mistake. On the one hand they have often failed to
realize that freedom is indivisible and that freedom cannot be expected by the employer unless he is willing to have this condition
apply equally to his employees. On the other hand many businessmen have preached free enterprise as though the words concerned only commercial operations. This modification of a general
principle has resulted in a distortion of that principle in behalf of
selfish personal interest.

The evidence of this distortion is spread wide on the pages of

American history. Time and again, those who argued for competition have, in practice, leaned toward monopolistic operations. Advocates of the free market have worked openly and surreptitiously for high tariffs and other governmental favors. During the period of the National Industrial Recovery Act, businessmen, with honorable exceptions, indorsed and supported controls of production and prices that completely invalidated the tenets of free enterprise, even in the narrow commercial sense of the phrase. As defenders of a philosophy of liberty, the record of many captains of American industry is uninspiring.

In *Economics in One Lesson*, Henry Hazlitt points out that: "Everything is produced at the expense of foregoing something else." He is not talking in strictly material terms. "Costs of production themselves," says Mr. Hazlitt, "might be defined as the things that are given up (the leisure and pleasures, the raw materials with alternative potential uses) in order to create the thing that is made." [28]

This thought merits deep consideration. The tremendous accomplishment of the American people has brought great rewards, in comfortable, easy, and often luxurious living. But it is equally true that the accomplishment represents great sacrifice. Precisely because our energies have been so concentrated on physical production, they have necessarily been directed away from spiritual production. In the United States the material conditions of men have been so improved that, compared with other lands and other times, we live like princes. That means responsibility, for each and every beneficiary of free enterprise, to efface abuses degrading to humanity.

Among European Socialists, confused and baffled by the well-being of the average American worker, it has been habitual to argue that the United States lags far behind in social legislation. The European background of servitude to the State obscures the fact that social legislation is a sign of retrogression, not progress. It should be obvious that there has been widespread individual failure if humanitarianism has to be enforced by disciplinary gov-

[28] P. 114.

ernmental action. The inevitability with which a planned economy leads on to the police State is now widely recognized in this Republic.[29] What must be recognized more clearly is that the American system, because it has relied on individual decency rather than State compulsion for its moral direction, is ethically far more advanced than English or European practice.

The major reasons for the inroads that feudalistic European thinking has made upon the more advanced American social philosophy are not obscure. In part they trace to the excesses of the free enterprise system. On the one hand the very exuberance of its operation has countenanced a "boom or bust" psychology. The restraints upon it have not been those of intelligence, but rather the enforced contractions resulting from gross overexpansion.

This absence of self-control has itself led to the illogical conclusion that there is something inherently desirable in the State controls made inevitable in Europe by the historically entrenched position of vested interests. And that conclusion has been assisted by the deterioration of philosophical thinking in the United States. The curious failure of Americans to appreciate, or even to understand, the significance of their institutions further explains the widespread surrender to European ideas that are not properly applicable to American civilization.

Decay in American political thinking has been forwarded by the very fact that the original American political thought was so brilliant. This thought was embodied in a political instrumentality—the federal Constitution—so well wrought, so firm, and yet so flexible that it has served the people whom it governs for over a century and a half of dramatic change and almost incredible development. But precisely because the organic law was so well drafted the thought behind it has ceased to have any real significance for many of us.

[29] Two books of European authorship have greatly helped to forward this recognition: *The Road to Serfdom*, by Professor F. A. Hayek; and *Ordeal by Planning*, by Professor John Jewkes. The latter tells us (p. 207) that in England, in 1947, inspections of private homes—the Englishman's castle—were authorized by seventeen Ministries and carried on, without search warrants, by 10,916 officials.

Nobody has ever given a better reasoned consideration to this phenomenon of doctrinal decay than did John Stuart Mill in the essay *On Liberty*. If an opinion is not held with conviction, he points out, it soon loses vitality. It must be constantly tested and re-examined, in the light of changing circumstance, in order to preserve its power:

> . . . not only the grounds of the opinion are forgotten in the absence of discussion, but too often the meaning of the opinion itself. The words which convey it cease to suggest ideas, or suggest only a small portion of those they were originally employed to communicate. Instead of a vivid conception and a living belief, there remain only a few phrases retained by rote; or, if any part, the shell and husk only of the meaning is retained, the finer essence being lost. The great chapter in human history which this fact occupies and fills, cannot be too earnestly studied and meditated on.[30]

The American system of government is based on principles that are eternal. But failure to review and reconsider those principles constantly has played into the hands of men who would identify them with the "horse and buggy" era. It goes unnoticed—until too late—that "streamlining" the "horse and buggy" ends by taking Man back to the era of the chariot. And the ease with which the accomplished demagogue can practice deception is due not so much to the lure of his oratory as to the shocking lack of any critical faculty among the electorate.

A part of the blame for this situation must go to the narrow conception of free enterprise that has been allowed to dominate. It is not enough that this system has shown unprecedented capacity for producing material goods. If free enterprise cannot balance this flood of production with an equally impressive moral output, then it and the Republic designed to promote enterprise on the part of free men will go down together.

[30] Ch. 2.

Chapter 9

The Fundamental Challenge

On the well-grounded basis of its free agriculture American civilization has so far successfully sustained an extremely rapid urbanization. While this has created serious problems, it has not yet fundamentally injured the distinctive character of the original political accomplishment. The strength of our civilization is attested by the abuses it has withstood.

In Western Europe, the feudal inheritance accounts for the different line of development. With few exceptions, proving the rule, we find that concentration of power, under centralized command, is the constant factor of political evolution in all of the Continent west of the Elbe River. Everywhere in this area, with appropriate local differences, the economic background was tenant farming under rigid manorial control. Then the walled city, virtually unknown in North America, emerges as the center of productive activity. And gradually the townspeople rally to the support of centralized government, seeking to establish that condition of free contract which is automatically outlawed by feudal status.

Thus, the State was entrusted with absolute power as the only agency that could suppress the Estate. That was a grim struggle, and because of its difficulty the eventual sense of accomplishment was real. Unfortunately, the evidence of change obscured the fact that there had been little fundamental progress. For State and

Estate are merely different forms of status. In either aspect, status automatically limits freedom and is inimical to liberty. A cynical French proverb sums up the Western European experience: *Plus ça change, plus c'est la même chose.*

But a study that seeks to examine the character and prospects of American civilization can no longer stop with the differentiation from Western Europe. There is a third pattern, developed gradually but logically on the great steppes of central Russia, which citizens of the Republic can now no longer ignore. The tempo of Slavic development has been slow, but is not the less influential for that reason. The fact that the glacier moves imperceptibly does not mean that it is motionless. As de Tocqueville before him, so Amiel noted its ruthlessness in his famous *Journal.* On July 1, 1856, this Swiss professor wrote:

> What terrible rulers the Russians would be if ever they should spread the night of their rule over the countries of the south! They would bring us a Polar despotism,—tyranny such as the world has never known, silent as darkness, rigid as ice, insensible as bronze, decked with an outer amiability and glittering with the cold brilliancy of snow,—a slavery without compensation or relief.

Few Americans possessed either the political vision or the historical knowledge necessary to foresee what was certain to result from the destruction of the German and Japanese barriers to Slavic expansion. In the heat of the apocalyptic conflict the Russian glacier simply dissolved, becoming an irresistible inundation. Confronted with a postwar political vacuum, to West and East, the Soviet system naturally expanded to fill the empty spaces. And it was wholly appropriate that the ruins of Berlin, bomb-shattered symbol of the destruction of Western Europe's urbanized civilization, should focus the first determined American effort to confine the enormous force that American political ineptitude had done so much to unleash, to our own deadly peril.

So, at the close of World War II the impact of Soviet Russia, on Western Europe and the United States, became the one outstanding political problem for thoughtful men. The general American reaction to this impact took three forms: (1) an honest effort to understand what lies behind the dynamic of Russian Communism; (2) a somewhat panicky attempt to ally the more humane cultures of Western Europe and America in opposition to the "Polar despotism"; (3) a resolute endeavor to reanimate the spirit of American civilization so that it would not crumble away under the attack of an aggressive political philosophy, the more potent because of its coldly diabolical motivation.

The second and third of these reactions were inherently contradictory. But they proceeded simultaneously because both were instinctive. To prevent either co-operation with Western Europe, or the American Renaissance, or both, from ending in failure, it is necessary to emphasize the importance of the first, and most objective, of the three reactions. We must examine the philosophy of Communism, and the form that it has taken as a result of centering in Russia. That involves consideration of the distinctive pattern of Russian civilization. To this background, as we shall see, the doctrines of Karl Marx were easily applied.

II

In the introductory chapter of his *History of the Russian Revolution* Leon Trotsky gives a penetrating, though perhaps prejudiced, analysis of some of the "Peculiarities of Russia's Development." He asserts categorically that political and economic development in Russia have followed a line of evolution distinctly different from that of Western Europe, on the one hand, or from that of the American colonies on the other.

In Russia the condition of freedom was absent throughout the Middle Ages, both on the land and in the towns. Says Trotsky:

> The meagerness not only of Russian feudalism, but of all the old Russian history, finds its most depressing expression in the absence of real medieval cities as centers of commerce and craft . . . The old Russian cities were commercial, administrative, military and manorial —centers of consumption, consequently, not of production.[1]

[1] *Op. cit.*, p. 7.

Despite the vast expanse of arable land, there was even less freedom of enterprise in the Russian countryside. The rise to power of the Romanov dynasty, early in the seventeenth century, was followed by the literal enslavement of the peasantry. It is noteworthy that this process was coincident both with parliamentary limitation of the power of the monarchy in England and with the establishment of new institutions of local government in the American colonies.

The Pilgrims landed on Plymouth Rock in 1620. Five years later a ukase in Moscow provided that if a landowner killed a peasant belonging to another landowner, the murder would be expiated by surrendering an equally healthy peasant to the lord who had suffered the loss of his own slave. In other words, the man was recognized by law as property and only as property. Peasants could be sold at will, but under a law of 1642 it was forbidden to sell land without the peasants who worked on it. In 1646 all time limit for the recovery of a fugitive serf was abolished. And in 1664 the Czar ordained that any landowner sheltering a fugitive must surrender four peasant families of his own as compensation to the owner of the errant serf.[2]

The backwardness of Russia's rural development, says Trotsky, "is sufficiently indicated in the fact that serfdom, born at the end of the Sixteenth Century, took form in the Seventeenth, flowered in the Eighteenth, and was juridically annulled only in 1861." That reform, prompted by the poor showing of Russia's slave soldiers in the Crimean War, came too late to save the Romanov dynasty from its eventual obliteration. And the Emancipation was too close, in time, to the breakdown of 1917 to permit the development of a vital liberal tradition, as distinct from the great contribution of many individual Russians to the growth of liberal thought.

In 1861 there were nearly fifty million serfs in Russia. The children and grandchildren of these slaves were to some extent vulnerable to the far more dreadful tyranny of Bolshevism. In that connection we should note that the intensive communist

[2] Sir Bernard Pares, *A History of Russia* (Fourth Edition), Ch. IX.

8 *THE POWER IN THE PEOPLE*

propaganda among American Negroes is based upon belief that
any people with a near background of enslavement can easily be
enslaved again.

While Western Europe enjoyed a flowering of urban civilization, and while America was building the strong agricultural basis
of its own distinctive development, power of every form was in
Russia centralized in a corrupt and tyrannical court. Of this au-
tocracy the Orthodox Church was merely an appanage. Trotsky
points out that: "The church never rose in Russia to that commanding height which it attained in the Catholic West. . . . The
bishops and metropolitans enjoyed authority merely as deputies
of the temporal power. The patriarchs were changed along with
the Czars." Then, in a very illuminating passage, he concludes:

> The insignificance of the Russian cities, which more than anything
> else promoted the development of an Asiatic State, also made impossible
> a Reformation—that is, a replacement of the feudal-bureaucratic or-
> thodoxy by some sort of modernized kind of Christianity adapted to
> the demands of a bourgeois society.[3]

The absence of any Reformation in Russia helps to account for
the nonnational character of the Russian State, which in turn has
proved most helpful to the supranational doctrines of Communism. In Western Europe, Protestantism stimulated the rise
of nationalism. In the United States, the absence of any State
church at least retarded the religious and crusading aspects of
nationalism. But though Russia was spared the passionate excesses
of clerical fervor, those who worshipped were also deprived of the
spiritual stimulus of intense individual faith. When Luther was
making his famous refusal to recant, before the Diet of Worms,
the Russian monasteries were arguing over ritualistic detail.
Should the blessing be given with two fingers, representing the
duality of Christ, or with three fingers to symbolize the Trinity? [4]

[3] *Op. cit.*, pp. 6-8. Sir John Maynard points out (*Russia in Flux*, p. 4) that
since there was no Reformation there could be no Counter-Reformation, "so that
Russia missed an educative influence such as the later and reformed Roman clergy
exercised in the West, while her own clergy neither studied nor taught."
[4] Pares, *op. cit.*, p. 158.

III

It was the conclusion of Karl Marx that capitalism paves the way for Communism, and that the proletariat could most easily achieve political power in the highly industrialized nations. Consequently, the initial triumph of Communism in Russia is often cited as evidence of fallacies in Marxist thinking. Of interest here is the fact that when the Communist Manifesto was first published, in 1848, it was immediately translated from the original German into English, French, Italian, Flemish, and Danish. Fifteen years elapsed before the first Russian translation, made by Bakunin, was brought out—in Geneva.

Communist writers, wedded to the theory of economic determinism, have been at pains to explain why the bourgeoisie were not first ploughed under in Germany or England, as Marx anticipated. Trotsky makes the important point that while industrial development came slowly in Russia, its development in the late nineteenth and early twentieth centuries was highly concentrated. "Russian industry in its technique and capitalist structure stood at the level of the advanced countries, and in certain respects even outstripped them." Certainly the proportion of the population employed in industry was relatively small, and the percentage of industrial workers engaged in small Russian enterprises was in 1914 only half the percentage similarly employed in the United States. "But the giant enterprises, above 1,000 workers each, employed in the United States 17.8 per cent of the workers and in Russia (in 1914) 41.4 per cent." [5] In other words, there was more than sufficient "Big Business" in Czarist Russia to make the transition to Big Government an easy one.

Students of the Russian Revolution will recall the important part played by the personnel of the huge Putilov plant in Petrograd, where the Bolsheviks quickly established communist cells to direct the political activities of the 40,000 employees.[6] More basic to the triumph of Communism in Russia, however, was the long tradition of centralized authority and the absence of any

[5] *Op. cit.*, p. 10.
[6] *Cf.* Trotsky, *op. cit.*, p. 421 ff.

well-established pattern of local government. When the minority of Bolsheviks dissolved the Constituent Assembly by force, groups like the Putilov workers turned blindly to the nascent authority that was aggressively seeking to take over—the well-disciplined and supremely confident Bolshevik Party. Russian workers and peasants did not make the Communist Revolution. They simply followed the relative handful of intellectuals who were aggressively prepared to fill the vacuum caused by the collapse of the Old Regime.

Emphasis on economic factors has tended to conceal the ripeness of Czarist Russia for political change. It was merely a matter of turning from a decrepit to a vigorous tyranny. And that explains why the political changes brought to Russia by Communism have been of a secondary rather than a primary nature. The convinced Communist firmly believes that his creed is the harbinger of the future. But the heritage of Russia's absolutist past hangs heavily over those who have seized control of that country's government. "If one were called on to name a single dominant element in Russian history, from the Middle Ages to the present time, it would be the unlimited power of the ruler." [7]

To a much greater extent than is generally believed there has been an essentially unbroken continuity between the czarist and communist regimes. At the time of the Emancipation, effort was made to transform the serf into a free peasant proprietor. Excepting Western Russia, however, ownership of land ceded by the nobility was not vested in those who actually tilled the soil, but in the village community as a whole. "The control of the commune was substituted for the authority of the lord." [8] This meant that the leveling tendency of serfdom carried over into the relatively brief period of emancipation, from 1861 to 1917. As Sir John Maynard emphasizes, ". . . equality made a stronger appeal than freedom: a fact which explains some things which would otherwise be unintelligible in the more recent history of Russia." [9]

[7] William Henry Chamberlin, *The Russian Enigma*, p. 19.
[8] E. Lipson, *Europe in the Nineteenth Century*, p. 96.
[9] *Op. cit.*, p. 27.

Under Lenin's New Economic Policy (1921) the peasants were temporarily allowed to own the land promised them at the time of the Revolution. But this tolerance of free enterprise was short-lived. In 1928 the Central Committee of the Russian Communist Party decided to push on with the collectivization of agriculture, and did so on the basis of the collective village ownership of czarist days. The provisional move toward private ownership of land was reversed. "By 1940 . . . 25,000,000 small individuals had been replaced by 236,300 *Kolkhozi,* or collective farms." [10] Sir Bernard Pares points out that as a part of this policy: "A new system of internal passports was introduced—a revival of a creation of Peter the Great, which had been one of the most odious features of the old serfdom." [11]

Many other "features of the old serfdom" have been restored in Russia by Communism. The censorship of the press and the suppression of individual opinion are developments of czarist laws which were much less onerous because much less effectively enforced. If political advance is measured by progressive emancipation of the individual from controls arbitrarily imposed upon him by others, then the communist government of Russia can only be defined as completely reactionary, for its restraints are akin to those imposed by the most tyrannical Czars. The basis of communist political thinking is czarist, but the techniques of Communism are far more efficient in the imposition of tyranny, and far more ruthless in the punishment of any who attempt to protest the omnipotence of the centralized dictatorship. "Nothing more strikingly illustrates the comparative efficiency of the present regime than the success with which subversive doctrines, as distinct from mere criticism of methods and details, are kept away from the public." [12]

[10] Chamberlin, *op. cit.,* p. 180. For particulars, see Alexander Baykov, *The Development of the Soviet Economic System,* Ch. XII.

[11] *Op. cit.,* p. 507.

[12] Maynard, *op. cit.,* p. 87.

IV

Lenin has been quoted as saying: "It isn't a question of Russia at all. I spit on Russia. . . . This is merely one phase through which we must pass on the way to a world revolution." [13]

Nevertheless, it *is* a question of Russia, because it is from the downtrodden and ill-informed Russian people that the Communist Party, in Russia and elsewhere, derives strength for its determined assault upon faith in individual liberty, and upon the economic system of free enterprise through which that faith is made active in the daily life of mankind. Russia is the powerful physical body that has been made subservient to the evil spirit of Communism.

Integration of communist doctrine with the absolutist traditions of czarist Russia was a historical accident, but one of those accidents so logical, and so natural under existing circumstances, that the word becomes a misnomer. Given the sequence of the first two world wars, the determination of the German leaders to destroy the Russian State, finally, the measures actually taken to create a political vacuum in Central Europe—then the shrewd manner in which the Kremlin has seized its opportunities is wholly understandable. Charles I had no intention of promoting an American republic; nevertheless, he greatly advanced that end. Franklin Roosevelt certainly did not mean to set the stage for conflict between the United States and Soviet Russia; but his third term as President had that effect.

It was Lenin's achievement to take control of the machinery of the old Russian State when it finally broke down—partly because of bureaucratic incompetence; partly because of the weak and vacillating character of the last Czar; partly because the centralized direction was too rigid to withstand the strain of World War I. It was the achievement of Stalin, who vowed at Lenin's bier "to strengthen and expand the Communist International," [14] both to regiment the Russian people so that they could withstand

[13] In a conversation with George Solomon, later director of Arkos, cited by David Shub, *Lenin*, p. 268.

[14] *Pravda*, January 27, 1924.

Hitler's attack, and shrewdly to take advantage of Anglo-American diplomatic blunders for the promotion of world revolution.

In one of his moving but flamboyant wartime speeches, Winston Churchill asserted that he was not called to preside over His Majesty's Government in order to liquidate the British Empire. Stalin never forgave the great English leader who said contemptuously, on January 20, 1940, that: "Everyone can see how Communism rots the soul of a nation." And to Stalin's personal effort is attributable much of that British imperial liquidation, which was not averted by Churchill's words, which was indeed unconsciously forwarded by his work.

Americans, more apt to read headlines than to reflect on the often ironic lessons of history, have been slow to grasp the enormous implications for their country in the catastrophic smash of the little Nation-States of Western Europe; the simultaneous rise of Communism as a political force of the first magnitude. Forgetful of their past, and showing little insight as to their future, the American people have twice let themselves be maneuvered into military alliances and essentially suicidal European conflicts of a nature more likely to destroy than to preserve the States with which we were allied. There is only one ally to which American military aid has been of any lasting benefit. That one was the ally resolutely pledged to destroy the American political and economic system.

The close of World War II saw the world divided between two Great Powers—the United States and its dependencies; Soviet Russia and the countries governed by communist proconsuls dependent on the support of imperial Moscow. In political and economic importance, no other nation is any longer in the same class as these two, and it is sadly improbable that the currently enfeebled States can regain the power which they have lost—a loss both relative and absolute.

The outcome of World War II made it certain that conflict—latent or active—between the United States and Russia would be the overshadowing issue of the postwar era. What, then, are the similarities, and what are the fundamental differences, between these two political organizations—much more than Nation-States

—in each of which the dominant leadership firmly believes that its way is best for all mankind?

V

In the first place, both the United States and Russia are non-European nations. They are non-European not merely by geographical location, but also in their fundamental cultures. While European thought has deeply affected both Russia and the United States, the former has remained predominantly Asiatic, and the latter has become distinctively American, in both social and political practice. Or, in alternative wording, both the Russian and American civilizations are *sui generis,* rather than imitative. These distinctions are likely to become more pronounced now that the influence of Western European culture, which for three centuries worked to integrate America, Europe, and Asia, has been so tragically dissipated. The civilization of Western Europe no longer greatly influences the United States and Russia. On the contrary, it is greatly influenced by them.[15]

A second mutual characteristic of the United States and Russia arises from the fact that the government of each is based on revolutionary principles. No Western European government of the prewar period operated under an organic law designed to embody a distinctive political theory. In every case European governmental forms evolved not as a result of careful constitutional architecture but by the method of trial and error. Even when political revolutions seemed successful, as in England in 1648, France in 1789, Italy in 1860, and Germany in 1919, the constitutional experiments were before long swept away by restorations of one kind or another. The American Revolution of 1776 and the Russian Revolution of 1917, however, have both been successful in establishing governments tailored to political theory. And those political theories are in each case deeply, though divergently, philosophical.

Finally, American and Russian political theories, even though sharply antagonistic, are nevertheless similar in being directed

[15] Cf. Edward H. Carr: *The Soviet Impact on the Western World.*

against the supremacy of the National Socialist State as it has evolved, through State conflicts of increasing intensity, on the common feudal basis of Western Europe. In sharp distinction from Socialism, the political theory of Communism, no matter how little fulfilled in practice, is that after the successful proletarian revolution "a special repressive force, a State, is no longer necessary." To quote the familiar assertion of Friedrich Engels, the close friend and collaborator of Karl Marx, "The State is not abolished, it withers away." [16]

In view of the rigorous controls exerted by the Soviet government over practically every aspect of Russian social life, it is tempting to cite Engel's oft-quoted prediction as a classic example of political myopia. Whatever else may be "withering away" in Russia, it certainly is not the State!

But authorized communist spokesmen, well-trained in the philosophy and dialectics of their revolutionary creed, find no difficulty in reconciling the present supremacy of an all-powerful Russian State with the anticipation of an international order in which the traditional Nation-State of Western Europe will eventually disappear. The present era, by social revolutionary reasoning, is the transition period from capitalism to Communism. During the transition, that State which is the seat of communist power must make itself physically stronger than any of the necessarily rival capitalist States, all of which will eventually be overthrown. Temporarily a State becomes strong—though the process is eventually fatal—by subjecting all economic and social organization to the dictatorial will of its officials. Therefore an important technique in the transition to Communism is to promote National Socialism, and thereby weaken free enterprise, in rival States which are slated for communist control. The State is to be killed, like a Strasbourg goose, by overfeeding—hypertrophy of function.

It is not sufficiently realized that Marx, and Engels as his ardent collaborator, specifically urged a steady augmentation of State power as the most effective preliminary to the establishment

[16] Quoted and expounded in *The State and Revolution*, by V. I. Ulianov (Lenin), Chapter I, Sect. 4.

of Communism. "The first step in the revolution," they explain in the Communist Manifesto, is "to centralize all instruments of production in the hands of the State, i.e. of the proletariat organized as the ruling class."

Then Marx and Engels, writing in 1848, list ten measures that all Communists should ceaselessly advocate, primarily because they "necessitate further inroads upon the old social order." The ten steps to Communism, listed in the Communist Manifesto as "pretty generally applicable," are quoted below. The reader may note for himself the extent to which a spurious "liberalism" has adopted communist doctrine.

1. Abolition of property in land and application of all rents of land to public purposes.
2. A heavy progressive or graduated income tax.
3. Abolition of all right of inheritance.
4. Confiscation of the property of all emigrants and rebels.
5. Centralization of credit in the hands of the State by means of a national bank with State capital and an exclusive monopoly.
6. Centralization of the means of communication and transport in the hands of the State.
7. Extension of factories and instruments of production owned by the State; the bringing into cultivation of waste lands, and the improvement of the soil generally in accordance with a common plan.
8. Equal obligation of all to work. Establishment of industrial armies, especially for agriculture.
9. Combination of agriculture with manufacturing industries; gradual abolition of the distinction between town and country, by a more equable distribution of the population over the country.
10. Free education for all children in public schools. Abolition of child factory labor in its present form. Combination of education with industrial production, etc.[17]

The attested feasibility of the communist program must be appreciated in order to get at the real meaning of Engel's asser-

[17] *The Communist Manifesto*, Section II; pp. 30-31 in 1939 (Eleventh) Edition of International Publishers.

tion that with social revolution the State "withers away." In turgid language Lenin explained the seeming contradiction:

> As a matter of fact, Engels speaks here of the destruction of the bourgeois State by the proletarian revolution, while the words about its withering away refer to the remains of *proletarian* statehood *after* the Socialist revolution. The bourgeois State does not "wither away" according to Engels, but is "put an end to" by the proletariat in the course of the revolution. What withers away after the revolution is the proletarian State or semi-State.[18]

In the same context Lenin explains that a necessarily parallel communist objective is the eventual elimination of political democracy, along with the "Bourgeois State." Incidentally, this explains why the Soviet government can make no compromise with democracy as the word is understood by most Americans. In Lenin's words:

> . . . it never enters the head of any of the opportunists who shamelessly distort Marx that when Engels speaks here of the State "withering away," or "becoming dormant," he speaks of *democracy*. At first sight this seems very strange. But it is "unintelligible" only to the one who has not reflected on the fact that democracy is *also* a State and that, consequently, democracy will *also* disappear when the State disappears. The bourgeois State can only be "put an end to" by a revolution. The State in general, i.e. most complete democracy, can only "wither away."

The essential point is made clear for everybody in the Preamble to the Statutes of the Communist International, adopted in Moscow in August, 1920, as follows:

> In order to overthrow the international bourgeoisie and to create an International Soviet Republic *as a transition stage to the complete abolition of the State* [italics supplied], the Communist International will use all means at its disposal, including force of arms.[19]

[18] Lenin, *op. cit.*, International Publishers, New York, 1935, p. 17.
[19] The full text of these Statutes is conveniently reproduced in *Blueprint for World Conquest*, HUMAN EVENTS, INC., 1946.

VI

The most sympathetic attempt to find principles in common, as between Russian and American political theory, is doomed to failure. No American who has given any thought to the subject—excepting only Anarchists and Communists in our midst—is anxious to see our particular form of State *abolished*, though many would indorse change in one or more constitutional particulars. Nevertheless, a very large number of patriotic Americans completely fail to realize that if our State is increasingly permitted to dominate social organization—in such fields as education, religion, industry, commerce, finance, agriculture, pensions, and medical care—this Republic will be destroyed.

No convinced and forthright Communist, on the other hand, will deny that his major objective in life is to assist in undermining all capitalist States, of which the United States is by far the strongest representative. There are many ways in which that end can be accomplished, aside from the contemplated "force of arms."

Economic strength can be undermined by continuous communist-inspired strikes. Social strength can be diminished by a constant centralization and enlargement of governmental functions, the great majority of which are unproductive and consequently serve to weaken the economic basis by the cumulative effects of regulation and taxation. Moral strength can be adversely affected by deliberately confusing the meaning of words, so that an advocate of dictatorship becomes a "Liberal" and any forthright opponent of totalitarianism a "Reactionary," or even "Fascist." National unity can be destroyed—very easily in the unsure American amalgam—by covertly encouraging racial and religious hates: Jew against Gentile; Protestant against Catholic; Negro against White; foreign-born against native; and always, of course, employee against employer. For startling evidence of the extent to which domestic collaboration is utilized in work of this sort, reference may be made to the 1946 Report of the Canadian Royal Commission on the atomic bomb espionage case in that country.

But we no longer need to look abroad for evidence, and preliminary documentation, on communist plotting.

On the national stage a great deal of communist intrigue and subterfuge could for a long time be kept concealed, though with increasing difficulty as the "fifth columns" became more active and better organized. So it was in the international field, in the form of open conflict for dominance over shattered Europe and chaotic Asia, that the appallingly fundamental character of Russian-American rivalry first became unmistakably apparent.

Any positive American aim in postwar foreign policy has been extremely difficult to locate and identify. Except for support of the United Nations, dubiously assuming permanent Russo-American agreement, it would seem that the Roosevelt Administration fought the last war primarily as an end in itself; not as a means to any intelligible long-range national purpose. But the Russian objective, additional to self-defense, was never concealed from any who took the trouble to study Communist documents. The consistent aim has been to enlarge the Union of Soviet Socialist Republics, as first established by Paragraph 2 of Article One of the Russian Constitution adopted July 10, 1918. This said: "The Russian Soviet Republic is organized on the basis of a free union of free nations, as a federation of Soviet National Republics." [20]

Federal union is the mechanism whereby the communist leadership expects to achieve eventual international unity, replacing the quasi-feudal anarchy of the old State system. In the words of the 1920 Theses of the Communist International, "Federation is a transitional form towards the complete union of the workers of all countries." [21] And Russian membership in the United Nations, as the Russian representatives in that organization certainly never attempted to disguise, always has had as its primary purpose the blocking of any international action that might retard the extension of Soviet imperialism. While the United Nations is still ostensibly a going concern, and while the Third International was ostensibly dissolved in 1943, the latter

[20] The translation is that published in *The Nation* (New York) of January 4, 1919.
[21] Quoted in *Blueprint for World Conquest*, p. 121.

and not the former was made the effective and positive agency of Russian postwar foreign policy.

The success of this policy was such as to make its further aggressive application virtually certain, wherever and whenever circumstances permit. In Europe alone no less than eleven formerly independent nations—Albania, Bulgaria, Czechoslovakia, Estonia, Finland, Hungary, Latvia, Lithuania, Poland, Romania, Yugoslavia—were quickly either incorporated into the Soviet Union, or made satellites of its policy. Large parts of two other former States—Austria and Germany—were cleverly kept under indefinite Russian occupation. In every remaining European country, excepting only Ireland, Portugal, and Spain, a powerful Communist Party worked continuously in the Soviet interest. In Asia, even aside from China, organized communist infiltration has been at least equally well-organized and successful. It has made notable headway in Latin-America. Eventual disclosure of the world-wide revolutionary objective did not flatter the intelligence of those Americans who attempted to argue, against all the evidence, that the Russian political design was merely to rectify a frontier, or to obtain a couple of warm-water ports.

In the development of Communist imperialism we see what is actually meant by the "withering away" of statehood, as predicted by Engels and interpreted by Lenin. All of the characteristics of statehood have, of course, been lost by the former Baltic Republics, even though their past independence is still given *de jure* recognition by the United States. Scarcely less pronounced was the surrender of independent sovereignty on the part of those former States, like Poland or Czechoslovakia, governed by the Communist Party and incorporated in the Russian "bloc." Only in Yugoslavia was there any strongly nationalistic opposition, on the part of the local Communist *Gauleiter*, to the diminution of State sovereignty.

Thus, democracy and the State have been simultaneously eliminated in nearly a dozen European countries, as Lenin bluntly said would be the case. But the central Russian State itself "withers away" only in the sense that it becomes increasingly the headquarters of an international rather than a national bureaucracy.

Saxons, Albanians, and Chinese are now governed from Moscow almost as definitely as are Ukrainians, White Russians, and Georgians. In this manner the potentially democratic Nation-State has given way as an institution to the spreading nucleus of a Communist World-State. And the latter is more inimical than national centralization—hostile though that is—to the traditional American pattern of spontaneous social development and local self-government.

The apparent similarities between the United States and Russia are therefore seen, on close examination, to veil differences so profound as to guarantee steadily increasing conflict and steadily decreasing co-operation. These differences are accentuated by the collapse of the European State system, and rendered inescapable by the crusading zeal of Marxist fanaticism. The communist objective of world revolution was by itself calculated to bring Russia and the United States into eventual conflict. But as long as Russia remained blocked off by a powerful Germany and Japan, and as long as the foreign policy of the United States was predominantly "isolationist," this conflict could be regarded as a remote threat. At the end of 1945, however, only fragments of States remained along the vast Russian periphery. Soon, on a frontier stretching from Korea to Bavaria, an interventionist America was maintaining conscript troops, and pouring forth its substance, in a Herculean effort to "contain" the very forces that our own "diplomacy" had so light-heartedly released.

Viewed in the light of inescapable facts it is indeed strange that the gross fiction of Soviet-American co-operation could continue to deceive anybody for even the few months after the last war during which the mirage lingered in American—not in communist—minds. Eventually there was no alternative to the bitter realization that the defeat of the Axis accomplished far more toward jeopardizing than toward preserving the security of the United States. What William Graham Sumner had called "Blessed Isolation" was indeed abandoned. In its place, unwittingly and unwillingly, the American people had accepted imperial burdens that strongly imply the passing of their Republic.

This unhappy outcome explains why so many patriotic and farsighted Americans viewed President Roosevelt's casual adventure into the last war with such grave misgivings. And the absence of reasonable foresight on the part of that administration further explains why American foreign policy under Mr. Roosevelt's successor has been necessarily an almost unbroken record of frustration and confusion, leading only to an alliance directed against a major wartime ally.

VII

As Rome and Carthage, twenty-two centuries ago, so Russia and the United States today face each other with mutual suspicion and distrust, not across the narrow Mediterranean Sea, but wherever their respective spheres of influence touch, from Austria to the Aleutians. The rivalry of these two Great Powers is not like the quasi-feudal antagonisms of the little Nation-States of nineteenth century Europe, jockeying to see which could capture a province or acquire a colony at the expense of another. Now the play is for control over what remains of the Victorian empires. Military occupation, economic coercion, and political loans have replaced the more suave diplomacy of the past. By our own insistence the doctrine of neutrality is ruled out so that, as in the Mediterranean world of the third century B.C., every important principality must again take sides in order to prove itself "peace-loving"! And now there is more than physical power at stake. For each of the two colossi is an embodiment of a political philosophy fundamentally antagonistic to that of its opponent. As Lenin envisaged the struggle:

> . . . either the Soviet Government triumphs in every advanced country in the world, or the most reactionary imperialism triumphs, the most savage imperialism which is out to throttle the small and feeble nationalities and to reinstate reaction all over the world. This is the Anglo-American imperialism which has perfectly mastered the art of using for its purposes the form of a democratic republic. One or the other. There is no middle course.[22]

And in his conclusion, Lenin was correct. On the one hand there is the assertion, in the Declaration of Independence, that

[22] *Selected Works,* Vol. XXIII, p. 292.

"all men . . . are endowed by their Creator with certain unalienable Rights." On the other hand there is Lenin's statement that "we do not believe in God" and therefore "we repudiate all such [religious] morality that is taken outside of human class concepts." [23] Between these diametrically opposite viewpoints there actually *is* no middle course. No man can have a half-belief in God and a half-belief in a system that denies God. In the showdown every man must either accept or reject "the first and great commandment," reported in two of the gospels in almost identical language:

> Thou shalt love the Lord thy God with all thy heart, and with all thy soul, and with all thy strength, and with all thy mind; and thy neighbor as thyself.[24]

Since liberty is an important political idea, this study, concerned with liberty, has throughout endeavored to separate the emotional and the intellectual content in all words dealing, directly or indirectly, with all political ideas. In that spirit we may tolerantly consider Lenin's assertion that an underlying American purpose is "to reinstate reaction all over the world." Perhaps there is nothing more "reactionary"—in the accurate sense of the word—than a firm belief in God. All men who believe in principles are reactionary, in the sense that they react with conviction in behalf of certain standards of conduct. And a people whose system of government is based on old-established ethical principles, embodied in binding constitutional form nearly two centuries ago, may properly be called a "reactionary" people. The fact that loose usage has given the word a disagreeable emotional content will not worry any thoughtful man. The research chemist does not recoil from an unpleasant odor; and the political scientist soon develops a similar immunity to attempts to influence his thinking by the offensive use of words.

But because we may assume superiority to the verbal chicanery of Communism, it does not follow, in the developing struggle between the United States and Russia, that all the enlightenment

[23] *Ibid.*, Vol. XVII, pp. 321-22.
[24] Luke 10:27; Matthew 22:37.

is on our side and all the obfuscation on the side of our opponents. The ideological cleavage is not so simple.

No American of this era can take credit to himself because three centuries ago men who were wise and brave decided that power of every kind should be distributed. No Russian under the Soviet yoke is discredited because his forebears could not prevent the concentration of power that has come to be characteristic of that country. The credit will go to the Russians if they can break their tyranny. The discredit will be for Americans if they lose their liberty.

We may profitably remember that the Constitution of the United States legalized human slavery for its first three-quarters of a century, and even authorized continued importation of slaves during the first two decades of the Republic. Moreover, there are many Americans who attest their willingness to accept political dictatorship, if the State will only furnish them with periodic handouts and otherwise show continuous benevolence in the ordering of their lives. There was more than a grain of truth in a sardonic observation made shortly before this country entered the last war: "Frequently, in the United States, it is not totalitarianism but Russian or German—in general, 'foreign',—totalitarianism that is being objected to; a 100 per cent American totalitarianism would not be objectionable." [25]

On the other hand, there is no denying that Russia under Communist rule has made substantial material progress in many lines. This advance was particularly pronounced after the dictatorship passed to the control of Stalin, described by a sympathetic English historian as possessing "a shrewd and eminently practical common sense which, with experience, mounted more and more to high statesmanship." [26] Again, offsetting American advocates of totalitarianism, there are undoubtedly many Russians who would revolt against that system in their own country if there were the slightest prospect of success for such a rising. Even highplaced members of the Communist bureaucracy are constantly

[25] James Burnham, *The Managerial Revolution*, p. 153.
[26] Pares, *op. cit.*, p. 499. A careful analysis of production in the U.S.S.R. is found in Baykov, *op. cit.*

proving this, often at the cost of life, by breaking with or fleeing from the Soviet tyranny. By contrast we see a substantial number of native-born American Communists more or less openly renouncing the Stars and Stripes in favor of the Hammer and Sickle.

The love of liberty, it may be said again, is not a characteristic of nationality, or race, or sex. It is an individual birthright, which many a free American would nevertheless sell for a mess of pottage, as under NRA. It is also an inbred spiritual craving, which many an oppressed Russian would give his life to satisfy, as at Stalingrad.

VIII

The necessarily continuous struggle to "secure the Blessings of Liberty" is fundamentally a domestic rather than an international problem. Yet every aspect of the internal problem is now rendered more acute by the rivalry of a potent counterrevolution against the liberal tradition. Because the dynamics of this counterrevolution are directed from Moscow, a constant political and governmental tension between the Soviet Union and the United States is henceforth to be anticipated. The ostensible dissolution of the Comintern in 1943 has in no way vitiated the international aspirations of Communism; and the abandonment of isolationism by the United States has greatly strengthened the imperialistic trend that has been increasingly apparent in our history during the past half-century.

The issues between the two super-States are political only in the larger, philosophical sense of the word. Neither Russia nor this country covets any territory or any material possession of the other in its quality as a State. But each seeks to win the mind and soul of its adversary. The hostility is ideological, not national. It was foreshadowed by the challenge to authoritarian government proclaimed in Philadelphia on July 4, 1776. And the latent issue was joined when the last war destroyed the Nation-States that until then had served as a barrier to the spread of communist ideas.

It is therefore wise to abandon the fond illusion that the better we understand Soviet Russia, the easier it will be to establish amicable relations between the two countries. Precisely the opposite is to be expected. As knowledge of Russia, past and present, becomes more widespread, there will be a more general realization that its people have never been able to free themselves from arbitrary concentration of authority. The coming of Communism has merely capped the climax of the dominant Russian tradition by denying that there is *any* authority superior to that which men can impose on other men. Under Communism, as practiced in Russia, it is not possible to render unto God the things that are God's, for the simple reason that Caesar has usurped all that once was dedicated to God. As the full implications of this are examined, admiration for Russian techniques is scarcely likely to gain ground in American minds. Increasing antagonism is much more probable.

But, as appreciation of the fundamental nature of the cleavage broadens, it may well have the happy effect of causing Americans to take stock of the intangible values that are their own heritage, and to move these from storage into more active commerce. Inherited ideas deteriorate, if they are regarded merely as an inheritance. The weakness of a written Constitution is that the thought behind it becomes dim, unless perennially revived. As the generations succeed each other the organic law may easily come to command more outward reverence than inner conviction. As John Stuart Mill said of any received opinion, "unless it is suffered to be, and actually is, vigorously and earnestly contested, it will, by most of those who receive it, be held in the manner of a prejudice, with little comprehension or feeling of its rational grounds." [27] The worth and validity of American political principles are now being aggressively challenged by the philosophy of governmental planning. As a result, the American faith in self-government has become less perfunctory; more vital. For this unintentional service, we should be grateful to the Kremlin.

[27] *On Liberty*, Ch. 2.

IX

It is proper to emphasize again that the Soviet system of dictatorship is theoretically transitional to what Karl Marx called "a higher phase of Communist Society . . . [when] it will be possible to pass completely beyond the narrow horizon of bourgeois rights, and for Society to inscribe on its banners: from each according to his ability; to each according to his needs!" [28] But it is equally desirable to emphasize that if this semimystical vision is ever realized, it will involve not only the liquidation of the State as we know it, but also the liquidation of all the democratic social institutions that our form of State was designed to safeguard. Once more in Lenin's words:

> It is consistently forgotten that the destruction of the State means also the destruction of democracy; that the withering away of the State also means the withering away of democracy.[29]

By no cross section of humanity, anywhere, is this aphorism more "consistently forgotten"—or ignored—than by Americans who believe that Communism is compatible with democracy as limited, and therefore safeguarded, in the United States. Since all the classic literature of Communism is filled with denunciations of democratic theory, and since there is little evidence in Russian history, before or since 1917, of any substantial faith in the underlying principles of democracy, this widespread misconception is disturbing.

The most plausible explanation would seem to be a feeling that since Communist Russia fought Nazi Germany, and since the latter was undoubtedly a dictatorship, therefore it must follow that there are strong democratic leanings in Russia. Perhaps this rationalization was necessary, because of the fact—too distasteful for honest admission—that American men and money were used to strengthen a system dedicated to the destruction of this Republic. But to alleviate that distasteful situation by pretense that Communism is democratic, when every major communist author-

[28] Quoted by Lenin, *The State and Revolution*, p. 79.
[29] *Ibid.*, p. 68.

ity is on record in opposition to this "bourgeois" principle, has been a pathetic intellectual performance.

Actually—and it is one of the characteristics that make Russia so formidable—its present governing system is fundamentally aristocratic, in that word's literal meaning of the "best rule." There is no question that the Communist Party in Russia is intended to be an intellectual elite. Indeed, it was the partial fulfillment of this aim that made the communist performance so superior to that of the Nazi Party, where loyalty to a neurotic mystic rather than to an intelligible philosophy was made the criterion of membership. And there seems little doubt that, by rigorous mental conditioning, frequent purges, and "Stakhanovite" rewards, the level of Slavic efficiency has been perceptibly advanced.[30]

The idea that the bureaucracy in the service of the State should be a technical and managerial elite is, of course, not of Russian origin. This "Cameralist" theory was brought to a high state of perfection by Bismarck's Germany and can be traced back in Prussia at least to the absolutist rule of Frederick William. At the close of the Thirty Years' War, this "Great Elector" found conditions as favorable to the substitution of State for private enterprise as is the case in the same territory three centuries later. It was from the experience of the very competent Prussian Civil Service, supported by the philosophic arguments of Hegel and Marx, that Communist Russia developed the idea of completely comprehensive State planning and State management. To the historian it will, therefore, seem wholly logical if Russia incorporates into its own bureaucracy a formidable leaven of the efficient German managerial class, left with no alternative livelihood in a country even more ravaged and broken than it was at the time of the Treaty of Westphalia.

The political significance of "The Managerial Revolution" has been examined in the important book of that title, written by a philosopher of inquiring mind who believes that "people, for the

[30] This controversial question is given careful and objective examination in Baykov, *op. cit.*, especially Chs. XIII and XVIII.

most part, do not want to know what is going to happen," but who nevertheless in 1940 decided to attempt some prediction. It is still appropriate to consider the validity of one of his observations, made during the period of the Nazi-Soviet pact:

> The Russian boundaries advance towards the West. At the same time, economic and social relations with Germany increase. German technicians, managers, move into the Russian industrial enterprises . . . This infiltration of German managers is a larger step in the road toward fusion of European Russia with the European center. We may be sure that the completion of the fusion, under whatever nominal auspices it comes, will find Russia subordinated to the European center, not, as the spinners of Bolshevik nightmares tell us, the other way round.[31]

For those whose primary objective is the defense of American political theory, it makes singularly little difference how a fusion of Russian manpower and German technical skills develops, if we are forced to conclude that this merger is probable. The important issue today is whether the union that Hitler failed to achieve by force is going to be accomplished by Stalin in a more subtle manner. German and Russian political thought are at least as similar as English and American. The Western school has been more profoundly influenced by Christianity and therefore has always been inclined to emphasize liberty. The Eastern school, now under the tutelage of Communism, is profoundly authoritarian. The Republic will have to prove, by means more impressive than its leadership in atomic weapons, that it has the better way. It is far easier today to denounce Communism than it is to be contemptuous of its strong foundation of deeply intelligent thought. And we may be sure that the American way of life will not and cannot be preserved if we place sole reliance on such superficial means of defense as those for which the military takes responsibility. Indeed these weapons are very apt to backfire.

Is the contemporary American indifference to political theory a reflection on the importance of that subject, or on the quality of our

[31] Burnham, *op. cit.*, pp. 225-6.

current thinking? It is not easy to follow through on a train of political thought. But it certainly should not be difficult to realize that man's social behavior is determined by his conception, confused or clear, of the functions of Society. This, in turn, is decided by the rules for Society which the State, as the repository of physical power, lays down.

Chapter 10

To Maintain the Republic

When there is an unresolved problem around the house, in the factory, or in the community, the natural American impulse is to "do something about it." This pioneer instinct of a practical and energetic people continues, in spite of frustrations. Because the roots of self-help run deep in American soil, there is reason to believe that this characteristic can be reanimated.

But a figure of speech drawn from our agricultural background is misleading. In the vegetable realm the recovery of vitality is seemingly automatic. When spring returns, year after year the sap runs strong. Seeds germinate; the tender green emerges; buds form; and in due course the cycle of the seasons brings first the flowering and then the harvest.

There is no such procession in the field of political life. There is growth and decay, but they are not seasonal. If there is any immutable law that determines when and how a civilization shall fall, where and under what circumstances another shall emerge, the operation of this control is as yet beyond detection and, so far as our current knowledge goes, is not predetermined.

When the last page of the last history has been turned; when all the instances of stupidity have been examined and all the acts of folly have been tabulated, the record of human achievement is still so heroic as to be almost incredible. In their own image, men make their communities and mold the political pattern of their lives. The will cannot always remove obstructions. But if the will weakens, then there is no way through.

Admittedly, circumstance does much to determine whether a particular Society shall move forward, toward the Celestial Country, or remain behind in the City of Destruction, "for want of a change in mind and will." John Bunyan personified the moral factors in his immortal allegory of *The Pilgrim's Progress*. Arnold Toynbee extended this classification to make a comprehensive examination of handicaps and stimuli in his consideration of "Challenge-and-Response." [1]

There are obstacles, internal and external, so tremendous that the individual scarcely seems culpable when, like Pliable, he turns back apprehensively from the Slough of Despond. Nevertheless, there are others, like Christian, who persevere. The countless instances of weakness are offset by the many illustrations of strength. A wealth of evidence indicates that human failure is as often the result of an inadequate as of an overpowering challenge. Adversity itself is an incentive.

At no place and in no time has the response to challenge been more pronounced and more persistent than on the American Continent since the sixteenth century, between the latitudes that now bound the United States. Undoubtedly response is partly due to climatic conditions that encourage a maximum employment of human energy. It is partly due to a long heritage of voluntary co-operation, habitual in this land ever since the first colonists formed self-governing societies for their pilgrimage to a New World. Finally, Americans have responded successfully to challenge because their institutions were designed to facilitate that achievement.

Our study has attempted to analyze the deeper political reasons for American accomplishment. And consideration of the various causes has served to emphasize the significance of the result. So far, maximum challenge has always brought adequate response from the people in whom the power of this Republic rests.

There is no really convincing reason for discouragement over the confusion that has followed the disaster of the two World

[1] *A Study of History*, Vol. II.

Wars. Rather, it should be stimulating to a United States which has gone soft in many ways. But victory in the struggle ahead will not be automatic. It will be a problem of brains as well as brawn. It will be a matter of reanimating the ideals of the Republic, rather than of denouncing those that oppose it. And such a renaissance requires an individual rebirth; a continuous effort of self-improvement which no bureaucracy can ever direct or enforce, because it is a matter of personal self-government.

The spiritual strength of the Republic will not be automatically or mechanically renewed. Spring will return to this land of liberty, not with the vernal equinox, but only with the vitality of restored ideals.

II

It was a penetrating mind that first described the early stages of Russian-American antagonism as a "cold war." For the doctrines of Communism have the chill of ruthlessness, and those of laissez-faire capitalism are devoid of the warmth of human kindness. Yet it would be disastrous to view this rivalry as nothing more than a conflict of materialistic philosophies. We know that the true Russia is bigger than Karl Marx, and we know also that the American Republic is not immured by Wall Street. The ideals and traditions of the Republic are not primarily economic. The means which it employs are capitalistic. But the means are not the end. Good will counts heavily in the American balance sheet.

The United States is not unique in world history merely because of its unparalleled material prosperity, still less because of its modest cultural accomplishment. What makes the Republic distinctive is the confidence that it places in Man's ability to plan for himself; its deep-rooted mistrust of governmental planning.

Of course there is nothing distinctively American in the belief "that men may rise on steppingstones of their dead selves to higher things." This was the moving principle of Athenian thought; this is the deathless element in the appeal of Christianity. The virtue of the Republic is not that it originated the idea of self-improvement, but that it embodies a political system directed to that end.

The individual's ambition to advance himself, by personal effort, is the most obvious and deep-rooted of American characteristics. This restless aspiration is certainly closely associated with the pure spirit of liberty. Indeed, we have suggested that this spiritual restlessness *is* liberty, from which all our material blessings flow. To trammel that spirit, arbitrarily, is to strike at something fundamental and basic to the American identity.

Hostility to regimentation is written into the Constitution. But these formal limitations on arbitrary government are the result and not the cause of an attitude that is expressed in our social as well as our political institutions. Except for slaves, during the period when the practice of slavery was accepted, the satirical exhortation of Charles Dickens, in *The Chimes*, had no cogency, and therefore no sting, for Americans:

> O let us love our occupations,
> Bless the squire and his relations,
> Live upon our daily rations
> And always know our proper stations.

It is not proper, but actually gross impropriety by American standards, to recognize any "station" as more than a temporary halting place. The strength of the country—its energy, its vitality, its dauntless will to accomplish—is simply a manifestation of this dynamic attitude. But restlessness can also be a source of weakness. And the less the imposition of status, the greater the dependence of the individual on guiding principles of some kind. Without this concentration his life has no focus, is literally dissipated, and becomes a mere kaleidoscope of essentially purposeless activity.

Many criticisms of American customs and practices may be disregarded as inconsequential. The boisterous, untidy, aggressive equalitarianism of the country is not indicative of a lack of culture, but represents the formative stage of a new culture in which even crude self-assertion is deemed preferable to artificial status. In the republican scale of values the dignity of Lincoln was not lessened by uncouth manners, and the shallowness of Beau Brummel was not concealed by the meticulous adjustment of a cravat. Always the test of worth in America has been a matter of objective, and cultivation of appearance has never served to compensate for absence of aspiration. But there is little or no respect for the man whose objective is revealed as one of mere self-aggrandizement. For such aggrandizement is at the expense of others, and therefore antisocial—by contrast with that self-development which enlarges personality in recognizing and expanding the interest of others.

The American experiment boldly leaves most of this important field of human behavior to individual discretion. The State in this country traditionally demands only a certain rudimentary schooling and the observance of a few traffic lights. Relatively little is *verboten*. Therefore, American society has always been the more insistent on conventional conduct, because Society knows that controls are necessary but is antagonistic to their application by the State. Supervision of the individual by Society, however, has long since ceased to be dictatorial, with the result that the individual in America is at liberty to develop his own philosophy of life in a manner that seems reckless to those reared in the tradition of status. If we were more aware of the unusual nature of this form of civilization, we would also be more aware of what it entails in the matter of personal contribution.

Clearly this Republic demands of its citizens something more than, and quite other than, industrial and commercial enterprise. Indeed, if we are concerned with "free enterprise" in only the narrow sense of the term, then much that is vital to the Republic is dead already. Self-aggrandizement is not at all the same thing as self-development. The most damaging charge that has been leveled at the capitalist system does not come from the communist camp. It is the essentially Christian indictment of the materialistic concept of free enterprise. "For where your treasure is, there will your heart be also." [2] We cannot minimize the validity of the accusation that industry "has come to hold a position of exclusive predominance among human interests, which no single

[2] Matthew 6:21.

interest, and least of all the provision of the material means of existence, is fit to occupy." [3]

III

That searching criticism, by a thoughtful English Socialist, is not easily dismissed. It helps to explain why the British Labour Party achieved political power. The appeal of Socialism, especially to the young, is not in its own virtue so much as in the deficiency of capitalism in spiritual qualities. The demonstrable advantages of the free market are not fully persuasive to those who are repelled by materialism. And the finer the intelligence, the more strongly it will revolt against attempted "conditioning" by techniques of high-pressure commercial advertising.

Even if they were less pronounced, the defects of an acquisitive Society should be frankly considered and confronted. For these defects serve to divert the attention of honest idealists from the far greater danger to the individual that lurks behind the architectural drawing of a benevolent Welfare State. Reliance upon the fancied panacea of State planning makes socialistic doctrine worse than futile. It also inclines the individual Socialist to be the unwitting, and often unwilling, tool of the more subtle techniques of Communism. There would have been less of this unintentional preparatory work for Communism, if the Pharisees of capitalism had not been so narrowly self-righteous.

Under our republican form of government the blessings of liberty have on the whole been widely distributed and deeply appreciated. In consequence, socialistic doctrine made relatively little headway in American thinking, even while it was capturing that of Western Europe. Much of the credit for this must go to the conscientious leaders of American business who, despite all efforts to discredit them as a class, have in the main been primarily interested in placing their creative and administrative talents at the service of Society. Through the exercise of these talents huge fortunes have certainly been amassed, and often not too scrupulously. But, just as notably, these same fortunes have been chan-

[3] R. H. Tawney, *The Acquisitive Society* (English Edition), p. 241.

neled into educational, cultural, and philanthropic undertakings, to an extent for which there is no parallel in any other country.

The European experience, primarily because of the feudal background, has been different. Under primogeniture it was not even possible to "alienate" an estate in order to endow a college or charitable institution. So one must conclude that the socialistic evolution was all but inevitable in Europe. There, the State arose as an instrument in which power *had* to be strongly centralized in order to crush the pretensions of privileged Estates.

The centralization of government as supreme overlord was to be expected when the nobility formed one Estate, the clergy a second, and when "the people" as a whole were lumped together in a *Tiers État*. This arbitrary and indeed indefensible arrangement was fertile soil for Rousseau's conception of an omnipotent democratic State, based upon "natural right" and presumably responsive to something glibly called the "general will."

Socialism was the political doctrine to be expected from the condition in which a "lower class," frankly labeled as such, was immutably subordinated to established privilege. "What is the Third Estate?" asked the famous pamphlet of the Abbé Sieyès, as the clouds of the French Revolution gathered in all their ominous density. Sieyès answered his own question with the extremism which extremism itself always so tragically induces. The Third Estate, he said, is "Everything!" Then: "What has it been until now in the political order?" Sieyès' own answer: "Nothing!" Finally: "What does the Third Estate demand?" "To be Something!"

Karl Marx merely elaborated the third answer of the Abbé Sieyès, and logically. If the Third Estate—or "Proletariat," as Marx preferred to say—*is* "Everything," then it may and properly should demand to *be* everything: "Dictatorship of the Proletariat."

The tragedy of Europe is illuminated by Sieyès' oversimplified rhetoric, as developed with less political caution and more intellectual courage by Marx. This revolutionary assumption, with regard to the Third Estate, suggests why unlimited power was given to representative assemblies; why democratic States then

became socialistic States; why socialistic States finally fell easy
victims to the new concept of a supranational Communist dictatorship. Napoleon and Hitler and Stalin are not just curious or
vicious historical accidents. They are the natural products of a
definite sequence of political thinking. We shall have such products in this country, also, unless our political theory is maintained
on the wholly different plane to which the founders of the Republic directed it. Even so, the American Republic will not endure, unless its citizens fight consistently against that monopolization of power implied by the assumption that a single Estate—
Nobility or Clergy; Business or Labor—is "Everything."

Fortunately that vicious premise has always not merely seemed
false, but, until recently, has also been alien to the great body of
American thought. Here there has never been a first or second
Estate, so that for Americans there is no reality to the argument
that a nonexistent Third Estate is "everything." Certainly there
was slavery under the Republic, long after that institution ceased
to exist in Western Europe. But very few Abolitionists ever
argued that those in servitude were properly "everything" in the
political order, and therefore should be placed in supreme power
when emancipated. Indeed, the essential decency of the country
recoiled in horror when, during what Claude G. Bowers called
The Tragic Era, the former slaves were temporarily awarded
legislative power in the southern states. Republican leaders themselves were appalled by the coincident Negro proclamation that
"Jesus Christ was a Republican." [4]

This miserable postscript to the Civil War actually emphasized
the validity of the Republic's fundamental canon—that emancipation by act of government always fails, unless balanced by individual emancipation from folly and excess. Europe has had
similar horrifying saturnalia. It is the only word to describe the
degeneracy into which the French Revolution slipped. But the
history and tradition of Europe are such that men have continued
to be more disposed to rely on arbitrary status, and less disposed
to emphasize personal responsibility, as a solvent of their difficulties.

[4] Bowers, *op. cit.*, p. 361.

The greatest danger to the Republic lies in the increasing tendency to abandon the American in favor of the European political philosophy. The fundamental lesson of revolutions needs to be learned again. It is that a concentration of political power which aims to liberate men from oppression almost invariably ends in oppression as great or greater than that which is removed. Our own Revolution, for reasons which have been set forth, is the exception that proves this rule.

IV

The chain of events that tends to produce dictatorships can be generalized, starting at any place, in any period, when circumstances have placed people in a condition where they have "nothing to lose but their chains."

Then a demand for governmental reform arises, stimulated by eloquent men who emphasize abuses and promise improvement— if they are placed "in power." By that phrase is meant unfettered control of the machinery of the State, as the repository of physical force.

With bows and arrows, or with ballots, or bullets—the difference in procedure is important but does not necessarily make any difference in the outcome—the existing, intolerable government is overturned, and the reformers are installed. To carry out their promises these new rulers must then proceed to enlarge the powers of government. And what they give to the favored will, for the most part, be taken from the disfavored. The acquisition of political power facilitates a redistribution of accumulated wealth. It does nothing—of itself—to create new wealth.

But deprivation of the privileged in behalf of the underprivileged is almost certain to be a disillusioning process for the latter. Some of the redistributed wealth evaporates; some of it sticks to the fingers of those who arrange the transfer; some of it is necessarily taken by the essentially unproductive machinery of redistribution—by the military, taxgatherers, administrators and the like. So only a fraction of the generous assurances made before the change of government will actually be fulfilled.

In consequence, there is disillusionment among those who have gained little or nothing, promoted actively or surreptitiously by those who have lost a great deal. And after a time the revolutionary government will itself be turned out, unless it is disposed to suppress the opposition by naked force. If willing to do this, the government is already a dictatorship, without authority in the correct sense of the word. And if the revolutionary government has achieved power by force, or trickery, its leaders will be strongly disposed to use the same devices to retain their grip on power. Therefore, the *method* of change—whether by *coup d'état* or free election—becomes a matter of fundamental importance.

The unchanging character of this cycle has long been recognized by political philosophers, and the effort to make its operation less negative has followed three different lines, leaving the Anarchists out, not because their political thought is unimportant but because it mistakenly denies any validity to the State as an institution.

In generalities, there is first the conservative attitude. This reasons that conditions are not really as bad as pictured by "agitators," and that abuses in the existing order are at least preferable to the risks of revolutionary overturn. Such an attitude is naturally pronounced among older people and among those whose personal situation is more comfortable than that of the majority of mankind. Those who are naturally lethargic are also habitually conservative, regardless of personal circumstance. Moreover, extreme conservatives are even disposed against peaceful change through the agency of elections, because they doubt the wisdom of a choice determined by counting noses.

In the second place, there is the political reformer, who reasons that the risks of revolution are outweighed in balance by evident evil in the conditions of the period. The reformer is admirably impatient with injustice, but is usually disposed to believe that improvement can be imposed by governmental fiat. Thus, the political reformer is more likely to be a Socialist, placing great confidence in the coercive power of the State, than a Radical who really seeks the root of social ailments. To the reformer, cure is generally more important than diagnosis, and reflection does not seem to be a prerequisite for action. Therefore, the more extreme reformers, for reasons quite other than those which impel the Conservative, also tend to mistrust elections, which seem a slow and uncertain method of correcting evils.

The third general category is that to which the title of Liberal properly applies. It is a middle of the road position, and, as we have pointed out, one in which the emotional factor is subordinated; therefore a position that is not easy for men to maintain. The instinct of the Liberal is neither to defend the *status quo*, nor to assume that change is necessarily progress. He seeks to solve the present problem in the light of principles that he knows to be eternal, and according to methods that he believes will be practical. Having faith in mankind, the Liberal logically favors the representative form of government. The method of election, by universal adult suffrage, on balance seems to him the most practical way of attaining and maintaining representative government.

Confronted with the political cycle outlined above, the Conservative, the Reformer and the Liberal all three exhibit characteristic reactions. The Conservative opposes governmental change; the Reformer welcomes it; the Liberal favors such change as seems to him necessary to advance the establishment of some tested moral principle.

This means that while the Liberal is more slow than the Reformer to indorse change, he is more sure than the Reformer to make it effective. And it means that while the Liberal may be as opposed to a particular change as the Conservative, he is less likely than the Conservative to regard political alteration as inherently undesirable. When a revolution succeeds, the Conservative is likely to become a Reformer—a counterrevolutionist. And the Reformer is then likely to become a Conservative, defending the new system regardless of its shortcomings.

But the Liberal remains a Liberal. He continues to be as critical of the new government as of the one that has been ousted. He knows that the fundamental difficulty does not focus in opinions, whether of the Right or of the Left. The Liberal knows that the

one enduring political folly is to concentrate in the hands of ambitious men power that they do not have the restraint to exercise
wisely. He knows what Saint Augustine recalled at a time not
unlike the present—when Rome had been sacked by Alaric and
his Goths—that the greatest glory of any civilization is to accomplish what concentration of power must always render difficult:
"To spare the lowly and strike down the proud." [5]

V

So, in the political cycle, the Liberal has focused his attention
on the problem of how change can most satisfactorily be made
innocuous. It is not a matter of opposing change because "things
are not so bad." It is not a matter of welcoming a turnover because "it's time for a change." The problem is how to determine,
first that there is an intellectually impressive case in behalf of
any proposed political change, and *second* that the judgment of
citizens can be honestly exercised in deciding the issue.

It is the remarkable skill with which this problem has been resolved in the United States that makes the Republic so worthy of
appreciation. Of course, the constitutional guaranties of freedom
of speech and press have not insured that spoken opinion shall be
temperate, or that written opinion shall be well informed. But
they *have* insured freedom of expression to opinions of every
kind, and only out of that clash can men hope for anything ap-
proximating truth. The Republic bravely assumes that individuals can, on the whole, discriminate between sense and nonsense;
that all of the people cannot be fooled all of the time.

If this assumption is granted, then the device of free elections,
conducted at regular terms, in a manner that takes account of
varying local circumstance, is as effective as any method that can
be designed for the choice of representative lawmakers. Again
the axiom is that the individual desires to discriminate intelligently. Election procedure in the United States certainly does not
insure that legislators shall be enlightened, any more than freedom of speech insures that public utterances will be illuminating.

[5] *Parcere subjectis et debellare superbos.* Virgil, *Aeneid:* Bk. VI, l. 853.

But no system of government can improve the quality of the individuals whom it governs. This they must do for themselves, with the aid of an Authority which is higher than that of the State. Political government can make it possible for men to secure the blessings of liberty. But self-improvement is, and must always continue to be, an individual matter.

Free speech and free elections are great achievements of the liberal mind—achievements that have always been bitterly opposed, that have been partially won for mankind through centuries of trial and error, at the cost of patient, resolute uphill struggle. But, of themselves, they are not enough. There must be other, positive, restraints upon the power of the State. For if these are lacking, it will be found that men unwittingly surrender their hard-won gains. And even when the power of the State is restrained, and held in check by an independent and wise judiciary, it is still continuously essential that men learn to restrain themselves. We "rest all our political experiments on the capacity of mankind for self-government."

The Liberal is one who recognizes that self-restraint is more desirable than imposed coercion. And the Republic is unique in history because its form of government is based upon and embodies that belief. Among Americans, past and present, the proportion of those who can properly claim to think and act as liberals is probably no greater than could be found elsewhere. The human seed, as scattered by nature, seems fairly uniform. And there is no single line of human thought or endeavor in which an honest and well-informed American is likely to claim that his countrymen have shown themselves biologically exceptional.

But the American soil was more clement toward liberalism than that of any other country. And that soil was first cultivated at a time and under conditions particularly favorable for the growth of liberal doctrine. To emphasize that point this study has explored beyond the American frontier, as it exists politically and historically. And as one reflects upon the role of this Republic in history, one must humbly conclude that within it lie some of the attributes of Saint Augustine's City of God. For all its worldliness there is in the United States something not of this world. Remove that element, and the experiment of the Republic loses the attributes that have really made it great.

Others have sensed this—more readily than many Americans. Sir Henry Maine, as one example, was not the type of man to praise lightly or lavishly. He could refer bitingly to "the nauseous grandiloquence of the American panegyrical historians." But he could also discern, in the same essay, that: "The Constitution of the United States of America is much the most important political instrument of modern times." And, writing in 1885, Maine could conclude that the success of American political institutions has "arisen rather from skillfully applying the curb to popular impulses than from giving them the rein. While the British Constitution has been insensibly transforming itself into a popular government surrounded on all sides by difficulties, the American Federal Constitution has proved that, nearly a century ago, several expedients were discovered by which some of these difficulties may be greatly mitigated and some altogether overcome." [6]

The real reason for the success of those "expedients" is that they were not merely expedients. They were an application of essentially Christian principles to the practical problems of Man in Society.

VI

It was the triumph of the liberal mind, reaching its highest political attainment in the writing of the Constitution of the United States, to break the vicious circle that until then had always restored dictatorship in the train of revolution against dictatorship. This accomplishment, however, will not be sustained unless its full significance is more widely appreciated. Of late years deification of the State has destroyed liberalism in countries where it was always weak, and threatens its survival in the United States, where it is still strong. The threat is the more dangerous because it is advanced under the mask of a spurious "liberalism." Those who have no training in political theory succumb easily to this deception.

[6] *Popular Government*, Preface, pp. xi-xii.

Nothing that advances the power of the State over Society, thereby subjecting the individual to the State, can properly be called liberal. The "nationalization" of an industry could possibly be advocated sometimes on economic grounds, but never philosophically by those who believe in human liberty. Other factors aside, the mere increase in numbers on the governmental payroll itself endangers the continuation of representative government.

An ever expanding bureaucracy ties the personal interest of a great army of jobholders to the political fortunes of the group managing the State. This group is in turn encouraged by the size of its mercenary following to speak with increasing assurance in the name of "the people." The stage is then set for the entrance of the monolithic party which seeks to absorb the power in the people, identifying party welfare with general welfare. When that essentially dictatorial party has once seized power, in the modern State, it will not permit itself to be dislodged. On the contrary, this monstrous perversion of party government spreads like a cancerous growth through the whole fabric of Society. The social units—church, school, trade union, co-operative, employers' association, professional organization, athletic club, and eventually even the family itself—are "regimented" into the "totalitarian" State. Society in all its aspects is subordinated by the State, and the individual finds that his entire life is directed and confined by State controls.

But the State is an artificial creation. People lived before States were formed, and people go on living after States have been destroyed. For two centuries the people of Alsace could be shifted back and forth, from French to German sovereignty, with reasonable happiness under either political allegiance. That was because their natural dependence was on social institutions, which can prosper regardless of the pattern on the flag that waves over them. Only when rival States destroy each other, after first sucking the blood of social institutions in vampire fashion, is the individual left helpless amid a rubble of the homely attributes that made his life.

Then the poor creature, regardless of his language, his color, or the measurements of his skull, is easy prey for Communism. That supertotalitarian doctrine appeals to him, not because of his nationality but because of his humanity. It provides an attachment to which he can cling when the State, after it has destroyed Society, has itself "withered away." To those who have seen the fabric of their lives destroyed, their social institutions undermined, their State humiliated, the appeal of Communism is extremely potent. Its hypnotic effect will not be exorcised either by economic homilies, or by threats of atomic warfare. Only a greater and more vital religion can exorcise an avenging passion, which is the more resolute because it has been nourished on despair. And those who are without faith themselves need not expect to win converts by doling out dollars or mobilizing armies. Such measures may be useful to support a faith already vital. They can never rekindle a flame which has expired.

VII

The flame of the Republic has not expired. But it burns more dimly than it did. And now that two States which are more than States stand face to face across a prostrate world, the spirit that animates American civilization must be revived. This should be the easier because there is nothing occult about the American way. Its underlying theory is as simple as that of a gasoline engine. All that is necessary is to apply to matters political the same objective, unemotional, critical faculty that Americans utilize instinctively in matters mechanical.

Such application will soon convince us that much of our confusion stems from our failure to understand and guard against the dangerous degenerative tendencies inherent in democratic action. "There is no word," says Sir Henry Maine in his caustic essay on *The Nature of Democracy*, "about which a denser mist of vague language, and a larger heap of loose metaphors, has collected." The force of that observation is certainly not lessened by the skillful manner in which the Communists have exploited the American tendency to speak of "democracy" as though it were simultaneously an objective, a procedure, and a panacea.

Because of the general misinterpretation of this word symbol, it cannot be too strongly emphasized that "democracy"—reduced to political compass—is merely a form of government that enlists the participation of many people as opposed to a few. Therefore, the more democratic the system of government, the more insistently it must stipulate that political decisions shall be made by a majority, in which the most careless and uniformed opinion has equal weight with that which is thoughtful and closely reasoned.

Unless its natural tendencies are very carefully restrained, a system of this nature is inevitably suicidal. Unless the philosophic importance of "states' rights" are recognized, emphasis on popular government is certain to enlarge the functions of centralized government. And deference to majority opinion is equally certain to make aspirants for political office promise more than they are able to perform. Thus hypocrisy becomes a characteristic of democratic government, while a steady proliferation of governmental agencies is its functional consequence.

This means that the direction of the State becomes simultaneously less forthright and more powerful. As the centralized State gains in power, the management of its affairs becomes more attractive to ambitious men, who become more unscrupulous not merely because of their ambition, but also because it is almost impossible to placate a majority without being unscrupulous. Thus the disinclination to abandon office, when once secured, becomes stronger. And the most practical way to remain in office is to identify one's party with the public welfare. This, of course, involves governmental "publicity."

At the outset, governmental publicity is always justified on the grounds of "informing" the taxpayer on the manner in which his money is spent. It seems unnecessary for bureaucracy to emphasize that the tax rate must be again increased—a very little— merely to provide this information. Then it is discovered that the information itself can scarcely explain, unless it also defends, the doings in the bureaucratic labyrinth. Moreover, if there is unfriendly criticism from abroad, the government should properly have a "Voice"—not for itself, of course, but for the Nation, with which to answer back. So, almost imperceptibly, the day of the "Ministry of Enlightenment" is at hand.[7]

Governmental propaganda does not proceed far before it begins to propagandize for the party that controls the machinery of government. When that happens, tyranny is just around the corner. In the United States, prior to the New Deal, administrative officers really regarded themselves as such. They had nothing of a revolutionary character to put over, and throughout the country reformist sentiment was concentrating on specific abuses. Moreover, any drift toward governmental dictatorship was checked by the constitutional provisions restricting popular government in the United States. The Fifteenth, Seventeenth, and Nineteenth Amendments certainly weakened these restrictions, while the Sixteenth Amendment, giving Congress the power to tax incomes, paved the way for an enormous development of centralized authority. These changes, however, were of themselves insufficient to break down the federal structure, to which the Democratic Party continued to give at least nominal allegiance until its national convention of 1948.

In Europe, on the other hand, a definite theory and philosophy of governmental aggrandizement had been entrenched for centuries. Private enterprise had long been denounced as something inherently evil. That "public" ownership would somehow prove essentially more moral was blandly assumed. Even before the New Deal, doctrinaire European Socialism was making headway in the United States, especially in allegedly "intellectual" circles. And for the gains made by diluted Marxism, there were two major reasons. One was the general failure of the colleges and universities to give any adequate instruction in American governmental theory, as distinct from structure. The other reason was the connected American tendency to regard Western European political thinking as being somehow more "advanced" than that of the United States. To these causes must be attributed the conclusion that it was an American "duty" to ally this country

---

[7] For an important study of developing administrative propaganda in the United States, see "Reports of the Committee on Expenditures in the Executive Departments," 80th Congress, 2nd Session.

with Western Europe against Central Europe in the essentially feudal conflicts among the Nation-States of that Continent.

Because these feudal conflicts were also futile, in respect to the true objectives of this Republic, it became necessary to bamboozle the American people with emotional slogans calculated to baffle analytical thinking. The most absurd, and therefore the most damaging of all, was the one that declared it an American purpose "to make the world safe for democracy." Nobody, certainly not President Woodrow Wilson as its sponsor, has ever explained what this phrase means. But the damaging suggestion was that the American system of government is undesirable. For obviously the outstanding characteristic of our whole system of checks and balances is its intent to make the United States safe *from*— not for—democracy.

So the natural centralizing tendencies of political bossism came to be strengthened, in the Republic, by theoretical advocacy of the Welfare State, as it had developed in Europe. For the first time, in this country, a considerable stream of opinion began to run in the direction of governmental tyranny. The stream grew to a torrent with the suffering and confusion engendered by the depression that brought the New Deal to power. Even without another war, always a potent means for expanding centralized authority, the roots of the American tradition were being eroded. By 1936 this tendency had gone so far that President Roosevelt could attempt to subordinate the judiciary to the executive, and could simultaneously say to a member of the House Ways and Means Committee, in words that might well have been used by Charles I: "I hope your committee will not permit doubt as to Constitutionality, however reasonable, to block the suggested legislation." [8]

Apparently the long travail of the seventeenth and eighteenth centuries had been in vain. Apparently the American Revolution had failed, less swiftly but as surely, as the two earlier attempts in England. It seemed as though the Republic had merely served to elongate the vicious circle that restores dictatorship after a rev-

[8] Quoted by Garet Garrett, *The Revolution Was*, p. 23.

olution designed to overthrow dictatorship. It seemed as though Alexander Hamilton had spoken hollow rhetoric in saying: "It belongs to us to vindicate the honor of the human race."

VIII

Now, in a way that was certainly unexpected by the American people, the chance for recovery has come. And the seemingly irrelative manner of its coming must make men feel that the Republic really has that "protection of Divine Providence" on which the signers of the Declaration placed "firm reliance."

World War II had three great historical results, written so large that they became almost immediately obvious to all. In the first place, the civilization of Western Europe was so thoroughly blasted as to eliminate any lingering feeling of American cultural inferiority. It is impossible to be deferential, as contrasted with sympathetic, to one's dependents. In the second place, the United States became simultaneously conscious of its material strength and its spiritual weakness. The duality of the discovery was salutory. It was impossible for Americans to be arrogant about winning a war in which their representative government proved utterly incompetent to make its stated ideals effective. In the third place, the sharply contrasting success of the Communist leadership had a humiliating but helpfully invigorating effect on American thinking. To use a much abused word, it really became necessary to "evaluate" our political instruction. So, fundamental reconsideration of our educational practices, and of the philosophic thought that alone gives animation to education, was certain to result from the celerity with which the United States proceeded to lose almost all the long-range objectives for which its people had so gallantly fought.

Between these three results of World War II there is an important linkage. This connection must be seen if the postwar disillusion of the American people is to prove constructive, and if the lives and treasure that were so lavishly expended are not to be altogether wasted. There is a moral underlying the crash of Europe; the blundering of America; the expansion of Asiatic tyranny as directed from Moscow. And that moral emerges from the analysis of this book.

For historical reasons that have been outlined, the civilization of Europe has never—since the fall of Rome—been truly liberal. It has never subordinated political considerations to the spiritual development of Man as a creature endowed with an immortal soul. The civilization of Europe has focused on political status. And for over a thousand years the major European effort has been concentrated on making men conform to politically enforceable status—first under the Estate, then under the State, now under Communism.

Because of the feudal heritage, private enterprise of every sort has long been regarded in much of Europe with suspicion. The very name of "bourgeois" has always been flavored with contempt. The "middle class" was suspect alike by those to whom status assigned either more or less privilege. Sir Henry Maine discerned the absurdity of this long since, when he observed that: "The movement of the progressive societies has hitherto been a movement from Status to Contract." [9] The word "hitherto" was prescient. Maine was well aware that in Great Britain the progressive movement could easily become retrogressive—from contract back to status. And that has happened.

The law of free contract is, of course, the law of the free market. Both arose in response to the effort to reconcile liberty and authority. In the Republic, under liberal leadership, this reconciliation was made effective. Elsewhere, a starkly reactionary movement, away from contract and back to status, prevails. This means the loss of freedom; the triumph of force masquerading as authority.

Liberalism must give primary importance to productive enterprise, because without production the most humane theories of distribution are meaningless. But for centuries the European producer was satirized as something almost uncouth. An absentee landowner was paradoxically more "cultivated" than those who actually cultivated his soil; to take royalties from coal production

[9] *Ancient Law* (Pollock ed., 1930), p. 182.

was socially more distinguished than to extract this important mineral; to chase a fox, in the company of one's peers, was to reach a pinnacle of social attainment to which no "tradesman" could properly aspire. So Monsieur Jourdain could be ridiculed as *Le Bourgeois Gentilhomme,* and Old Jolyon Forsyte, "in whom a desperate honesty welled up at times," felt compelled to insist that his pig-raising forebears were "yeomen." And "he would repeat the word 'yeomen' as if it afforded him consolation." [10]

In consequence, European liberalism was never really sure of itself. It was always oppressed by status. First the Estates showed ill-concealed contempt toward all who were not born to the purple. When this became intolerable, the State was called in to control the Estate. But in the process the centralized State itself assumed the right to assign a subordinate role to everyone. In both cases status ruled, and the producer, the necessary prototype of liberalism, was subordinated to status.

Under such regimentation, whether feudal or socialistic, liberalism must languish. For the liberal must be sure of himself and must be free from status. The creed is not to be confused either with the condescension of an enlightened aristocracy or with the well-meaning tyranny of a bureaucracy run rampant. The man who accepts a title that is not functional cannot be a true Liberal, because in claiming nobility he tacitly asserts a fictitious superiority to his fellowman. And even the moderate Socialist must mistakenly assume that the State has a magical power to make men better than they are. Americans understand this instinctively. The idea of honoring a Lincoln by calling him "Sir Abraham" is repulsive. The idea of an economy stabilized by governmental control of wages is almost equally grotesque.

Status is unquestionably pleasant to a certain type of mind. Americans are by no means immune to its appeal. There were many who hated to relinquish status at the time of the Revolution. Many sought to retain it, through the institution of slavery and in other ways, under the Republic. Through monopoly power,

[10] John Galsworthy, *The Forsyte Saga,* Part I, Ch. I.

both organized Business and organized Labor have tried to re-create the privileged Estate. Many would now like to see a new form of status established in America, through a governing elite or managerial class of "planners." They are the most subtle fellow travelers of Communism.

The American tragedy lies in this continued flirtation with the seductive principle of status, which is merely a pleasant name for slavery. The Russian triumph centers in the skill and determination with which it has subordinated all the forms that status may take to the single centralized dictatorial status of a governing elite. This is seemingly democratic, because any man with ability can hope to become a member of that elite. It is intelligent, because it discerns the artificial nature of nationalism. It is powerful, because for all its social waste Communism can focus a physical strength greater than that of any single nation, excepting only our own. It is ruthless, because Communism has religious fanaticism without Christian moderation, and because its respect for the individual is limited to the service that he can give within the status assigned to him.

The rise to power of this philosophy has at last shaken many Americans out of their complacency and their pitiful concern with the purely material advantages of contract. The insidious undermining of liberalism is resulting in a re-examination of the principles on which liberalism must take its stand. The effort to destroy Christianity has stimulated reconsideration of the truths for which Christ stood. It is reasonable to expect that this maximum challenge will produce a maximum response.

IX

In his essay on "Self-Reliance" Emerson tells us that: "Travelling is a fool's paradise. We owe to our first journeys the discovery that place is nothing." Thus it is with the difficult journey which we now conclude. It has led us back to our original assertion. This Republic is distinctive in all history for one outstanding reason. Its government is based upon, and is designed to strengthen, a moral code of honorable individual conduct. In Emerson's words:

> It is only as a man puts off from himself all external support, and stands alone, that I see him to be strong and to prevail.

As with its people, so with the United States. To depend on others is a sign of weakness, not of strength. To demand security, from one's own or other governments, is to forfeit liberty. The strongest country in Europe is little Switzerland, which never formed a military alliance and never submitted to domestic tyranny. The empires around it rise and fall. The Swiss Republic, strong and clean as its snowcapped Alps, endures.

The United States has developed a civilization of its own, and no apologies are needed. This civilization owes much to Europe, but it is different from that of Europe. Owing something also to Asia and to Africa, the American way of life is nevertheless basically dissimilar from anything those continents have produced. In this country men have stood alone, unfettered by status, unhampered by the State, contracting with each other in an essentially free Society. So standing, men have grown strong, and have prevailed. They have prevailed because it is only when Man stands alone that he rises above himself, hears the still small voice of conscience, and hearkens to the Authority of his Creator. Then, paradoxically, he is no longer alone. "And yet I am not alone, because the Father is with me." [11]

The American civilization is neither mature nor fully stabilized. Its pains, therefore, are those of growth, not dissolution; of strength, not weakness. This civilization will continue to grow as long as it is based on the assumption that people are generally honorable and trustworthy, simply because of their humanity.

That is what most Americans mean when they loosely use the word "democracy." Of course, a faith in human goodness is not at all the same thing as democracy, which, as an abstraction, means the "rule of the people" and, as a political system, means the unrestricted majority rule that our Constitution so carefully forbids. But a belief that Man is honorable for himself is Christian

[11] John 16:32.

and liberal and inspiring. It is democratic to the extent that it opposes the privileges and restrictions of status. And for a civilization based on that belief there will be a bright future, so long as the people retain the power that is in them.

Because it has faith in the individual, American civilization is hostile to any seizure of power from the people, and is particularly hostile to the seizure of this power by centralized government. From the assumption that Man is honorable comes the conclusion that self-government is desirable. To assist self-government the American is expected willingly to accept the conventions and reasonable regulations of a free Society. But he is also expected to oppose resolutely all arbitrary government by the State. The power is in the people. They must retain it.

The average American is, at least vaguely, conscious of the importance of the tremendous Revolution, finally accomplished in this country, whereby men threw off the slavery of status. He believes that other peoples can similarly achieve freedom, if they so desire. But the most that any government can do is to set people "at liberty." The State can stabilize the condition of freedom, and that is its sole excuse for being.

Liberty is from God, and men must develop their liberty from within. It cannot be doled out by governmental agencies. To create a political dictatorship in America, on the specious pretense of liberating others from their particular dictatorships, would be to destroy the whole achievement of the American Revolution. And that is the way in which the Republic is most likely to be destroyed. That is what Washington meant when, in the Farewell Address, he asked: "Why quit our own to stand upon foreign ground?"

In the field of charity, of companionship, of trade and intellectual intercourse, no ground is foreign to Americans and no man is a foreigner. There has never been a people whose natural instincts are less "isolationist." Mixed blood and mingled origins dispose Americans to think well of men as men. They are happily not disposed to think well of governments as governments. The fundamental American faith responds to association of men—

everywhere. It has no confidence in associations of governments —anywhere.

For essentially the same reason, Americans mistrust empire. Common sense tells us that the Republic was never designed to run an empire. Imperialism requires centralization of power, and all the political institutions of our federal union were carefully planned to make that centralization difficult. To become an empire, the United States must cease to be a Republic. Of course, this could happen here, as it happened in Rome. But it is hard to detect any popular enthusiasm for the imperial role. Sent overseas, the chief desire of the average American boy is to do the assigned job as quickly as possible and then "come home."

One may believe that this homing instinct will continue, as long as home is significant to Americans. And if it ceases to be significant, we are lost. For after all, the homely things are those in which the American people take most pride; of which they have most to offer. It is not accidental that the outstanding esthetic contribution of the Republic has been in the field of domestic architecture. Probably there is no American ambition that runs deeper and is more pervasive than that of "making a home."

And that is what the student of American history and American institutions would infer, even if he had never set foot upon American soil. For in the home are first instilled those lessons of self-government and of voluntary co-operation for the common good which the Republic expects of its citizens; without which the Republic will not endure. It is the home that first molds the conduct of the individual. It is in the home that he first learns to appreciate the nature of liberty. It is the home, and not the palace of potentate or proconsul, that has determined and will continue to determine the character of American civilization.

In recent years Americans have been abroad, in more than the literal sense. We can stay abroad, or we can come home. We shall never make the world safe for democracy. But we can keep and continuously strengthen the power in the people, here at home. Only thus will the light of this Republic continue to shine before mankind, as a beacon unique in history.

Select Bibliography

Because of the scope of this book, its bibliography is necessarily selective. Space considerations alone prevent mention of many important works of reference in the broad terrain disclosed by a survey of American political philosophy.

The criterion of selection has been to facilitate better understanding, on the part of the general reader, of the principles underlying the American system of government. No book without some value in this direction is listed. But the compiler is well aware that there is no reference to many studies which could properly be included.

Most of the titles named are available in the better public and college libraries. More specific guidance for the reader has been attempted in two respects. With some temerity a line of personal valuation is included. There is also classification of the utility of the source to the present writer. Two asterisks indicate that the particular work of reference has been indispensable; one asterisk means that the source has proved suggestive or otherwise definitely instructive; unemphasized mention means that the volume cited has been occasionally helpful.

A number of sources quoted in this volume are omitted from the bibliography. In the case of the New Testament, inclusion would be superfluous. In some secondary cases, also, the footnote identification by itself is sufficient reference. Conversely, this bibliography includes a number of titles which have not been utilized in a manner requiring citation in the text.

The publisher, and particular editions, are identified whenever desirable for purposes of guidance. And because each chapter of this book is written as a unit, the bibliographical references have been made to conform to the chapter arrangement. This procedure is admittedly somewhat arbitrary, for many of the sources have been useful in more than one chapter. But the breakdown by chapters should assist the reader who wishes to go more deeply into various phases of the subject.

Chapter I

* ACTON, JOHN EMERICK EDWARD DALBERG: *The History of Freedom and Other Essays;* especially valuable for its refined critical faculty, not less stimulating because of conclusions which are often highly controversial (Macmillan, 1909).

* DE MONTESQUIEU, CHARLES DE SECONDAT: *De l'Esprit des Lois.* This classic is available in various translations. I have used the French text in the "Collected Works," Guettier edition, Paris (An IV de la République Française).

** FARRAND MAX (editor): *The Records of the Federal Convention,* Revised edition (Yale University Press, 4 vols., 1937). This is the definitive record of the Constitutional Convention, supplementing Madison's reports and correcting them wherever later evidence warrants; indispensable for thorough study of American governmental origins.

** HAMILTON, ALEXANDER; MADISON, JAMES; JAY, JOHN: *The Federalist.* This famous contemporary commentary on the Constitution remains unique in the field of political analysis. Perhaps the most satisfactory of the innumerable editions is the "Sesquicentennial" (1937), promoted by the Carnegie Corporation of New York, with introduction by Professor Edward Mead Earle.

HEGEL, GEORG WILHELM FRIEDRICH: *The Philosophy of History.* I have used the Sibree translation, but if possible these remarkable lectures should be read in the original German.

** LEGISLATIVE REFERENCE SERVICE OF THE LIBRARY OF CONGRESS (compiler): *The Constitution of the United States;* annotated and with citations of cases construing its provisions as decided by the Supreme Court to January 1, 1938. This invaluable compendium is published in one volume by the Government Printing Office, Washington, D. C. A new edition is scheduled.

** MADISON, JAMES: *Reports of Debates in the Federal Convention;* the fundamental source book on the actual framing of the Constitution. The edition used in this study is that published in three volumes by Allston Mygatt, Mobile, 1842.

** MILL, JOHN STUART: *Essays,* especially *On Liberty* and *Representative Government.* Nobody who seeks to understand the political meaning of liberty can afford to neglect these essays, first published in 1859 and 1861 respectively. The Oxford University Press edition (1912) is recommended.

* PLATO: *The Dialogues,* translated and edited (5 vols.) by Benjamin Jowett; *The Republic* (Vol. III in Oxford University Press edition) and *The Laws* (Vol. V) of course cannot be overlooked.

SANDBURG, CARL: *Abraham Lincoln; The Prairie Years* (2 vols.), *The War Years* (4 vols.); excellent biography (Harcourt, Brace).

* SPENGLER, OSWALD: *The Decline of the West.* These "Perspectives of World History" are important not only for their erudition and insight, but also paradoxically, because the reasoning is often completely alien to the main body of American political thought. The George Allen and Unwin edition (London) is the authorized translation by Charles Francis Atkinson.

* TOYNBEE, ARNOLD: *A Study of History,* the first six volumes (Oxford University Press). This heroically ambitious inquiry into the rise and fall of civilizations has been condensed into an authorized one-volume edition, satisfactory for the purposes of the general reader.

Chapter II

* BEARD, CHARLES A. AND MARY: *The Rise of American Civilization* (2 vols.); a thorough survey, with emphasis on economic forces, of national development up to the year of publication (Macmillan, 1927).

* BEARD, CHARLES A.: *The Republic;* a searching symposium on the Constitution, in the Socratic manner (Viking Press, 1943).

* BRANT, IRVING: *James Madison* (4 vols., of which only the first two had been published by Bobbs-Merrill prior to the completion of the present book); very comprehensive biography; thoroughly reliable as well as readable, with much emphasis on the nationalist strain in Madison's thought.

** BRYCE , JAMES: *The American Commonwealth* (Macmillan, 2 vols.) Although outmoded in details, this famous study by an eminent English statesman is still essential reading for serious students of American politics.

* CAIRNS, HUNTINGTON: *Law and the Social Sciences;* the chapter on "Political Theory" is of particular interest (Harcourt, Brace, 1935).

CHINARD, GILBERT: *Thomas Jefferson;* a standard biography (Little, Brown), especially interesting because of the French background of the author.

* DICEY, A. V.: *The Law of the Constitution;* a classic study of English Constitutional Law. The eighth (1915) edition (Macmillan), with its comprehensive and luminous introduction, should be utilized. The chapter on "Parliamentary Sovereignty and Federalism" is especially important for American readers.

MALONE, DUMAS: *Jefferson and His Time.* The work as a whole is designed to have four volumes, of which only Vol. I, *Jefferson the Virginian* had been published (Little, Brown) prior to the completion of the present book.

NOCK, ALBERT JAY: *Jefferson;* a stimulating biographical essay (Harcourt, Brace, 1926).

* OLIVER, F. S.: *Alexander Hamilton.* This "Essay on American Union" is more than an interesting biography, from an English viewpoint. Putnam has published an American edition.

* PAINE, THOMAS: *Rights of Man* and *Common Sense.* Both of these essays are in Vol. I of the two-volume Foner edition of *The Complete Writings of Thomas Paine,* an excellent compilation published by the Citadel Press, New York, 1945.

VAN DOREN, CARL: *Benjamin Franklin;* excellent biography (Viking Press, 1938).

VAN DOREN, CARL: *The Great Rehearsal;* a popular and readable account of the drafting and ratifying of the Constitution (Viking Press, 1948).

* VINOGRADOFF, PAUL: *Common-Sense in Law;* a short but illuminating study of the principles underlying legal arrangements (The Home University Library).

Chapter III

BUELL, AUGUSTUS C.: *William Penn* (Appleton, 1904); a balance to the Comfort biography, cited below. Mr. Buell concludes, of Penn: "Sometimes he was a great statesman; at other times he was a great Quaker; but he was never both at the same time."

* CATLIN, GEORGE: *Story of the Political Philosophers;* an encyclopedic study, gracefully written and useful to all who are interested in political theory (Whittlesey House, 1939).

CHANNING, EDWARD: *Town and County Government in the English Colonies of North America;* a careful study of local government.

COMFORT, W. W.: *William Penn;* readable biography, excellent on Penn as a Quaker but deficient in presenting his political importance (University of Pennsylvania Press, 1944).

FISKE, JOHN: *The Discovery of America* (2 vols.); continues to be standard.

** GARDINER, S. R.: *Constitutional Documents of the Puritan Revolution;* essential source material (Oxford University Press).

GARDINER, S. R.: *History of the Commonwealth and Protectorate;* standard for reference.

** HOBBES, THOMAS: *Leviathan.* There are many editions. I have used that published by George Routledge & Sons (London, 1894), with introduction by Henry Morley.

* LABAREE, LEONARD W. (editor): *Royal Instructions to British Colonial Governors* (2 vols.). This American Historical Association study is a mine of valuable documentary material for the period covered (1670-1776).

** LOCKE, JOHN: *Essay Concerning the True Original Extent and End of Civil Government.* There is a good edition, with thoughtful introduction by Professor William S. Carpenter, in the Everyman's Library. The *Essay Concerning Human Understanding* and the *Letters on Toleration* should also be consulted in Locke's *Collected Works.*

* MAITLAND, F. W.: *The Constitutional History of England;* a series of lectures which, in the words of H. A. L. Fisher, will always be notable for "the union of high speculative power with exact and comprehensive knowledge of detail" (Cambridge University Press).

* MILLER, JOHN C.: *Origins of the American Revolution,* a popular and scholarly study (Little, Brown, 1943).

** MILTON, JOHN: *Prose Writings.* The definitive edition is that published by the Columbia University Press, in 18 volumes (1931-38) plus two-volume index (1940). The Modern Library Edition, *Complete Poetry and Selected Prose,* of John Milton, contains some of the more important political essays, including *Areopagitica,* as also the Everyman Edition. There are many good biographies of Milton; that by Mark Pattison, in the English Men of Letters Series, has been useful for the present writer.

MORLEY, JOHN: *Oliver Cromwell;* excellent biography, which may be supplemented by that of John Buchan (later Lord Tweedsmuir) with the same title.

* ORTON, WILLIAM AYLOTT: *The Liberal Tradition;* an impressive statement of the principles underlying "the noblest of political philosophies" (Yale University Press, 1945).

PARKMAN, FRANCIS: *France and England in North America* (9 vols.); graphic historical narrative, now superseded in some details by later scholarship.

** PROTHERO, G. W.: *Select Statutes of the Reigns of Elizabeth and James I;* a carefully edited source book of constitutional documents for the period immediately preceding the Puritan Revolution (Oxford).

* ROBERTSON, C. GRANT: *Select Statutes, Cases and Documents, 1660-1832;* contains the more important English constitutional source material for the period covered (Methuen, London).

* THWAITES, REUBEN J.: *The Colonies.* This little book, in the Epochs of American History Series, is a good introductory study.

* TREVELYAN, GEORGE M.: *England Under the Stuarts;* good and easily readable general history of the period (Methuen, London).

* WINTHROP, JOHN: *History of New England,* 1630-49 (2 vols.); indispensable for thorough research in the period.

* WOODHOUSE, A. S. P. (editor): *Puritanism and Liberty.* Contains well-selected documentation of the Puritan Revolution in England. The introduction is excellent (J. M. Dent & Sons, London).

Chapter IV

BALLAGH, JAMES C. (editor): *The Letters of Richard Henry Lee* (2 vols.); useful for advanced students.

* BURKE, EDMUND: *Speeches and Letters on American Affairs.* The Everyman Edition contains both the speech on *Conciliation with the Colonies* and the famous address *To the Electors of Bristol.*

** DE TOCQUEVILLE, ALEXIS: *Democracy in America* (2 vols.). The most satisfactory edition for the general reader is that with introduction by Phillips Bradley (Alfred A. Knopf, 1945). The foreword by Harold J. Laski is controversial. This translation, based on that of Henry Reeve, is also subject to some criticism, as will appear on comparison with the original French.

* HILL, HELEN: *George Mason;* good biography, especially important for its careful analysis of the States' Rights viewpoint (Harvard University Press, 1938).

JAMES, MARQUIS: *The Life of Andrew Jackson;* reliable and entertaining biography (Bobbs-Merrill).

* JEFFERSON, THOMAS: *Commonplace Book.* The original manuscript can be consulted in the Library of Congress. A satisfactory edition is that edited by Gilbert Chinard (Johns Hopkins Press, Baltimore, 1926).

PARTON, JAMES: *Life of Thomas Jefferson;* first published in 1874 and superseded by later biographies, but still interesting for reasons other than its vehement partisanship.

* POLLOCK, SIR FREDERICK: *History of the Science of Politics;* a short but brilliant study, based on lectures delivered in 1882.

** ROUSSEAU, JEAN JACQUES: *Du Contrat Social.* This should be read in the original French. The best contemporary edition is that published by Constant Bourquin, Geneva, with critical introductory essay by Bertrand de Jouvenel.

Chapter V

** ARISTOTLE: *Politics.* The edition used is the 1920 Oxford, translation by Benjamin Jowett; introduction and analysis by H. W. C. Davis, who reminds us that this classic embodies "theories of perennial value, and refutations of fallacies which are always re-emerging."

BELLOC, HILAIRE: *The Servile State;* first published in 1912 and interesting for its prophetic power (reprinted by Examiner Books, New York).

BOURNE, RANDOLPH: *The State;* an interesting essay, definitely anarchistic. Obtainable, with other anarchist writings, from the Resistance Press, Cooper Station, N. Y.

* CASIRER, ERNST: *The Myth of the State.* This study by a Swedish philosopher is not less important because written during World War II. Published posthumously (Yale University Press) and perhaps for that reason imperfectly edited.

* CORWIN, EDWARD S.: *Liberty Against Government.* As the title suggests, this challenging book examines liberty as a juridical concept, enforceable by courts against other branches of government. Published by the Louisiana State University Press, 1948, a decade after the same author's *Court Over Constitution* (Princeton University Press) which has also been utilized.

* DE JOUVENEL, BERTRAND: *Power.* Translated by J. F. Huntington. Hutchinson, London, 1948.

* ELIOT, THOMAS S.: *The Idea of a Christian Society.* Three important lectures, delivered in March, 1939, and taking as their point of departure "the suspicion that the current terms in which we discuss . . . political theory may only tend to conceal from us the real issues of contemporary civilization." The American edition is by Harcourt, Brace.

* FRAZER, SIR JAMES GEORGE: *The Golden Bough.* For the general reader the one-volume abridgement (Macmillan) will be satisfactory. The condensation has been done so skillfully that reference to the full twelve-volume edition will seldom seem essential.

* HOCKING, WILLIAM ERNEST: *Man and the State;* thought-provoking, but unnecessarily discursive and lacking in unity (Yale University Press, 1926).

KROPOTKIN, PETER: *The State.* Written as a lecture, in 1896, this famous essay survives as the primary thesis of modern philosophical anarchism (Freedom Press, London, 1920).

* MACHIAVELLI, NICCOLO: *The Prince* and *The Discourses.* The Modern Library edition is excellent.

* NOCK, ALBERT J.: *Our Enemy the State;* a stimulating appetizer for all who seek to understand the nature of the subject discussed. Republished in 1946 by the Caxton Printers, Caldwell, Idaho.

** OPPENHEIMER, FRANZ: *The State.* This brilliant political study is simultaneously readable, brief and profound. The authorized translation (Vanguard Press) by John M. Gitterman is wholly satisfactory, except that it lacks an index.

* PARETO, VILFREDO: *The Mind and Society* (4 vols., Harcourt, Brace, 1935). This tremendous treatise on "General Sociology" remains difficult reading, in spite of the superb editorial treatment by Arthur Livingston. But it cannot be ignored by any thorough student of representative government.

* SPENCER, HERBERT: *The Man Versus The State.* These remarkably prescient articles were first published in the *Contemporary Review* (London) in 1884. There is no more acute analysis of the thesis that "increase of freedom in form" can lead to "decrease of freedom in fact."

Chapter VI

* BURCKHARDT, JACOB: *Force and Freedom.* In 1943 Pantheon Books published the first English translation of this classic by an eminent Swiss historian. The introductory essay by James Hastings Nichols is a valuable appraisal for any who are unfamiliar with Burckhardt's work.

* COLE, FRANKLIN P.: *They Preached Liberty;* significant excerpts from the sermons of New England Ministers during the late Colonial period. The collection (Fleming H. Revell) is made with a view to throwing light on two vital questions: Where does liberty originate? What are its obligations and results?

* CROCE, BENEDETTO: *Politics and Morals*. A good English edition of these important essays is the Castiglione translation (Philosophical Library, Inc., New York).

* MADELIN, LOUIS: *The French Revolution*. From the viewpoint of political theory this is an outstanding study in its field. Crowned by the French Academy, in 1911, the excellent English translation is published by Heinemann, of London.

ORTEGA Y GASSET, JOSÉ: *The Revolt of the Masses;* more readable, less pedantic and less controversial than Spengler, whose thought is often paralleled. The authorized English translation was published (1932) by W. W. Norton, also publisher of the same author's less important: *Toward A Philosophy of History*.

* PENN, WILLIAM: *Collected Writings*. The Everyman Edition contains both the famous "Essay Towards the Present and Future Peace of Europe" and the "Fruits of Solitude."

*WILLOUGHBY, WESTEL W.: *The Ethical Basis of Political Authority;* a scholarly attempt to state "criteria for testing the right of particular States or Governments to exist" (Macmillan); see also the same author's earlier book: *The Nature of the State*.

Chapter VII

**AQUINAS, ST. THOMAS: *Basic Writings;* an excellent edition is that edited by Professor Anton C. Pegis (Random House, 1945). Careful students will profit from Walter Farrell's: *A Companion to the Summa*.

* AUGUSTINE, ST.: *De Civitate Dei*. The Everyman Edition (2 vols.) is a revised edition of the famous Healey translation and has an important introduction by Ernest Barker.

BAILLIE, JOHN: *What Is Christian Civilization?* A fundamental question briefly but searchingly posed by a former Moderator of the Church of Scotland (Scribner).

* FOX, GEORGE: *Journal*. There are many editions of this classic. That of 1901, edited by T. Ellwood, has been utilized.

GAEVERNITZ, G. VON SCHULZE: *Democracy and Religion*. The "Swarthmore Lecture" for 1930 (Allen and Unwin, London).

* GOMPERZ, THEODOR: *Greek Thinkers*. The authorized (4 vols.) translation, by Laurie Magnus and G. G. Berry, of the lifetime work of the great Austrian classicist (John Murray, London, 1906).

* HAMILTON, EDITH: *Witness to the Truth.* Profound scholarship shines through the simplicity of these essays on personal Christianity (Norton).

* JONES, RUFUS M.: *The Quakers in the American Colonies;* an interesting historical study which is unfortunately less well-known than other books by this great contemporary interpretator of Quakerism.

MARITAIN, JACQUES: *L'Humanisme Intégral.* The English translation of this important book is called *True Humanism.*

** NUTTALL, GEOFFREY F.: *The Holy Spirit in Puritan Faith and Experience.* This important historical study is additionally interesting for advanced students because of the "synopsis of argument" included in each section (Blackwell, Oxford, 1946).

* OATES, WHITNEY J. (editor): *The Stoic* and *Epicurean Philosophers;* containing in one volume, with a general introduction by the editor, the complete extant writings of Epicurus, Epictetus, Lucretius and Marcus Aurelius, in standard translation (Random House, 1940).

* WELLS, HERBERT G.: *Mind at the End of Its Tether.* Published by Didier, 1946, to whom acknowledgment is made for permission to quote.

Chapter VIII

AUSTIN, JOHN: *Lectures on Jurisprudence* (5th edition, 1885). This careful political analysis, in the Hobbes tradition, leads to the conclusion that political sovereignty is not a matter of law, but of fact.

* BEER, MAX: *A History of British Socialism* (2 vols.). An Austrian scholar examines the way in which: "From the thirteenth century to the present day the stream of Socialism . . . has been largely fed by British thought and experiment" (London, G. Bell & Sons, 1920).

* BRANDEIS, LOUIS D.: *The Curse of Bigness,* being the miscellaneous papers of Mr. Justice Brandeis (Viking Press). The collection is so heterogeneous that the student would be well advised to consult first *Brandeis and the Modern State,* by Alpheus T. Mason (National Home Library Foundation).

GEORGE, HENRY: *Progress and Poverty.* This classic, of which there are innumerable editions, cannot be ignored by any objective student of "free enterprise."

** GIBBON, EDWARD: *The Decline and Fall of the Roman Empire.* The Modern Library Edition (2 vols.) is adequate. The most desirable edition of this classic is that published by the Heritage Press (3 vols.), with critical introduction by J. B. Bury, beautifully printed and adorned by the Piranesi etchings.

** HALLAM, HENRY: *View of the State of Europe during the Middle Ages* (3 vols.). The fifth edition, John Murray, London, 1829, has been utilized. Few historical works have stood the test of time better than this study.

** HAYEK, FRIEDRICH A.: *The Road to Serfdom.* This is a careful post-war analysis of the actual effect of Socialism on liberty and freedom. It is well supplemented by John Jewkes: *Ordeal by Planning*, a case study of English post-war experience. See also L. von Mises: *Omnipotent Government.*

* HOBSON, JOHN A.: *The Evolution of Modern Capitalism* (Revised edition, Walter Scott, London, 1916); a lucid and objective study in economic history.

* MARX, KARL: *Capital.* I have used the Glaisher edition, London, 1920, translation by Moore and Aveling. This tremendous work is far too readily derided by many who have never even read it.

** SMITH, ADAM: *The Wealth of Nations.* The Modern Library Edition, with analytical introduction by Professor Edwin Cannan, is excellent. An interesting and valuable condensation of this classic—"simplified, shortened and modernized"—has been made by Arthur Hugh Jenkins: *Adam Smith Today* (Richard R. Smith, New York).

** TAWNEY, R. H.: *The Acquisitive Society.* A great deal of the strength in contemporary indictments of Capitalism stems, consciously or unconsciously, from this brilliant essay (London, G. Bell & Sons, 1921).

Chapter IX

* BAYKOV, ALEXANDER: *The Development of the Soviet Economic System;* an admirably objective and comprehensive study of state planning in the U.S.S.R. The comprehensive bibliography is invaluable for advanced studies (Cambridge University Press; American edition (1948) by Macmillan).

* BURNHAM, JAMES: *The Managerial Revolution;* a brilliant, if journalistic, attempt "to elaborate a descriptive theory able to explain the character of the present period of social transition." Reference may also be made to this writer's: *The Struggle for the World* (John Day, New York).

*CARR, EDWARD HALLETT: *The Soviet Impact on the Western World;* a preliminary, but important, analysis of Communist influence on the intelligentsia of Western Europe (Macmillan, 1947).

CHAMBERLIN, WILLIAM HENRY: *The Russian Enigma;* a balanced interpretation, not less valuable for having been published (Scribner, 1943) during the honeymoon period of wartime Russo-American alliance.

**CHAMBERLIN, WILLIAM HENRY (editor): *Blueprint For World Conquest;* fundamental documentation of the Communist International (Human Events, 1946).

*DALLIN, DAVID J.: *The Real Soviet Russia.* An acknowledged authority here examines the seamy side of life under Communism. Mr. Dallin's *Russia and Postwar Europe,* also written during the war, is equally forthright. These are Yale University Press publications.

DOBB, MAURICE: *Russian Economic Development Since the Revolution.* This study, published in 1927, is out-of-date in many respects, but remains useful for its analysis of Soviet economic policy during the first years of the Revolution.

**MARX, KARL AND ENGELS, FRIEDRICH: *The Communist Manifesto.* The International Publishers edition is reliable and obtainable at every Communist bookstore.

MAYNARD, SIR JOHN H.: *Russia in Flux;* a careful examination of the Soviet period. The American edition (Macmillan) is edited and abridged by S. Haden Guest.

*PARES, SIR BERNARD: *A History of Russia.* The fourth edition (Knopf, 1944) brings this sympathetic study down to the post-war period.

*SHUB, DAVID: *Lenin.* This vivid and penetrating biography is by a former member of the Russian Social Democratic Party. It is carefully documented and has an appendix with important quotations from Lenin's *Works* (Doubleday, 1948).

SOROKIN, PITIRIM A.: *Russia and the United States.* This emotional study has a continuing value primarily because it senses and emphasizes the underlying strength of Soviet Russia as an "original sociopolitical innovation" (Dutton, 1944).

*TROTSKY, LEON: *The History of the Russian Revolution.* The Simon and Schuster edition, translation by Max Eastman, contains the three volumes of this remarkable book within single covers.

**ULIANOV, V. I. (Lenin): *The State and Revolution.* There are many textual variations in different editions of this Communist classic, as Lenin is continuously revised to fit exigencies of the party line. I have used the English edition, published by the British Socialist Labour Press in

1919 and the "revised translation" of International Publishers, New York, 1935.

Chapter X

* ADAMS, BROOKS: *The Law of Civilization and Decay;* antedates, and in a measure anticipates, Toynbee but has curiously received less consideration from American readers than either Toynbee or Spengler. The Knopf edition (1943) has introduction by Charles A. Beard.

BEARD, CHARLES A.: *The Economic Basis of Politics;* lectures originally delivered in 1916; a new chapter is added in the Knopf (1945) edition.

BOWERS, CLAUDE G.: *The Tragic Era;* readable and careful history of the twelve years following the death of Lincoln, when "the Constitution was treated as a doormat." The Blue Ribbon Books edition contains an excellent bibliography.

** BUNYAN, JOHN: *The Pilgrim's Progress.* There are innumerable editions of this immortal allegory. Unfortunately, some lack the author's apology: ". . . nor did I undertake thereby to please my neighbor; no, not I. I did it mine own self to gratify."

* HUME, DAVID: *Essays* and *Treatise of Human Nature.* The Everyman Editions of both are satisfactory.

** MAINE, SIR HENRY SUMNER: *Popular Government;* including the famous essay on the "Constitution of the United States." The careful student will also familiarize himself with Maine's *Ancient Law.* The original American editions of these classics are by Henry Holt.

Mayer, J. P. (and collaborators): *Political Thought; The European Tradition.* The introduction to this pre-war study (Viking Press, 1939) is by R. H. Tawney.

Index